Dear Senator

Dear Senator

A MEMOIR BY THE DAUGHTER OF STROM THURMOND

ESSIE MAE WASHINGTON-WILLIAMS
and WILLIAM STADIEM

ReganBooks
An Imprint of HarperCollins*Publishers*

A hardcover edition of this book was published in 2005 by ReganBooks, an imprint of HarperCollins Publishers.

HarperCollins books may be purchased for educational, business, or sales promotional use. For information please write: Special Markets Department, HarperCollins Publishers Inc., 10 East 53rd Street, New York, NY 10022.

First paperback edition published 2006.

Designer: Laura Blost

Photo insert credits: Pages 1–4, top photo on 6, pages 8, 10, 11, 15: courtesy of author. Pages 5: courtesy of Clemson University. Lower photo on 6, pages 7, 9, 14: courtesy of Time Life pictures/Getty Images. Page 12: courtesy of Senate Historical Society. Page 13: courtesy of Olan Mills. Page 16: courtesy of Jonathan Alcorn.

The Library of Congress has cataloged the hardcover edition as follows:

Washington-Williams, Essie Mae, 1925–
Dear senator : a daughter's memoir / Essie Mae Washington-Williams and William Stadiem.
p. cm.
ISBN 0-06-076095-8
1. Thurmond, Strom, 1902—Family. 2. Washington-Williams, Essie Mae, 1925– 3. Thurmond, Strom, 1902—Relations with women. 4. Thurmond, Strom, 1902—Relations with African Americans. 5. Daughters—United States—Biography. 6. Racially mixed people—United States—Biography. 7. Legislators—United States—Family relationships—Case studies. 8. Southern States—Race relations—Case studies. I. Stadiem, William. II. Title.

E748.T58W37 2005
973.9'092—dc22

2004061387

ISBN 13 978-0-06-076142-4 (pbk.)
ISBN 10 0-06-076142-3 (pbk.)

06 07 08 09 10 RRD 10 9 8 7 6 5 4 3 2 1

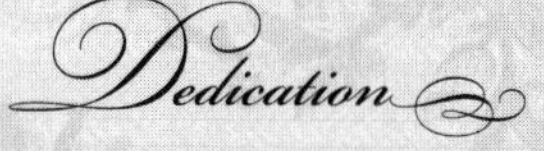

Dedication

Dedicated to my children, grandchildren, and great-grandchildren. My legacy to you is the discovery of your lineage. Continue the journey of life, love, and family. Endure the hardships, and embrace the future. Judge not the ethnicity of the person, but scrutinize the character.

I love each of you. God bless all of you.

In loving memory of my mother, Carrie Butler Clark,

my father, James Strom Thurmond,

my aunt, Mary Washington Bowman,

my uncle, John Henry Washington,

my brother, Willie James Clark, and

my cousin, Calvin Franklin Burton.

Acknowledgments

One of the great joys in excavating a life is the wonderful cast of characters you meet in the Big Dig. I would like to single out the following very special individuals for their time, their insights, and for their unforgettable Southern hospitality: Jack Bass, Barry Bishop, Thurmond Bishop, Daniel I. A. Cohen, Butler Derrick, Carrie Lee Early, Bruce Elrod, Gordon Farmer, Tex Fuller, May Ouzts Green, Donna Kendall, Hon. Matthew Perry, Bettis Rainsford, Catherine Ray, Peg Rivers, Deborah Rosen, Tom Tisdale, Ginna and Jay Waddell, and the staffs of the Strom Thurmond Collection at Clemson University and the South Carolina Historical Society in Charleston.

Special thanks to Bridie Clark for her devotion to this project and her editorial inspirations; to Robert Edmonds, for his invariably sage counsel; and to Peter Miller, whose unique fusion of zeal and weal takes agenting to a different level and a better place. Above all, I must thank Frank K. Wheaton, "the kid from Compton," without whom this book would never have come to pass. His intelligence, humor, and compassion, combined with his utterly fearless commitment to justice, have been essential in securing Essie Mae Washington-Williams's place in history and in the hearts of this country.

William Stadiem

Santa Monica
October 6, 2004

Contents

Dear Senator

CHAPTER ONE
Summer of '38

I ALWAYS THOUGHT I had a fairly normal childhood, until I found out my parents weren't who I thought they were. I grew up in Coatesville, Pennsylvania, a small town in the hills along the Brandywine River on the threshold of the rich farmland of the Amish country. We were only forty miles from Philadelphia, and the main line of the Pennsylvania Railroad ran through our town. And yet Philadelphia might as well have been the moon. That was the Big City. Coatesville was nowhere, but for a little girl it was everywhere—it was all I had and all I knew. Coatesville was what was considered a one-horse town, but that horse was a very powerful steed called steel. The Lukens Steel Company dominated everything about our town. Its dozens of soaring smokestacks dominated the skyline. They were our own skyscrapers. Even the smoke belching from those enormous stacks was a point of pride, not pollution. That pungent, thick, black soot meant the mills were working full blast, that the little town was booming. It was the smell of money.

Like most men in Coatesville, my father, John Henry Washington, worked for the steel mills. Bethlehem Steel and Worth Brothers Steel had huge plants in Coatesville, but the colossus was Lukens Steel. Like an industrial octopus, Lukens had devoured its rivals and made them its own. The matriarch of the business was a legendary local character named Rebecca Lukens, known as "The Woman of Steel." She was an independent woman, far ahead of her time, a Pennsylvania version of a steel magnolia. Rebecca was the driving force behind the expansion of her family's Brandywine Iron Works into an international powerhouse. She was one of the first women in America to run a major company, and her daughter married a man named Huston. When I was growing up, the Hustons were Coatesville's first family. They lived in a grand manor house called Terracina and were to Coatesville what the Kennedys or the Rockefellers are to America. Despite the small size of the town (15,000 people), I never met a Huston, and, by the same token, I never aspired to become a woman of steel. American women today have those sort of huge "have it all" ambitions, but growing up black during the Great Depression, I was perfectly happy to dream about becoming a nurse. That was a pretty big deal at the time, and I was more ambitious than most.

My mother, or at least the woman who I thought was my mother, kept house, while daddy worked on the assembly line. Mother had worked as a picker in the cotton fields of South Carolina and said that was enough hard labor for two lifetimes. I had a half-brother, Calvin Burton, who was my mother's son by a previous relationship, which I later learned was not an actual marriage. Calvin was seven years older than I, and by the time I was thirteen, in 1938, he had left home to live in New York City. I had fantasies of following him there, to become a nurse in a big city hospital, but these were only fantasies. At thirteen, I still hadn't gotten to Philadelphia.

We lived in a small, two-story, three-bedroom row house in a neighborhood called The Spruces, named after the tree, which was populated by other black steelworkers. Most of them, like my family, hailed from the South. I had my own room, which seemed like a castle to me. The house was heated with coal stoves, and there was no running water or any bathrooms. We had to use an outhouse in the back and take tub baths in the bedroom using water we'd carry from an outside pump. It sounds primitive, but it seemed normal then, although the winters were awfully cold, and the day of the week the big sanitation trucks would come to clean the outhouses was the smelliest day you could imagine. We'd all try to stay away from home on that day. I remember visiting the home of a white girlfriend. The house wasn't any nicer than ours, but it did have an indoor toilet. It seemed like the ultimate in high technology at the time.

I'll never forget the wonderful dinners we'd have: fried chicken, biscuits, lots of fresh vegetables, and the sweetest pies made with local peaches, strawberries, apples, and plums. Every night was like Thanksgiving. My mother, who was tall and slim and a great cook, always wore a kerchief around her head. That seemed old-fashioned at the time, as did her habit of chewing tobacco and expelling it into a spittoon. I gathered that it was an old southern custom she'd brought with her. I didn't question her about it. In fact, I didn't tend to question things at all. My parents were of the "children should be seen and not heard" school. As a little girl I started out quite chatty, but one day my mother warned me "that mouth of yours can get you into trouble," after which I learned to keep it shut.

We never talked much at those fine dinners, partly because we were all listening to the radio all through the meal. That was our ear to the world. Despite all the bad news that seemed to be coming through the airwaves—the seemingly endless Depression, the rise of the Nazis in Europe, disasters like the *Hindenburg* airship explosion—the feeling around the table was very positive. My father, a handsome man who always came to the table after a hard, dusty day at the mills immaculate and smelling deliciously of soap and cologne, always said a blessing of thanks, for the food, for his job, for his wonderful family, and for funny or odd things, like Shirley Temple, or Charlie Chan, or Heinz ketchup. And then we'd listen to comedy shows like Edgar Bergen and his puppet Charlie McCarthy or the big band music of Benny Goodman. There wasn't much need to talk; the radio said it all.

And then came 1938—a big year for me for a lot of reasons. First of all, my parents got divorced. My father, apparently, was not only a hard worker but also a hard drinker, haunting the many taverns of our town, rarely during the week but frequently on weekends. Steelworking and hard drinking seemed to go hand in hand. Prohibition had ended in a big way, and there was a bar or "whiskey house" on every corner, many of which seemed to have been frequented by my father. There were no problems at home that I ever noticed, but there must have been plenty. One day, daddy was gone, and I never saw or spoke to him again. In keeping with my mother's philosophy of the fewer questions, the better, I never asked her about my father's departure, much as I would have loved to do so. Nor did she sit me down for a heart-to-heart about why he left. He was gone, and that was that. I missed the confident, comforting masculine presence of my father. He made me feel safe in an increasingly turbulent world. I felt lost without him but learned to keep that kind of emotion deeply to myself, and eventually the pain died down.

Not too long afterward, my mother remarried. My new stepfather, James Bowman, wasn't as tall or handsome as my real father, John Henry Washington, but he had the virtue, at least in my mother's eyes, of not drinking. He also was a devout churchgoer, which daddy was not. Because he was one of the rare people in the area who didn't work for Lukens Steel, James Bowman was outside of the hard-drinking steel-driving culture of Coatesville. He seemed a little dull, but my mother liked that. James Bowman had a job as a cement finisher for a local contractor. He built everything, from bridges to houses. I also called him daddy, although I never really felt that kind of bond. I warmed up to him when he moved us to a new house in the Newlinville area, named after the farmer who sold the land for the subdivision. We had a peach orchard as our back garden, and my stepfather himself installed a bath, toilet, and sink. To me, it was the ultimate in luxury. I felt like a little princess, every bit the equal of the lords of steel in their palace at Terracina. I enjoyed watching my stepfather work. I admired his craftsmanship. But he was more a man of deeds than words, and we never spoke very much. I became even more glad for that radio.

Nineteen thirty-eight was also a watershed year in that it marked the first time I had to attend a segregated school. Before this, my elementary school was completely integrated. There were thirty students in my grade, half black and half white, and we all got along fine. In our early years during the Depression, we all wore the same gray flannel "welfare uniform" and all ate the same rations of peanut butter and powdered milk. We were all poor, but we were together. Most of the whites were the children of eastern European immigrants who worked for Lukens—Poles, Czechs, Hungarians, Slavs, all with long "oski" names that were hard to pronounce. The other half were black kids whose families had moved to Coatesville from all over the South. My folks were from Edgefield, South Carolina, and there were dozens of other Edgefieldians around. I guess when one family found a place up north, they sent for their kin and friends, and a little community was born.

My friends were both white and black. In 1938, however, all the blacks in our county were herded into one huge regional junior high—for just one year of school—while the whites went to several others. I'm still not sure why they split us up. It had something to do with administrative efficiency, cost savings, whatever. This was the first time my black friends and I had ever been defined by our race. When school started, we found ourselves staring at each other, trying to make sense of it. But none of us said anything about it, even as a joke. Apparently, all of us had been raised in the same school of mouth-shut acceptance of the way things were. I think all of us were glad to be getting an education, and an excellent one at that. If anything, the all-black faculty paid more attention to us than the white teachers had. I never had more caring teachers. But there was no sense of black unity, no stirrings of what later became known as "black power." We were just a bunch of local school kids herded into a school where everyone happened to be black. We didn't have time to reflect on the deeper implications—the term was over in a flash. But it did make its mark.

When we entered the fully integrated regional high school, where there were 300 students to a grade, the lines had been drawn. I only had black friends. There were blacks on the sports teams, but none were allowed to be cheerleaders. The idea of having a white boyfriend, or girlfriend, would have never occurred to any of us. Although I had been held back in the first grade because of an awful scalp disease that afflicted all the kids in our neighborhood, I had been making up for lost time ever since. I had been at the head of my class each year in elementary school and would go on to be an honor student in high school. But that one year in junior high branded me, in my own mind, as a second-class citizen.

That feeling was reinforced by Coatesville. Although the thousands of blacks who had come up from the South may have seen Coatesville as a kind of promised land, offering good jobs and equality that just didn't exist below the Mason-Dixon Line (in Maryland, only twenty miles from us), the reality of Coatesville fell short of these ideals. Steelworker wages were low, and equality was a myth. Blacks could shop at Santee's Drug Store, but we weren't allowed to sit at the soda fountain and have their fabulous-looking ice cream floats and sundaes. Nor were we allowed to swim at the public pool. If we wanted to swim, we were told to go jump in a creek, quite literally. The YWCA was likewise off limits, which didn't seem like a good Christian attitude.

There were two movie theaters in town. At the Auditorium, we blacks had to sit in the "colored balcony," while at the Palace, we were sequestered in a cordon of narrow seats in the rear of the theater. I tried not to let it detract me from watching my favorites, Fred Astaire and Ginger Rogers, and heartthrobs Clark Gable, Errol Flynn, and Gary Cooper, but sitting up there in the auditorium made me feel strange about having girlish crushes on these white movie idols. If I couldn't even sit in a normal seat, how could Clark Gable respect me, or (in my dreams) love me? So my girlfriends and I had our own little protest by sneaking down into the white seats. Once the ushers caught us and ordered us back upstairs. I held up the line and demanded our money back. The ushers gave it to us, relieved to see us go. That may have been gutsy for a thirteen year old, but that was as radical as I got.

For the most part, however, I was happy. I had my family and my friends, I loved school, I had a private bathroom, and I could call my friends on our telephone. We had that radio on which I could listen to President Roosevelt and all kinds of serials, and we had a Victrola where I could play, over and over, Ella Fitzgerald's hit "A Tisket, A Tasket." I adored that song. I also liked "My Heart Belongs to Daddy," though at the time I had no idea how significant that title would soon become in my life. Outside of the house, aside from going to the movies, I enjoyed hiking in the beautiful woods around Coatesville, picking violets, blackberries, and hickory nuts, and I actually preferred the fresh creeks to any old swimming pool. I even made my own money in the summer, getting up at 4 A.M. to pick strawberries. If I filled fifty baskets, I would make a dollar, and that seemed like a fortune to me.

I joined the church at age twelve. My stepfather went to the AME Methodist Church every Sunday. Mother, like her first husband, was a member of the Bernardton Baptist Church in The Spruces, but wasn't very religious and liked to sleep late. So I went with my stepfather, at first to get out of the house, and later, because I loved singing the hymns, like "The Old Rugged Cross," "Just a Closer Walk with Thee," and "Amazing Grace." I soon joined the church myself, my mother's Baptist church, to try to get her to attend more often.

My mother, who didn't take churchgoing that seriously, was a bit surprised by my decision. How, she wondered, had I become so religious all of a sudden, and without her to inspire me? Nevertheless, she had a deep respect for the Lord. Because of her lax attendance, she wasn't sure she was "worthy" and she wasn't sure about my worthiness either, in that my conversion seemed to have come out of thin air. "You have to be ready to accept Christ," she told me. It was a major life commitment, not to be taken lightly. "I *am* ready," I answered. The Bible was all white, but so were the movies. I loved them both. The whiteness I just accepted, just like a lot of other things. Acceptance was our way of life, as there didn't seem to be much point, or hope, of trying to change the system.

The racial divide did become much more dramatic to me in the summer of 1938 because of a dreadful incident that shattered the normal calm of our town and forever changed the way I perceived Coatesville, even as a teenager, as a good and wholesome place to grow up. Helen Moore, a white teenager a little older than I was, had been walking in the woods near her South Hill neighborhood when she was attacked by a man. Coatesville didn't have that much excitement, so this was a big deal for us. The girl was unconscious. When she came to, she couldn't remember who attacked her. Everybody had a theory, everybody wanted to solve this mystery. However, within a short time the rumors started spreading that a young black man had attacked the girl and that he had raped her. Because my parents hadn't talked to me about the birds and the bees, I wasn't sure what rape was, but I had an idea, and it wasn't good.

The town went crazy over the black man, a steelworker, who was arrested and taken to the jail. Within hours, a huge mob of white people assembled on Main Street and began talking about lynching the suspect. They had guns, knives, and rope, and they meant business. There were hundreds of white men, maybe more. I remember my stepfather going a little crazy himself, though on the other side. "This ain't gonna happen again," he swore. I had no idea what the "again" meant.

My father had a brother who had a rifle that he used to shoot groundhogs, which we fried and ate. On that hot day in 1938, my stepfather and his uncle got that rifle and joined a mob of black men who went out to stop the mob of white men before they hanged the accused black man. My mother begged him not to go, warning him that he would get killed himself. I had never seen her so emotional, weeping and screaming. "Don't be a fool!" she entreated him. "They'll kill you and then they'll come kill *us*!" Suddenly I got scared, not just of losing my stepfather, but for my mother and myself as well. My mother thought I was in my room. When she saw me listening, she marched me back to my room and closed the door. Emotional outbursts were forbidden in this household, and certainly not for my eyes. So I holed up and listened to the screaming, followed by an endless silence. All I could do was shudder and pray for my family.

A few hours later, my prayers were answered. My stepfather returned with good news, which I heard that night only by eavesdropping, and later by gossiping with my friends. What I learned was that there had been a showdown on Main Street, right near the jail. It was something out of the Wild West, like I had seen in the movies. The Gary Cooper part was played by the Coatesville chief of police, a tall, brave, white man, who faced the two mobs and declared that justice had to be served and this was not the way.

What stopped everyone short was when the chief warned that Coatesville didn't need another Zack Walker. Coatesville, he said, had been the "shame of the nation." It would be even worse this time. The mere mention of the name

Zack Walker was like a magic password that somehow silenced the violent, white mob and vindicated the black one. The men all put down their weapons, and the crowds dispersed. The black prisoner was taken away to another city by the chief of police for his own protection. Within a week, another man was arrested who confessed to the rape of Helen Moore. He was white.

The "again" my stepfather had referred to got me very curious. And who was this Zack Walker? I had never heard his name mentioned before, but after this awful incident, he was all that folks in Coatesville talked about for months to come. It was the town's dark secret, and now it was out of the bag. In a way, I wish I had never known.

Zack Walker was the name of the victim of a horrible tragedy that occurred in Coatesville twenty-seven summers before, in 1911, but what happened seemed more out of Europe's Dark Ages or the worst barbarities of the Roman Empire, when Christians were fed to the lions. He was a young, black man from Virginia, who, like my family and so many other black southerners, was lured to Coatesville by the prospects of a good job and greater freedom than at home in Dixie. Like my father John Henry Washington, Zack Walker worked on the steel assembly line. His employer was Worth Brothers, later taken over by Lukens. Like my family, Zack Walker lived in The Spruces, then a shantytown for black workers. Nice houses like the one I grew up in were built in the Roaring Twenties, when the mills were at the height of their prosperity. It was a Friday in August, during the Harvest Home Festival, when Walker was walking home from a bar on Main Street. He was supposedly drunk; it wasn't at all unusual for workers, like my father, to celebrate "when the ghost walked," which was steelyard slang for getting your paycheck. Walker was carrying a gun, which, too, was not that unusual for steelworkers, especially as times then were much rougher than they were when I was a girl. Again, Coatesville wasn't Dodge City, but it wasn't that far from it.

Before he crossed the Brandywine Bridge that led across the river to The Spruces, Walker encountered two Polish steelworkers he knew from Worth Brothers, and, as a joke, fired his gun over their heads. It was all in fun—the kind of fun you might have in a steel town in 1911. However, it may not have seemed that amusing to Edgar Rice, a security guard for Worth Brothers, which stood right near the bridge. Rice, who had been a city policeman before he became a private one, may have forgotten that he was now in the private sector. Burly, powerful, and white, Rice pursued Walker across the bridge into The Spruces and tried to arrest Walker for carrying a concealed weapon. Drunk, afraid, and aware of his guilt, Walker tried to get away from Rice, but the security guard wouldn't relent. A struggle ensued. Rice drew his revolver and fired. Walker drew his own and fired back. In the end, Rice lay dead, and Walker fled to his cabin in The Spruces.

Officer Rice had been a minor local politician who had once run for constable and nearly won, despite being a Democrat in solid Republican territory. He was extremely well liked, and his death came as a terrible shock to Coatesville. When the Polish workers reported to the police that the tragedy had been ignited by Walker's firing his gun, all of Coatesville was quickly up in arms. Numerous search parties were assembled to locate and arrest the man quickly renamed "the black fiend." One of these posses, from the fire department, soon found Walker hiding in a tree. So terrified was the Virginian that he took his gun and shot himself in the face, hoping to end it all. But he failed. Instead, the badly bleeding man was taken to Coatesville Hospital, the place where I always dreamed of working at as a nurse when I grew up.

At the hospital, Walker, underwent emergency surgery. He was bandaged up like a mummy. When he awoke, he immediately admitted to police officers that, yes, he had shot Rice, but only in self-defense. Rice, acting far beyond his authority, had viciously attacked him, Walker claimed. He was simply trying to save his own life. No one in Coatesville, at least no one white, would buy Walker's alibi. The day after the shooting, August 12, in what amounted to an extension of the Harvest Home Festival, a huge lynch mob of over a thousand white men stormed the grand pillared portico of Coatesville Hospital. They smashed down the doors. Then, pushing aside nurses and orderlies too terrified to resist them, they found their way to Walker's room. To prevent any possible escape, the police had put him in a straitjacket and chained his leg to the footboard. The police at the hospital did nothing to quell the mob. None of them, though, had the key to Walker's chain. So the mob ripped off the footboard, and dragged Walker, blood gushing from his recent head surgery, down the halls and down the steep front steps of the hospital. Outside, a crowd, estimated to be 4,000—a great part of the town—cheered Walker's appearance and began chanting "Burn him! Burn him! Burn him!"

The mob then pulled Walker, his white bandages and straitjacket red with blood, nearly a mile through unpaved roads to the Newlin farm, the site of where I now lived. There they tied him to a wooden fence, created a bonfire of straw and hay, and set the man on fire. When the flame first caught, Walker begged his tormentors for mercy. He reiterated his claim of self-defense. Miraculously, he was able at one point to escape the inferno, even with the footboard still shackled to his leg. He must have seemed like a zombie and terrified the crowd. But they could not be swayed from their purpose. Someone beat him over the head with a stray fence post, and they tossed him back into the flames. Still he would not die. Apparently, he escaped a total of three times, until a group of men tied a rope around his neck and brought him back to the fire, like a lassoed steer to be branded. He once more begged them to spare his life, even though he wasn't white. In his final moments on earth, Zack Walker considered that mercy was reserved for whites, and none came for him. His pleas unanswered, the flames shot to the heavens, and Zack Walker finally died.

It was said that among the 4,000 cheering Coatesvillians were a number of blacks as well. These weren't the southern refugees, but the "old Negros," some who had been in the area since the Revolutionary War, and all who had been living there since before the Civil War. Their tenure gave them a kind of social status, a snobby thing. They looked down on the southern blacks, the "new Negroes," as low-rent interlopers in their Yankee heaven. It was one thing to resent their new neighbors, but it was still another to burn them at the stake. Something about the scene reminded me of the crucifixion of Christ, with the crowd cheering as the match was lit and the pyre ignited. This poor man was hardly Jesus, but he deserved better than this. He certainly deserved a fair trial or even an unfair one. Even witches got trials.

Soon after the near-lynching, following the rape of Helen Moore, one white boy at school proudly brought out a bone fragment that his father claimed came from the charred remains of Zachariah Walker. He showed it around as a great souvenir. I was disgusted. Apparently, the town vultures chopped up Walker's bones, his manacles, the footboard, and the rail fence to which he was bound, and sold them off at great profit.

I felt even more disgusted when I learned that the ringleaders of the murder all got off. Despite the fortune the state spent on the trials of these fifteen men, half of whom were teenagers, Coatesville juries acquitted every one of them. The only justice, if any, was a kind of divine retribution. A few months after the burning, Coatesville was stricken with its own plague, a major typhoid epidemic. Over thirty people died from contaminated drinking water, and hundreds more fell violently sick. The burning and the plague put Coatesville on the map as the American Sodom. Three decades later the blot had been forgotten, until the Moore affair unearthed Coatesville's disgraceful past.

That another black was nearly a martyr made me rethink everything about my happy youth, and the impact was especially strong in the context of being segregated for the first time. This period marked the beginning of my black consciousness. For the first time, it sunk in that being black was being different, and that white people, my friends and neighbors, could be capable of such vitriol and venom toward us. I never again felt completely secure. But despite this awful epiphany, at age thirteen I still had a youth to live and little choice as to where I lived it.

I was about to face an even greater revelation. One lovely, crisp fall day when the leaves were turning red and gold, soon after the Moore affair had shaken my world, a very beautiful woman came to visit us. My mother introduced her as her sister Carrie, and she was the most amazing woman I had ever seen. My mother seemed tall at five foot five, but Carrie towered above her by at least three or more inches. Because of this, Carrie called her sister

"Tiny." She moved and dressed like a fashion model—not that her clothes were fancy, but the way she carried herself in them was regal. She wore a plain cotton dress with a string of dime-store pearls, yet she looked as elegant as any of the rich swells in the Fred Astaire high-society films, as naturally aristocratic as Katharine Hepburn, living proof that a black woman could hold her own against any Hollywood ideals. My aunt was darker-skinned than my mother, and had thick, lustrous, wavy hair and coal-black big eyes that would light up any dark night. At thirteen, I was becoming aware of feminine beauty, and my new aunt had it in spades. I guess you might say I developed an instant crush on her.

Because she carried herself like a big-city sophisticate, I immediately presumed Aunt Carrie was visiting from New York City, which I thought was the ultimate in glamour. But she actually had just moved up north from Rock Hill, South Carolina, near my parents' home of Edgefield, which was nothing more than a name to me at the time. She was living in Chester, which was only an hour away from us. She had a seven-year-old son named Willie and was divorced from his father, who remained down south. The whole day Aunt Carrie was there, I couldn't take my eyes off her. Nor could she take her eyes off me, but I assumed it was because I kept staring at her.

I followed her into the kitchen to help prepare an early dinner before she had to take the train home. Even though I knew nothing about the South, I did know that my family always "ate southern"—fried chicken, sweet potato pie, candied yams, black-eyed peas, peach cobbler, and iced tea with enough sugar to run a confectionery. Aunt Carrie was busy making some kind of chicken salad, when she stopped what she doing and just looked at me for the longest time. I thought maybe I had done something wrong. Maybe she thought I was being too nosy, following her around the way I was. But then she gave me the sweetest smile.

"I'm your mother, you know," she said to me.

I was stunned speechless.

"Did you know?" she pressed me.

"No, ma'am," was all I could say.

"Let me give you a big kiss, Essie Mae," she said to me.

My eyes became riveted to the floor, my body paralyzed from moving an inch.

"Don't be afraid of me." She opened her arms in a huge embrace.

"No, ma'am."

"Don't you 'no ma'am' me, child. You're my daughter, my big, beautiful daughter," she said, and walked over and enveloped me in her embrace. It was the strangest moment of my life so far. It also may have been the happiest.

I was deeply confused. If this was my mother, what about . . . my real mother . . . her sister? I felt like I was on the quiz show *To Tell the Truth*: Will Essie Mae's real mother please stand up? Was this a joke? My people weren't jokesters. It was too late for April Fool's, yet I surely felt like one. And yet I was so taken with this new woman, too taken for it to be anything like a normal infatuation. Blood, mother's blood, had to be at work here. Aunt Carrie—I wasn't sure *what* to call her now—sensed my utter and complete confusion.

"This is awful to do to you," she apologized, "but I love you too much to keep my mouth shut. I just had to see you."

"But why . . . ," I stammered. "What happened?" I had always thought my parents had me back in South Carolina, then moved up to Coatesville when I was just a baby. I liked putting "Aiken, South Carolina" down as my birthplace whenever I had to fill in any papers. I had no idea where Aiken was and barely where South Carolina was, other than that it was a good place to get out of, at least for our people. It sounded exotic, and I liked that. But now talk about exotic. Here was a woman, the most beautiful woman on earth, who was claiming to be my mother. Assuming it was true, how special did that make me?

At this point my mother (that is, the woman who had been my mother until a few moments ago) entered the kitchen and saw the look on my face.

"Carrie! You didn't . . . did you?"

"I did, Tiny. I just couldn't keep it to myself. I'm so sorry."

"Well, the cat's out of the bag now, isn't it?" Mary said with a sigh of resignation.

"Tiny, you tell her," Carrie said, as if she required her sister's testimony to validate her actions at the time of my birth, behavior of which she was now ashamed.

"Your mother was quite young when you were born," said Mary, who was four years older.

"How old?" I blurted out, curious beyond the bounds of discreet behavior.

"She was sixteen," Mary answered, for Carrie was abashed into silence. "She had to work, and she wanted to finish high school, and she just wasn't ready to raise a child."

Sixteen, I marveled. I was thirteen. My mother had me when she was just three years older than I was. I couldn't imagine having a baby. I hadn't even had a date with a boy. I was even more mystified and awed by my mother's "sophistication."

"I couldn't care for you properly, baby," Carrie explained in a voice full of apology and remorse. "First I put you up with friends, but I felt more secure about you with kin than I did with anyone else. Thank the Lord, Tiny came though for us."

The story began to unfold. Carrie put me in the care of her sister, who was moving up north with her husband to a much better life than anything I might have had back in South Carolina. It was a giant sacrifice, Carrie said, but it was all about my welfare. Children were often "farmed out" like this among black families, Mary told me. It simply wasn't talked about. "Forget the birth and follow the love," Mary explained. I had never felt anything but love, pure maternal love from Mary, so I had no reason to doubt her. And now I had double the love, which was seemingly a good thing. But having two mothers did create some big logistical issues. Whom was I going to live with?

I slumped into a chair at the kitchen table. Carrie fortified me with iced tea, while Mary gave me a warm hug, as if to reassure me that she hadn't forsaken me. I had started to worry that Carrie would take me away to Chester, that my whole world was about to be turned upside down. After the near-lynching episode, I was disillusioned with Coatesville, but it was nonetheless my known world. I wasn't ready to leave it, even to be with this wonderful new creature that had just swept into my life.

As it turned out, I didn't have to worry. Carrie swept out of my life as quickly as she had swept into it. She had to get back to Chester, she explained, to take care of her family. There was no discussion of when I would go to visit them, if at all. Instead, all she said was, "See you soon, baby," with the implication that she would be coming to Coatesville, not I to Chester. Carrie kissed me goodbye on the lips. Mary had never kissed me on the lips, and there was something extremely voluptuous about the affection. I loved Carrie madly.

Only when she was gone did it hit me that I now had no idea who my real father was. It obviously wasn't the departed John Henry Washington. It wasn't my stepfather, to whom I could only get so close. I was intrigued by the notion of having a real father, someone I *could* get close to. Was it Carrie's ex down in South Carolina? I definitely had a need, but I was too young, too scared, and too conditioned at this point to ask any more questions. All I could do was sit back and see what the future would bring.

Nineteen thirty-eight had left me deeply insecure about both my community and my family. I had thought Coatesville was an all-American city, but if that was true, I wasn't at all comfortable about what America stood for. Likewise, I had thought my family was all-American as well, and that I was a pretty regular girl. Now I felt there was nothing regular about me at all, certainly not how I came into the world. At the time, I had absolutely no idea how unusual the circumstances of my birth would turn out to be.

CHAPTER TWO
Southern Exposure

IT WAS SIX MONTHS before I saw Carrie again, and it may have been the longest six months of my life. When I'd ask Mary about her sister, she'd dismiss my questions with a curt "She's living her life." I got the impression that Mary was feeling like a second-class parent. She could see how taken I was with Carrie, and that may have hurt her feelings, though it certainly wasn't my intention. "She may be your mother," Mary said to me one day in exasperation at my low mood, "but I'm the one who does the motherin'."

The next time Carrie came for a Sunday visit, she brought her cute, young son. While the boy was at the age where he needed his mother, I couldn't help being jealous that she seemed to pay more attention to little Willie than she did to me. I still wasn't sure whether Willie was my brother or my half-brother. If Carrie's husband James were my real father, he would have come up north to visit me. Wouldn't he? I tried to put my questions about my father's identity out of my head. There were already too many men in my life, and I hadn't even gone on my first date.

When Carrie went home that Sunday and kissed me on the cheek rather than my lips, as before, I felt rejected and frustrated. I went up to my room and put my Ella Fitzgerald record on the phonograph to drown out my tears. I cried myself to sleep. One of my biggest problems was that I had no one to talk to about my situation. Mary was too involved in the situation, and her own feelings were too sensitive. My stepfather wasn't the talkative type, and he didn't seem to be that involved. I would have loved to talk to John Henry Washington, who I had heretofore assumed was my father. He would have known everything, but that man was long gone.

As for my friends, for a long while I dared not say a word. I was ashamed of the whole situation. After the lynching disaster, I became very conscious of how black people were perceived. Drunken fathers who left their families, irresponsible mothers who abandoned their children, endless promiscuity—these were the negative stereotypes I picked up, and stereotypes I hated to hear. Yet here in my seemingly proper, all-American family were those same stereotypes come to life. These were secrets I was too mortified to share with anyone.

Finally, I did break the ice with a friend named Elizabeth Kennedy. Elizabeth was living with her grandmother. Her mother lived in Philadelphia, where she was able to find a better job than what was available in Coatesville. Elizabeth never saw her, and it didn't bother her a bit. "I've been treated so well by my grandmother, I have nothing to be dissatisfied about," Elizabeth said. Her attitude emboldened me to talk to her, and only her, about my two mothers. "There are a lot of broken homes around here," she tried to console me. "It's *normal* for us for your parent to be gone. It's not a bad thing. It's the standard thing. Remember, you're not alone."

Elizabeth wasn't miserable, but I still was—because I yearned to know my new mother. She had abandoned me once when I was little but I hadn't known it at the time. Now her second abandonment stung. The only salvation for me was to immerse myself in high school. After that one year of segregated junior high, I came back to a fully integrated high school, Scott High. The student body was fully integrated, but not the all-white faculty. That was yet another jarring experience after having only black teachers in the junior high. I missed those black teachers, most of whom had seemed far more interested in their students than the white teachers were.

Perhaps the white teachers were more involved with their white students, because they were far more likely to go to college than the blacks were. Hardly any of my black friends had hopes of going on to any higher education. One black boy, a few years older than I, got a scholarship to Penn State and was considered a local hero. I made excellent grades, mostly A's and a few B's, and was always on the honor roll. Yet no teacher or guidance counselor ever called me in to encourage me to go further with my schooling. So I encouraged myself and never lost sight of my ambition to go into nursing. The white friends I had in elementary school seemed to drift away at Scott High. That one year apart seemed to have forever separated us. We might have shared the same classes, but we never sat together in the lunchroom, and I was rarely invited to a white classmate's home as I often had been as a little girl.

I had my first boyfriend in high school, a tall, handsome football star named George Taylor, who was so proper and formal that he invariably wore a white shirt and necktie to school, which was unusual for people that age. Unfortunately, he dropped out of school in the tenth grade and joined the army, cutting short any possibilities of romance. A little heartbroken, I thereafter tried to stick to my books. There were a number of black players like George on the Scott High sports teams. That made it all the harder to understand why there could be no black cheerleaders. My best friend, May Ouzts, who was black but had a strange German name that was impossible both to spell and to pronounce, simply couldn't accept the restriction. If the male teams could be "mixed," which was our term for integrated, why couldn't the female cheering squad? May railed her complaint to anyone who would listen.

"We're sending you girls to school to get an education, not to be cheerleaders," May's father had told her. But May was a natural-born protester, ahead of her time. Her next stop was the high school administration. I'll never forget what Assistant Principal Muthard told May: "You girls can't be cheerleaders because you people don't have *bouncy hair*." May and I have laughed about that comment for the last sixty years.

Ever the challenger of rules, May found a black girl who happened to have very straight, thick, "bouncy hair," and encouraged her to apply for the cheerleading squad. Hair notwithstanding, she was also rejected. May went on to complain to our gym teacher, Miss Toomey, who could only laugh. "Don't go trying to change the world," she advised us. "Do your cheering in the stands. And be glad you can go there." After all, there were plenty of places that were off-limits to us in Coatesville, such as Ash Park, the city's main public recreational ground. The police would run us out, but prodded by May, we would often sneak in after dusk, just for the sheer devilment of it.

It was hard to comprehend what it would be like for us growing up in a place like South Carolina. Just that year, at the premiere of *Gone with the Wind* in Atlanta, Hattie McDaniel, who would win an Academy Award for her role in the picture, was not allowed into the theater for the film's world premiere. We might have been relegated to the back seats at the Palace, but at least we blacks in Coatesville could see Clark Gable kiss Vivien Leigh. More than a few of us wished we could be in his arms. Although people like Miss Tully probably thought that all black girls should identify with McDaniel's Mammy character, most of us secretly wanted to be Scarlett O'Hara, a subversive ambition in Coatesville or anywhere else in America.

I still couldn't get the deep mysteries surrounding my mother, Carrie, out of my mind. Imagine the joy I felt at the end of the school year, when Mary told me that Carrie had invited me to Chester to spend a month with her that summer. Carrie was looking after Willie all by herself and wanted me to help. So off I went on the Pennsylvania Railroad to Chester, for the biggest ride of my life thus far.

Chester, which was just outside of Philadelphia, was a much bigger city than Coatesville. There was lots of traffic, lots of neon, lots of black people who looked like they had fancier jobs than working at steel mills. Carrie lived in a tiny row house that did have its own bathroom, though not much more. She did housework for a living; even at those low wages, she didn't seem to lack money. Nor did she seem to want a new husband. She never talked about her ex or any men, good or bad. Men looked at her on the street, white men and black, and she'd smile back and make their day. Yet the entire summer I was there, she never went on a date.

Carrie was a remarkably good mother to Willie, maybe to make up for having abandoned me. She was with him constantly, never leaving him alone.

She was a magnificent cook, even better than her sister, especially when it came to desserts. Her triumph was a three-layer coconut-pineapple cake. We made that cake one evening and devoured every bit of it in one sitting. How she kept her beautiful figure, I'll never know, as I was getting slightly plump off her good meals. On Sundays, Carrie, Willie, and I would go to church with two more of my aunts who had moved to Pennsylvania from Edgefield. What a huge family I came from, and they all seemed to have fled the South. Carrie was much more religious than Mary, even more than my stepfather. She belonged to a Pentecostal Holiness Church, where the congregation would shout and testify in the style of the old revival meetings. It scared me at first how possessed my mother would become. I was used to my stepfather's relatively reserved Methodist ceremony, singing hymns, saying prayers, hearing a thoughtful sermon of life lessons, then going for the church social of ham and chicken and cake. The Pentecostals were primitive true believers, and Carrie was devout—although once we left the church, she never mentioned Jesus or religion at all. Stepping inside to services seemed to put her in a trance.

The same woman who would get lost in her faith could also get lost in the secular world. Carrie took Willie and me into Philadelphia several times. It was the first time I had been there or in any big city, and I was amazed. We went to see the Liberty Bell, Independence Hall, the Betsy Ross House, and other cradles of American civilization. In light of what happened to Zack Walker in Coatesville, these shrines left me a little cold. It seemed like someone else's country, a little less mine. That bit of knowledge was a dangerous thing, in that it was making me less patriotic than I should have been. And I wasn't really thinking about slavery. That subject had yet to come up in my life. It had never been discussed at home. I knew about the Civil War, but not much. But I knew about Zack Walker, and that was enough to disillusion me.

Carrie pushed me to pay attention. The world was going through some crazy times, with the rise of Adolf Hitler and his invasion of the Low Countries. He had just taken Paris. War was in the air. If anyone was an enemy of black people it was Hitler, with his Aryan "Master Race" theories. I remember how depressed my stepfather was when Joe Louis lost his boxing match to the German champ Max Schmeling, and how elated he'd been the next year when Louis beat the German in a rematch. He saw it as a battle of the races, black versus white, good versus evil. That victory, he said, did more for black people than anything Abraham Lincoln or Booker T. Washington ever did. Now I know he was carried away, but that's how symbolic that fight was in the tense prewar times.

As a teenager, the idea of world war seemed like something in the movies, but Carrie tried to give me some perspective on it. She knew a lot about politics and loved Franklin Roosevelt and anything Democratic. She was sure Roosevelt was going to save the world and wanted me to appreciate our democracy, which had started here in Philadelphia. "It's not *ours*, it's *theirs*" was what I wanted to say, but I didn't want to be negative to my peppy mother. Somehow she felt very entitled as an American, more so than I did, and more so than I thought any black person who knew the score would. She urged me to learn history, though she did say once that history up north was different from history down south. It took a few years for me to understand what she meant by that.

History was interesting, and a trip to the zoo was great, but shopping was better. Carrie took us to John Wannamaker's, which had to be the biggest store in the world, with floor after floor of treasures. I hadn't been on an escalator before, and Willie and I couldn't stop riding up and down. Carrie loved trying on clothes, and unlike our one nice ladies' store in Coatesville, the Parisian Dress Shop, where the Jewish owners would sell to blacks but wouldn't let us try on the merchandise, at John Wannamaker, the salesgirls just doted on my mother. They told her how fabulous she looked in everything, which was true. Even when she didn't buy anything, they treated her with such courtesy. "They say the customer is always right, honey. That's the way it ought to be," she told me. The biggest treat of all was when Carrie bought me a red silk dress with a hat to match and black patent leather shoes. I never felt grown up before that. My mother made a woman out of me.

At the same time, she made a child, her child, out of me as well. For me, the best part of our summer was sleeping in the bed with my mother. She would cradle me in her arms and kiss me like a baby, and she made me feel like one. I realized then that I had never before felt like anyone's baby, and I loved the feeling of being adored by a mother, a real mother. She told me how beautiful I was. "No one has ever told me that," I said.

"That's 'cause you've never been with your mother."

"I'll never be as beautiful as you," I told her, in total sincerity.

"You already are. Look at that skin of yours."

"What's so special about that?" I asked. "Yours is a lot softer," I said, stroking her arms.

"Yours is a beautiful color. You're so fair complected."

"Is that good?" I wondered, and she gave me a look that said, "What kind of crazy question is that?" It was true. My friends never complimented others on the beauty of their dark skin, only light. Those were the days before black was beautiful.

I held my arm up next to hers. I was many shades lighter. I hoped doing that might get her talking about my father, whoever he was, and how I got to be the way I was. But she didn't. Despite our closeness, I was still too much Mary's child to open my mouth and ask probing questions about Carrie's past. This relationship was too new, too shaky, too ephemeral. You could get in trouble by asking questions. That was Mary's warning, and I heeded it. I didn't want to risk breaking the magic spell I was under with my new mother. I didn't want to risk ever losing her again. So I just let her hug me and kiss me and love me, and that was all I could ever ask for.

"Boys are gonna go for you in a big way," she flattered me.

"I don't know about that," I squirmed, "I've got no use for boys."

"You will." She never lectured me, though, about the facts of life. Her deep religiousness seemed to overwhelm her extreme attractiveness. The way men looked at her, the way they were drawn to her beauty, she could have easily been a femme fatale, a sex goddess. But she wasn't, and was actually very prudish, never talking about men or sex or anything the scandal magazines like *Confidential* that you would see on the newsstands would feature in their headlines.

I knew after our month together that my relationship could never be the same with Mary again, and so did Carrie. But I still never called Carrie mother, nor Mary when I came back home. It didn't seem fair to either, so I excised the M-word from my vocabulary. It was hard to speak without it, but harder to speak with it. Somehow I managed.

Back in Coatesville, all I could think about was escaping. It was a matter of how're you gonna keep 'em down on the farm after they've seen Paris—or Philadelphia, in my case. To facilitate my escape I began to work as a nurse's aide during the rest of the summer at Coatesville Hospital. I felt very honored to have been chosen for this job, for there were no black nurses in the hospital, and I was the first black woman to have an aide position. Coatesville Hospital was the place where Zack Walker was dragged from his bed, footboard and all, to his fiery doom. Hence, there were some negative associations with the place. But I chose to go with the positive ones: I was bringing change to a place that needed it, and this job would be a wonderful resume item when I was ready to seek work in the world outside.

Coatesville Hospital was a very snooty place. The administration was resented in our black community because of the way they'd treated our one black physician, a wonderful man named Dr. Atkinson. Dr. Atkinson was from Georgia and was so light-skinned he could have easily passed for white. But he had no interest in social climbing, only in helping sick people, and Coatesville Hospital denied him their facilities to do so. I later would learn about the Hippocratic Oath, which Coatesville Hospital obviously suspended when it came to black patients, whom it would treat only in welfare wards, never in private rooms, and only by white doctors. All the blacks in Coatesville got together to build Dr. Atkinson his own clinic, by giving a series of chicken dinner fund-raisers. The result was a beautiful private hospital in a mansion on Chestnut Street, the fanciest street in town. Dr. Atkinson was the only black on that street, but the best testimonial to him of all was that he had a lot of white patients.

Dr. Atkinson's achievement gave me hopes for a nursing career in New York City. My aide job at Coatesville Hospital was the first step on what I knew would be a long road. To me it was a giant step. I earned the princely sum of twelve dollars a week and was issued a white uniform and white lace-up shoes. My jobs were to bathe patients and serve trays of food. My most indelible memory of the hospital was its ringing bells. Every patient had a bell, and every one seemed to be pressing it at the same time. I was thus always on my toes, answering one request or another. It made me feel important to be needed.

Despite the absence of black doctors and nurses, there were plenty of black patients, and I could tell they were happy to see me, a friendly face. My only friends at the hospital were the kitchen's black head cook and another outsider, a young Amish nurse named Hilda, who invited me to her family's home in Lancaster many times. Hilda was the kindest, most color-blind white person I had ever met. She turned around a lot of the negativity my exposure to Coatesville's secret shame over Zack Walker had engendered.

Back in junior high school, I found a teacher who cared a great deal about me. Ernest Warren, who taught music, sent me to a clinic for my eyes. He noticed that there was something wrong with way I always sat in the front row and still had a hard time seeing the blackboard. He asked me what kind of light I studied by. I told him by the streetlight outside my window. "Who do you think you are? Beethoven?" the music teacher scolded me and then kindly explained his reference to Beethoven's "Moonlight Sonata." It wasn't that I didn't have a lamp, but Mary made me go to bed at nine. Because I loved my studies, I wanted to keep reading, but I didn't want to get into trouble so I read by the streetlight.

Mr. Warren sent me to an eye clinic, where I was prescribed a hideous pair of round metal glasses. The moment I put them on, once I got over the shock of my appearance, I loved them. All of a sudden, I could see. I must have been nearly blind before, but I had no idea. Besides, I wasn't a complainer. When Mr. Warren asked me why I never went to the doctor, I explained Mary's philosophy about doctors: You went to the doctor only if you were miserably sick, at death's door. Otherwise, you took baking soda. He laughed. That man was my savior because he literally opened up the world for me.

I'm glad I had those glasses, because they enabled me to see South Carolina when I finally got my chance. After our summer together, Carrie, who was a bundle of energy, would come to see us nearly once a month, bringing Willie with her. She would always give me a treat, like taking me to the Parisian Dress Shop to buy me clothes or going with me to the Rocky Springs Recreation Park, an amusement park where they had a ride called the Jack Rabbit that always gave me a thrill. Once she gave me an even bigger one by taking me up for a ride in an airplane that cost her one dollar for half an hour. But my biggest thrill came when she and Mary, my two mothers, took me with them down to their birthplace in Edgefield. One of their beloved sisters had died. They wanted to go home to her funeral, and they decided it was time to show me where I had come from.

The four of us, Carrie, Mary, Willie, and I all assembled in Chester to go to the Pennsylvania Station in Philadelphia, where we would take the train down south. The station was like a great ancient temple, with soaring columns and brilliant shafts of sunlight streaming through the windows hundreds of feet above the bustling station floor. We were all dressed up, for in those days traveling was a special experience that demanded respect. The public address speaker called out the names of wonderful, exotic places I had never been to: New York, Boston, Cleveland, Chicago, Richmond, Savannah, Miami, Trenton, Rahway, and Albany. Crisply dressed black redcaps carried the fine leather bags of glamorous white people, women in silks, men in striped suits. It was all so grand; I felt I was at the gates of heaven.

The first part of the trip was very elegant, as we sat in a parlor car with those dapper, white people and the equally dapper and crisp black porters and conductors who served us all and watched the world go by, the big stone mansions of Philadelphia, the Chesapeake Bay at Baltimore, the huge white government buildings of Washington, D.C. We caught a quick, fleeting glimpse of the white marble temple that Carrie, our history expert, told us was the Lincoln Memorial. "Our friend who delivered us from evil," she said, quoting the scriptures as she often did. What I knew about Lincoln from school was that he had freed the slaves, won the Civil War, and been shot for doing so. He had to have been a wonderful man, I thought, considering the tomb they put up for him.

I soon came to wonder about Lincoln's legacy when we changed trains at Union Station. After the fancy parlor car we had started in, our new accommodations, to which we were herded, felt more like a cattle car. There were only blacks in these tattered seats. Half the windows wouldn't open, and the fans didn't work. It smelled awful. I was hungry and wanted a snack, but Carrie held me back. "This is a *southern* train," she said, meaning that blacks were segregated in the worst cars and weren't allowed in the dining car. Eventually, a black porter came through with a cart selling soft drinks and sandwiches, which we ate in our hot seats. Life wasn't fair, I thought, but I was far too excited to complain. I was on a trip, the first big trip of my life. So I was one lucky girl just to have any seat on this magical train. The whole journey reminded me of the song "Chattanooga Choo Choo," which was a big hit that year for Glenn Miller. I knew the words from the radio: "Nothing could be finer, when you're in the diner, than to have your ham and eggs in Carolina." This was *almost* like that, except we couldn't go into the diner. Well, nothing was perfect.

The train's first stop was Richmond, which Carrie pointed out had been the capital of the Confederacy, and near Appomattox, where Robert E. Lee surrendered to Ulysses S. Grant. I liked the ring and rhythm of those names. They sounded like warriors, though I didn't have an idea, aside from the notion of blue versus gray, exactly what they were fighting about. It made me look forward to the American history class we had the next school year. From the train Richmond didn't look that different from Philadelphia—lots of grand buildings with columns. Philadelphia was the Cradle of Liberty; Richmond, I guessed, was the Cradle of Slavery. Apropos of slavery, what I did notice was a lot of very sad looking black men just lolling about on benches at the train station. "What are they doing?" I asked.

"Just what you see. Nothing," Mary answered. "Waitin' to come north, where they can get a job."

As the train passed through the endless Virginia tobacco fields, I saw more and more scenes of these unemployed black men sitting aimlessly at all the whistlestop stations, with absolutely nothing to do. We didn't have scenes like that in Coatesville. All the men were at the mills working, busy doing *something*. The South seemed lazy and sleepy, I commented. "That's the nice part," Mary said.

Virginia gave way to the rolling hills of North Carolina and still more tobacco fields. "What's the difference between North Carolina and South Carolina?" I asked.

Carrie had a quick answer. "They call North Carolina the valley of humility between two mountains of conceit. The mountains are South Carolina and Virginia."

"Speak English, girl," Mary told her sister. "Where'd you get that stuff?" I was confused, too.

Carrie explained. "South Carolina and Virginia are both a lot fancier than North Carolina, at least they were until the war. They were full of big plantations and rich people. Because of all these hills we're looking at, North Carolina was divided up into a lot more farms. It was a state of small farmers, not big planters, so it didn't put on airs like the other two. And now North Carolina's a lot better off than South Carolina. Because those small farmers didn't have that much to lose and knew how to take care of themselves after the war, but the big planters in South Carolina had no idea what to do without us."

"Us?" I asked.

"The slaves."

I never thought about myself as a slave, or a descendant of slaves, but, as I said, this trip would open my eyes. "How do you know so much?" I asked Carrie.

"I had a wonderful teacher," she said.

"In high school?"

"Here and there," was all she would say. That cryptic answer would soon take on a whole new meaning.

The train reached Columbia very early in the morning after an all-night ride. We had been riding in that coach for over fifteen hours, and I had been too excited to sleep. The song went "Nothing could be finer than to be in Carolina in the morning," and I couldn't have agreed more. It was great to get off that train and smell the sweet magnolias, honeysuckle, and orange blossoms in the air. We took a cab to the bus station to transfer to Edgefield. Carrie, ever the historian, told us how General Sherman burned Columbia down on his bloody march from Atlanta to the sea.

"Why would he burn a whole city down?" I asked.

"To teach the rich folks a lesson," Carrie answered.

Columbia, the state capital, didn't look at all like it had been burned, or if it had, it was perfectly rebuilt. There were broad boulevards with huge plantation-style houses, with double-deck front porches and endless gardens. We passed the majestic state capitol, which was every bit as impressive as what I had glimpsed in Washington, D.C. Carrie pointed out a gray, stars-and-bars flag in front of the state house, flying next to Old Glory.

"That's the Confederate flag," she noted.

"Why do they let them fly it? Didn't they lose?" I asked.

"Not in *their* minds," Carrie said with a rueful laugh. "They sure love that war down here."

At the bus station, full of more sleeping black men, I was struck by the signs for two separate waiting rooms: White and Colored. Obviously, the colored room was shabby and crowded, the white room plush and empty. Thirsty, I was disappointed to find that the colored water fountain barely worked, and that the water wasn't refrigerated. Nobody was at the white fountain in that empty room, but Mary's look told me I dare not push my luck. We caught a rickety bus to Edgefield. I had plopped down with exhaustion in the first seat I could find, but Mary yanked me out of it as if it were wired with a bomb that could explode. I guess in a sense it was.

"You can't sit there," she snapped at me.

"Why not? It's empty," I replied.

Mary gave me a look of warning. "Don't be asking stupid questions," she ordered me, and I followed her to the rear.

On the hour ride to Edgefield, through rich cotton fields and peach orchards, Carrie explained to me about the segregation laws in the South. "They think we're still slaves," she said. "They can't seem to get over that we're not."

"That was eighty years ago. They lost."

"Stop saying they lost. They may have lost up where we live now, but down here they think things are the same. They think they won. And look around, child. Maybe they did."

"They must be weird people," I marveled, staring out the bus window at the decrepit cabins in the cotton fields where "our people" lived. They made the worst shacks in The Spruces look like the White House by comparison.

"It's so poor down here," Carrie said. "That's why we all left."

The bus sputtered into Edgefield. "What a dump" was my first impression. It was a tiny village of two-story stores centering around a square dominated by a tall obelisk. As there was no bus station, we were let out at the square. More silent, sad black men were standing around in the shade. None, however, were sitting on the benches in the square. A Confederate flag was flying, but not an American one. I looked more closely at the obelisk. It was the "Monument to the Confederate Dead, Erected by the Women of Edgefield County." Behind it stood a big building, the Edgefield County Courthouse, that did have a small American flag next to a larger Confederate flag. Across the way was the Edgefield Baptist Association. Aside from a small hotel seemingly misnamed the Plantation House (flying still another Confederate flag), the rest of the square was devoted to business. The store names didn't advertise their content, such as Ace Hardware or Magnolia Tool and Dye, but rather they announced the name of the proprietor. Strangely, most of the nearby stores seemed to have foreign-sounding names over their doorways: Jacob Rubenstein, Bully Rubenstein, Jonah Goldberg, Abram Daitch, Jacob Alstock, Israel Mukashy.

"Jews," Carrie said. "They have all the stores."

I thought we had a lot of Jewish merchants in Coatesville, but I never expected there to be so many in this distant outpost of civilization. "Here?" I sounded surprised.

"There's a lot of money in this little town," Carrie said. "Isn't that so, Tiny?"

"But not for us."

I was amazed that this little town had sent so many people up to Pennsylvania. Who could be left? Why would anyone stay? The only redeeming aspect of the place were the trees and flowers, all in bloom. The little hamlet smelled like the perfume counters of John Wannamaker. Otherwise, this was Nowhere, USA. Or Nowhere, United States of the Confederacy, as was more the case.

There were no taxis. There were no people, so how could there be? Carrying our suitcases, we walked down a long road called Buncombe Street toward where our relatives lived. We passed a grand, brick Baptist church, which seemed out of place for this hamlet, as well as a lovely stone Catholic church. Then the mansions began, and I suddenly became impressed. Carrie was right. There was a lot of money here in Nowhere. They all looked like Tara in *Gone with the Wind*, great plantation houses on tall sloping hills. Most of the houses were gleaming white, as if they had just been painted. Finally, I saw men at work, black men, gardening, planting, tending these imposing houses.

"Nine governors of this state came from this tiny town," Carrie said proudly, as if she could identify and draw sustenance from the statistic. "Leaders are born here."

"So they say," Mary added.

"Hush your mouth, Tiny. You were born here."

"Well, I left, and I don't miss it."

"I think it's nice to be home."

"Well, you would."

We walked on through the spring beauty of the place. One house was more dramatic than the rest, each a variation on the theme of a Greek temple, vast columns, vast porches, vast lawns. "Is everyone here a millionaire?" I blurted out.

"Nine governors," Carrie repeated her point.

"And 90,000 slaves," Mary made her own.

"That's the house of the man who started the Civil War," Carrie noted, pointing out another white temple on a high hill in the distance.

"Brookses," Mary added. "Bunch of hotheads."

"Did he kill Abraham Lincoln?"

Carrie broke out laughing. "What do they teach you in Coatesville, child? Lincoln was killed after the war was over."

"Next year we have a course."

"I hope so." Then Carrie gave me one of her little history lessons. "Preston Brooks was this rich cotton planter and war hero who was Edgefield's man in Congress. Big slave owner. He hated the Yankees, felt they were jealous of all he and his people had down here. The one he despised the most was the big Yankee Senator from Massachusetts, Charles Sumner, the chief antislavery man. Sumner knew it was wrong and wasn't afraid to say it. So one day Brooks went into the Senate and took his walking cane and beat Sumner near to death, right on the floor of the Capitol. Claimed he insulted South Carolina, so he nearly killed him. And he got away with it. Made him a hero down here. He was the king of this town."

"But how did it start the war?"

"Because it drew the line. It showed the southerners were ready to fight over this thing, fight and kill and stand up for their 'honor' . . ."

"Their honor," Mary sneered, "our backs."

"Preston Brooks drew that line and crossed it. After that the North hated the South and the South hated the North, and it was just a matter of time 'til it all blew up."

I was so impressed with how much my mother knew. Maybe the high school she went to down here was better than mine. Looking at the gracious mansions and all the black gardeners, I could see how the northerners might be both jealous and offended at the same time. I myself was offended when we turned off Buncombe Street onto a smaller road named Brooks Street after the senatorial assailant himself. If Buncombe Street was the façade of a Hollywood stage set, Old Buncombe, as this area was known, was the hard reality behind the glamorous façade.

Old Buncombe, which quickly descended from the high ground of the Greek temples into a steep gully, was a desperate shantytown of the kinds of unpainted wooden shacks and outhouses like the ones I had noticed with pity from the train. How could people live in such squalor? I wondered. I was about to learn firsthand, because the people who lived in these shacks were *my* people.

"This is it," my mother said.

"It" was a letdown, to say the least—a crumbling, unpainted wooden shack. A large woman wearing a headscarf like the one Mary wore around the house stepped off the porch to greet us.

"Well, I'll be," the woman said, giving me a big hug. "Come here, baby. It's been a long time. Come to your Aunt Bertha."

She hugged me, then Willie. Mary introduced us to this woman who was the sister of my two mothers, but who looked nothing like them. She was a country lady; they were city girls. The thought crossed my mind that maybe they might have gained weight and looked like her if they had remained down here.

Bertha, a Paul Bunyan of a woman, seemed to pick up all our bags at once and bring them into the house. At first glance, it seemed even more depressing inside than out, a dank cavelike single room subdivided with hanging sheets to create some cubicles where we might have privacy. There was no electricity, no running water, no phone, nothing. I thought how lucky I was back in the luxury of my home in Coatesville. As my eyes adjusted to the dark, however, I did see some amazing tattered antiques, big brass beds, a love seat, and some cracked gilt mirrors. They looked like ancient hand-me-downs from the mansions on the hill.

Bertha filled this shack with a spirit that took my mind off the surroundings. Like her sisters, she was a great cook, and she began feeding us cakes she had baked for us, which distracted me from the surroundings. That night we all huddled around an old wood-burning stove for warmth, as it got cold in that damp, wooded area behind the rich folks' homes. It was like camping out. As I had never camped out overnight before, I decided to be positive about the whole experience and look at it not as hardship but as an adventure. I did feel sorry for Bertha, though, and wished there were some way to get her to move up north with us.

As bleak as our surroundings were, the food was wonderful. We ate endlessly from that big stove: fried chicken, pickled collard greens, steaming fluffy biscuits with melting butter, my first taste of hush puppies, which were fried balls of corn meal designed to throw to the hounds to keep them quiet. They sure shut me up. I also tried Brunswick stew, which was made with squirrel meat. Since I had eaten groundhog in Coatesville, I wasn't too put off by the squirrel, but tried to pretend it was chicken. It was actually delicious and took our minds off the lack of other creature comforts.

The next day, we got all dressed up to go to my aunt's funeral—the very first funeral I'd ever attended—in a Baptist church further down the road. The building wasn't much more than a barn, but the spirit was like a glorious cathedral. Hundreds of people were there, all in their finest clothes, which, like their homes, were rather threadbare. Yet they had dignity, and what singers they all were. The hymns, which I loved to sing, were divine, but the part I couldn't handle was the open casket. I had never seen a dead person before and was afraid to get too close. Mary said I had to go pay my respects, despite not knowing my late aunt. So I walked up there and tried not to look. I still had nightmares about it for weeks afterward.

After the funeral all we did was eat, going to one house after another in Old Buncombe to meet with friends and relatives. All the neighbors would bring covered dishes as a show of respect, and we showed our respect by eating every bit of them. The day after the funeral, Carrie woke me up from a bad dream I was having about my deceased aunt's casket. "You've got to get up and get dressed," she told me in a whisper as to not disturb the others, who were sleeping. "And look 'specially nice."

I noticed through my bleary eyes how pretty my mother looked. She was all dressed up in a lovely frock, with pearls and earrings. I assumed we were going back to church for more services, but what my mother had on didn't strike me as mourning attire. She picked my nicest dress out of my suitcase, combed out my hair, and told me to put on makeup. "Too much lipstick," she scolded me, wiping some off. At sixteen, I wasn't very good in this department. I redid my lips, wanting desperately to please her. She was so beautiful, I felt I could never compare with her, no matter how hard I tried. I couldn't keep my eyes off of her. She was still a mystery woman to me.

I thought I was all ready, but my mother decided she didn't like the dress after all. "Too sad," she said.

"But aren't funerals supposed to be sad?"

"This isn't a funeral, darling," she said with that enigmatic laugh of hers. "I'm taking you to meet your father."

My heart started racing. In the three years we had known each other, the identity of my "real" father had never been discussed. Now was the moment of truth, and I was scared to death.

We walked up the steep hills of Old Buncombe to the paradise of Buncombe Street. The shacks were all quiet. The black world was sleeping. I kept wondering when my mother would turn so that I could meet my fate. At first I thought it might be one of the big white-columned mansions where this mystery man might be working as a butler to some rich family. But we kept walking down that dusty, oak-shaded road, straight into downtown. Maybe he was a barber or a porter in the Plantation House hotel, I thought, but we passed those establishments as well. I didn't dare ask my mother. I knew she wanted to surprise me, and she was doing a good job.

The men in the street seemed to notice and admire my mother, with her pretty clothes and that graceful way she moved. All of those men were black, working in yards, painting buildings, smoking cigarettes outside of the general stores. I suppose the South Carolina heat was too much for the white folks, whom I rarely saw outside. In any event, none of these men turned out to be my father.

Finally, we arrived at a one-story white building that housed a law office. Thurmond and Thurmond, Attorneys at Law, the sign said. That was it. My new daddy was a driver for a big-shot lawyer. We went up the steps and knocked on the door. A black servant in a white coat opened the door. I wanted to throw my arms around him, but he just looked at me blankly. Then he showed us into a grand office, stocked floor to ceiling with law books and diplomas, where my mother and I were left to stand alone in silence. My heart was pounding so hard I feared it might be audible. A few moments passed, and then a fair, handsome man entered the room—a little nervously, I thought, as he tipped over a standing ashtray. He wore a light blue suit and tie and looked every inch the lord of a plantation. He gazed at my mother a long time, then stared at me even longer. Finally, his stone face broke into a smile. "You have a lovely young daughter," he said in a deep, commanding voice.

I was speechless.

"Essie Mae," my mother said, with a big smile of her own, "meet your father."

I couldn't get out one word. This was even crazier than when I learned Carrie was my mother. Now I saw that my real father was a handsome, charming, and rich white lawyer. My first thought was whether Mary knew this and, if so, why she didn't tell me. My second thought was that I didn't know this man's name, my father's name. Thurmond and Thurmond, I remembered the sign.

"Hello . . . Mister . . . Thurmond," I stuttered.

"What do you think of our beautiful city?" he asked me.

"It's different from my home."

"This *is* your home, Essie Mae. You must think of yourself as a South Carolinian. This is a wonderful city, a wonderful state."

"Nine governors," was all I could say.

"Maybe ten," Carrie added cryptically, winking at the man, who smiled sweetly back at her.

"The Palmetto State. Do you know what a palmetto is, Essie Mae?" Mr. Thurmond asked me.

"No, sir."

"It's a small palm tree, what they call a cabbage palm, native to our state. Look here." He put his arm on my back, which gave me an electric shock, and led me over to a wall with portraits of white men in black judicial robes, embossed certificates, and a framed souvenir of what looked to be two sides of a large coin, which is what he pointed out to me.

"This is our state seal. See the palmetto, growing out of that fallen oak. That represents our great victory, from a fort built of palmetto logs, over the British fleet built of oak. That Latin phrase there *Quis Separabit* . . . do you know what that means?"

"No, sir."

"Take a guess, Essie Mae."

I looked helplessly at my mother, who couldn't suppress her laugh. "Your father used to be a schoolteacher," she explained.

Mr. Thurmond, which was the only name I had for him then, put his hand on my shoulder. "It means 'Who Can Separate Us?' "

I took the comment personally and was deeply flattered by it.

"And see the other side. See this beautiful lady." He pointed out the other side of the seal, a somewhat risqué image of a voluptuous woman in a diaphanous toga holding up a laurel twig. "That is Hope. And that Latin phrase is our state motto. *Dum Spiro, Spero*. When I breathe, I hope. Spiro, like inspiration, a deep breath. See? You must learn Latin, Essie Mae. It'll help you with a lot of things."

Instantly, I saw where my mother got all her inspiration and who her "wonderful teacher" had been. I also realized that this visit wasn't some spontaneous drop-in but had been planned. Yesterday, after the funeral, my mother took off for a few hours between house parties "to visit some old friends," she had said. Now I saw who the old friend was. When he pulled out two chairs to offer seats to my mother and me, his hand brushed over hers, and he held it there just a moment longer. Her eyes looked up and met his. They were in love, clearly in love. In that split second I could tell what was going on, and it was as strange to me as seeing aliens from another galaxy.

"I'm terribly sorry about your aunt," Mr. Thurmond said to me, condolences that were wasted, as I didn't know her. He had clearly already shared his sympathies with my mother. "She worked for our family. Wonderful lady. Fine seamstress. She made me shirts that will never wear out. It's a shame to lose someone so young." He then segued into a concern for me. He turned to Carrie and said, "I hope you're feeding her right. Diet is the key to longevity." Carrie avoided his gaze, perhaps embarrassed by all that Brunswick stew. So Mr. Thurmond turned to me and looked me up and down, like a prize cow. "I would stay just as you are, not another pound more. Be careful of that fried food, no matter how good it tastes. It can kill you. And drink plenty of water, at least three big glasses a day, one before every meal. That way you won't eat as much. And walk everywhere you can."

"He used to be a coach, too," Carrie interjected, and that made Mr. Thurmond laugh heartily.

We stayed together for about an hour. Mr. Thurmond loved to give little lectures, about health and fitness, about local history, about the state of the nation. He was very positive about President Roosevelt but concerned that the only way to deal with Hitler was to go to war to defeat him. He was glad Roosevelt had initiated a peacetime draft, but he bragged, "We don't need a draft in Edgefield. This is a town where the boys love to fight." This launched him into an address on the endless list of the heroes of Edgefield: William Travis and James Bonham, who fought at the Alamo; General Matthew C. Butler, a Civil War legend; Francis Pickens, Ambassador to Russia and courageous Civil War governor; Pickens's Russian-born daughter Olga Neva, who led her own army that drove the "carpetbag Yankees," as Mr. Thurmond called them, out of South Carolina in the dark days after the Civil War. "We call her the Joan of Arc of South Carolina. Do you know who that is?" he asked me, and, again, I was embarrassed to say no.

"That's what schools are for," Carrie spoke up for me.

"You study hard," Mr. Thurmond admonished me. Among the other Edgefield warriors he mentioned was a revolutionary soldier named Ouzts.

My ears pricked up. "I have a good friend in Coatesville named May Ouzts," I volunteered.

"Then her family must be from Edgefield, with that name," Mr. Thurmond said. I wanted to say, "but she's black," but I was afraid to say too much. I figured out that May's family must have been slaves that took their master's name. Then I thought back to the General Butler he just mentioned. Butler was my mother's maiden name. Her family must have been that hero's family's slaves. She was from slave blood, and here she was with master blood, and here I was, all mixed up in every way. I had never thought before about where we all came from, but that was just one of the revelations of this journey home.

Eventually, it was time to go. Mr. Thurmond would have kept talking, but Carrie said, "I know you've got important work to do."

Mr. Thurmond stood up and bowed cavalierly to both of us. Then he must have decided that wasn't "fatherly" enough, so he came out from behind his massive oak desk and shook my hand, then my mother's. Not a kiss, but the strongest, bone-crushing handshake I had ever experienced. He took a last, long look at me. "She has my sister Gertrude's cheekbones," he marveled. "Isn't she a lovely girl? You have a lovely daughter." It was a kind thought, but inside it hurt me. I would have liked to have heard him say, "*We* have a lovely daughter." As it was, it sounded as if I might never see this man, my mystery father, ever again. He never called my mother by her first name. He didn't verbally acknowledge that I was his child. He didn't ask when I was leaving and didn't invite me to come back. It was like an audience with an important man, a job interview, but not a reunion with a father. When he closed the door to his office, and we were standing out on the street near the main square with all the sleeping black men, it was as if it had been a dream, a crazy dream. I looked hard at the sign: Thurmond and Thurmond, Attorneys at Law." I now noticed the names on the bottom: "J. William Thurmond and J. Strom Thurmond."

"Which 'J' is he?" I asked Carrie.

"Strom."

"Is it true?"

"It is," she assured me, as we walked away from the office.

"Who is he?" I wanted to know.

"A lawyer, a judge, a very powerful judge," she answered.

"And who is J. William?"

"His father."

"Where is he?"

"He passed a long time ago."

"But his name is on . . ."

"You don't take down a name like his."

Carrie gave me her own genealogy lesson on my new family. Out of nowhere I had become southern aristocracy. The Thurmonds were perhaps the preeminent legal dynasty in South Carolina. Judge Thurmond's grandfather, George Washington Thurmond, was a Civil War hero who had fought beside the great General Robert E. Lee. After the Southern surrender at Appomattox, he supposedly walked all the way home across Virginia and North Carolina (just as in the novel *Cold Mountain*, but a much farther journey, and a real one). Judge Thurmond's father J. William ("Will") had served as the United States Attorney for South Carolina, as well as a justice on the South Carolina Supreme Court. He might have gone on to become Edgefield governor number ten but for a blot on his record: He had shot a man in cold blood in front of the law office I had just visited. He claimed it was a question of honor, and honor being a high stake in this family, as well as the fact that Thurmond was the law in Edgefield, he was acquitted of the murder charge. (My mind said *this* family rather than *our* family at this point; the paternal ground I had just stepped on was too shaky at this early stage to be claiming proprietary stakes.)

Instead of becoming governor, Will Thurmond became the brains behind the throne, the crown being worn by still another violent Edgefield man named "Pitchfork" Ben Tillman, a one-eyed, Latin-spouting, pro-lynching intellectual rabble-rouser who got his sobriquet by threatening to stab then-President Grover Cleveland, whom he ridiculed as "an old bag of beef," with a pitchfork—unless he treated the South with more respect. Tillman despised blacks only slightly less than he despised Yankees, and in fact lumped both groups together as culpable for all his state's endless economic problems at the turn of the century. Tillman was one of the state's great folk heroes, and Will

Thurmond was his chief advisor. "It was Ben Tillman who taught little Strom how to shake hands like that," Carrie told me.

"It nearly killed me," I said.

"It's supposed to show strength of character," she replied. "Weak handshake, weak man."

Strong men who lynched weak black men, I thought. How could the son of this architect of white supremacy fall in love with my mother, a black woman? "Is it safe?" was all I could muster in the way of a query.

Carrie shrugged, rather enigmatically. "Love is love. It's color blind. Besides," she added, "all that hate talk is just politics."

Then why aren't you two married? I wanted to ask, but I held my tongue. Instead, I asked how she and my father had met. She explained to me how she, as well as her recently deceased sister, had been working at the Thurmond home on Columbia Road, one that she promised to show me before we left Edgefield. Strom had graduated from Clemson University and was living at home while teaching classes and coaching football at the Edgefield High School. It was 1925. He was twenty-three. She was fifteen. She and her sister made beds, cleaned, and did basic housekeeping. "He was known for having an eye for the ladies, and he was handsome, as you can see. He was always running in the road, half naked, at the crack of dawn, because that was part of his health routine. I couldn't help but notice."

"And he noticed you?"

"Only after his brother did. Mister Will, that's what I called him, the big brother, was going to medical school, and he would come home and flirt with me like crazy. I think he saw too many cadavers. And Mister Strom would see this, and I think he got jealous."

"And the father? What did he say?"

"Big Mister Will. He was the nicest man you ever met. Always took an interest in me, always 'please' and 'thank you.' Sometimes he'd pick flowers and give them to me. Bought clothes for our whole family. Sweet as sugar, so the other stuff was just politics. He was no Simon Legree," she said, referring to the evil slave driver in *Uncle Tom's Cabin*. Mrs. Thurmond, on the other hand, she described as polite but cool and distant. "We didn't have that much to do with her. She was strict, very religious, very involved with the Baptist church." The church was just a block away from the Thurmond law office.

Carrie told me about the rest of the family and how nice they all were to her. In addition to big brother William, there was another brother, Allen George, who also became a doctor. "He flirted with me, too. Those boys sure liked women." They liked them so much they both became gynecologists. I found that a little weird, but not Carrie. She thought it showed how smart and motivated the whole family was. The sisters, an older one named Gertrude, whom my father said I resembled, and the twins, Mary and Martha, were all schoolteachers. "Everybody was educated. Everybody did something special with themselves. You don't often see that in one family, where every child makes you proud like that."

Strom Thurmond, Carrie said, got to know her by helping out in the kitchen and in the vegetable garden behind the big house. "He knew everything about fruits and vegetables. He taught agriculture in the high school and wrote articles in the papers. We'd go out to the orchards and pick peaches, and he'd know exactly when they were ripe and which ones would be the sweetest," Carrie said, impressed with the domestic skills of such a manly seeming man. "One thing led to another."

"But where? How? The mother . . ."

"It was a big house. These were busy people who were always out doing something. Love finds a way, darling." My mother was both proud and embarrassed at the same time.

We began walking back to Old Buncombe, to our reality. Having had a taste of fantasy, I wasn't sure I liked going back. It was Cinderella's gilded coach turning into a pumpkin.

"I thought he'd be a black gentleman," I said to my mother. "You never told me he was a Caucasian." I finally had my explanation of why I had the lightest skin in my family.

"He really liked you," Carrie said to me.

"Liked?" My disappointment in her choice of words was obvious.

"Loved."

"Does he love you?" I was bold enough to ask her.

"I hope so. I think so."

"Do you love him?"

"Yes."

"Does he have a wife?"

"No. He cares about me," she asserted.

"What can we do?" I asked her plaintively.

"Nothing." Carrie's high spirits vanished in an instant. "This is South Carolina."

My mind started racing about possibilities. I had never known of a mixed-race couple in Coatesville other than a neighbor in The Spruces whose father had moved to Reading and married a white woman. That was cause for enormous gossip among our neighbors; imagine what they would say about *me*. I did see several white men with black women in Philadelphia and remember feeling a little shocked just by that sight. Race mixing simply wasn't done. Black people had enough problems of their own. Falling in love with white people seemed to just be asking for trouble, enormous trouble. And now here I was, right in the thick of it.

Back at the cabin, everybody was excited to hear what had gone on. They all knew that I was going to meet my father, all except me, and they had kept the secret.

"We wanted to surprise you," Mary said.

To me it wasn't a pleasant surprise. What do you do when you meet your real father but may never get to see him again? I tried to play along, but I was still in shock. That night we went to church. I prayed that my mother and father could somehow be united. My mother was praying, too. Even though the Baptist services were far more restrained than at her Pentecostal church back in Pennsylvania, she was putting all her heart in her prayers and in the hymns. She was forever talking about being forgiven for her sins. Now I knew what her sins were, and I was the direct result of them. I was also paying for them in the worst way, and I'm sure she was, too. Maybe that explained why she had become so religious, much more so than her sister Mary. My mother Carrie and I both needed salvation. But in the society we lived in, what I was praying for would take a miracle.

The next morning, as we were packing to go back north, a black Ford arrived at our cabin. There was a black driver in a white coat, the same servant outfit that the butler at the Thurmond law office had been wearing. The driver got out and opened the door to the back seat. Out stepped a slender, well-dressed woman in a pink hat and a pink frock. She looked like she had taken a wrong turn into the slums on her way to a garden party at one of the mansions. I stood at the window watching, as my aunt went out to greet her.

"It's Mr. Thurmond's sister," my aunt said excitedly, "She's got a package for Carrie." My mother quickly combed her hair and fixed her dress and went out to meet her. They talked just a few moments. My mother then came back inside. The "package" turned out to be a long envelope. She opened it, and inside was cash, a lot of cash, in ten-dollar bills. There were 200 dollars in all, which was serious money in 1941. I had never seen so much money.

"This is from your father," she told me, "to pay for our trip." The woman, she said, was Mary, one of the twins. "I used to work for her," Carrie said.

All my relatives came in to ooh and aah over the money. If it was a lot for someone from Pennsylvania, it must have seemed like a million dollars to the residents of that desperate shantytown. Once I got over the fact that the gift had been made, I felt awful. Didn't Miss Thurmond want to meet her niece? She had to know who I was. Didn't my father want to see me again? He could have come, just as she did. Were they trying to buy my mother off so she wouldn't shame them in some way? Was there any love here, or was this some kind of hush money? I didn't ask. We sat in the back of the bumpy bus back to Columbia, then boarded another hot and segregated railway coach for the long trip back north. I stared at the cotton fields and the poor sleepy black men. I'm the daughter of a powerful white judge, I thought to myself. Why am I sitting here? Why am I, why is my family, why is anyone being treated like this? Then I went back into the filthy toilet, locked the door, and broke down into tears.

CHAPTER THREE
Reconstruction

I DIDN'T SEE or hear from my new father for nearly a year. It was so long that it seemed like that meeting with him had never happened at all. My mother went back to Chester, I went back to Coatesville, and life went on almost as before. I say almost because once something like the facts of your birth get into your head, you never can be the same again. In my darkest hours I began to look at all black people as victims and white people as oppressors, and everything in America struck me as grossly unfair. In my brightest hours, I began to look at myself as someone very special, an amalgam of all that was great about America. I had a brilliant white father and a beautiful black mother; was I not the golden child? Alas, the real Essie Mae fell somewhere between these two poles. I was too humble to be conceited, too meek to be a firebrand. My mantra was "accept," and accept I did, at least outwardly. Yet inside me was pure turbulence.

Because of Mary's conditioning me to keep my mouth shut, and because of the precarious and ephemeral nature of my relationship with my "new" parents, I always felt I was skating on very thin ice. On the other hand, I had no desire to get off the pond. I remained fearful, cautious, and deeply insecure. I was uncomfortable in the way I would have guessed that spies were uncomfortable, having to juggle different identities, present different façades. Yet I was also thrilled to have the chance to play this game, because these new parents were so intriguing, and because they were my *real* folks. What child could resist the idea of being with his or her real parents? Hence, I was in a perpetual state of anxiety. The only way to deal with all this disequilibrium was to ground myself in the obligations of school and work.

Working at Coatesville Hospital in my nurse's aide job that summer, I now became hyperaware of how second class the black patients were being treated, even here in the so-called enlightened North, our own Promised Land. It was the medical equivalent of those segregated train coaches in which we were forced to ride. The "poverty ward" where the blacks were treated was like a prison barracks. Even the food the black patients were given was extremely substandard. They got what was known as "the culls," nearly rotten vegetables and fruits that would otherwise have been "culled" to be thrown out. Sometimes when I was in the kitchen getting the trays to serve, I would try to switch the food so the blacks would have an equal opportunity at the string beans and squash and berries. I didn't once get caught, and I felt good, like a Robin Hood, trying to make things just a tiny bit fairer.

I went back to high school with a vengeance, determined to learn all about American history—not necessarily to please the secret father I might never see again but to understand him. Knowing that I had a white father somehow emboldened me to do things I would have never done before. One example of this got me into big trouble. I had a math class with one of our strictest teachers, Mrs. Wynn. I always got A's. There was one pretty blond girl named Gloria, a cheerleader whom all the boys liked, who just couldn't do math at all. She had the hardest time. She may have been the queen bee after class, at the soda shop I couldn't go to, but here in the classroom, she was an utter failure. I decided I wanted to help her. So during a big exam I sat next to her and turned my paper so she could copy my answers. She did, and even though she had never spoken to me before, after that exam, she gave me the warmest smile. It made me feel so good. On a less-than-noble level, helping this popular beauty gave me a sense of power, a sense of belonging to the elite sisterhood of the school. I felt sure Gloria would invite me into her inner circle, and given who my father was, I felt entitled to belong.

These feelings didn't last long. In grading the tests, Mrs. Wynn, with her eagle eye, noticed not only that Gloria had improved dramatically as a mathematician but also had given the same few wrong answers that I had. A furious Mrs. Wynn called me in and threatened to send me to the principal, who might have expelled me. I didn't tell her my true motivation. I gave her some line about trying to help poor Gloria, in an effort to "remember the neediest." Mrs. Wynn lectured me about everybody having to stand on her own feet, that if I could stand so nicely on mine, so could Gloria. The implication was that if a poor black girl could do well in math, it should be a piece of cake for the school's white princess. The idea that Gloria needed *Negro* assistance was beneath her and the school's dignity. I hung my head and apologized. Mrs. Wynn gave us both F's, though she never brought us in for a scolding together, and Gloria never did speak to me one way or the other.

Afterward, I stuck to my black friends and to my classes. I finally took my much-anticipated American history class. I was disappointed by how little I was taught about the South in general and South Carolina in particular. This was Pennsylvania, and the course was very biased, with lots and lots about Benjamin Franklin and the Revolutionary War and the Constitution, and not enough, for me, about the Civil War. Yes, the class spent several days on the Battle of Gettysburg, but the big hero here, after Abraham Lincoln, was a Pennsylvania congressman named Thaddeus Stevens. A New England–born lawyer who lived in Gettysburg, Stevens was one of the leading opponents of slavery. He was so annoyed with the Democrats for protecting the institution that he broke with his party and founded the Republican Party, whose hallmark was its commitment to emancipation. His chief ally in Washington was Charles Sumner, whom Edgefield's Preston Brooks tried to kill by caning on the floor of the Senate.

After the Civil War, Stevens and Sumner were the leaders of the faction known as the Radical Republicans, who led the impeachment proceedings against Lincoln's successor President Andrew Johnson on the ground that he was being too soft on his native South. What they couldn't do to punish Johnson, Stevens and Sumner did to the South as a whole, forbidding the old planter aristocrats, like the ones in the mansions on Buncombe Street, from holding office, and confiscating most of the diminished wealth they had left after the war. Stevens even tried to redistribute all the wealth to the former slaves, now called freedmen, but that was too radical even for the Radicals in Congress. He called the Confederate states "conquered provinces" and barely wanted them back in the Union. When he died, he was buried in a black cemetery in Lancaster. He put his body where his mouth was, to illustrate in death his credo of "Equality of man before his Creator."

Stevens seemed to me like a wonderful hero, well worth studying about. So was Charles Sumner, a Harvard lawyer who stood up for blacks before anybody else of his elite class did. In one book I read there was a lithograph by Currier and Ives in 1872 of the seven black members of Congress. To me it was unforgettable, these seven distinguished gentlemen, all in waistcoats and bow ties and mutton chops, looking every inch the leaders of the country that they were—for a brief shining moment. Three of the men were from South Carolina. One shared my birthplace of Aiken. All had been slaves. Now they were congressmen. It was a testament to hope and equality. And then it all vanished when, barely a decade after the Civil War, the Old South rose again and drove the Yankee occupiers out. Without the federal troops to restrain them, the Old Southerners terrorized blacks from exercising their newly won right to vote. And without the black vote, these distinguished black congressmen were unable to find reelection. Out of office, most of them went on to very sorry ends, as victims of financial frauds and chicaneries. Few ended up better than sharecroppers, like my poor family, virtual slaves. How did it happen? I had to know, and my high school didn't tell me.

I got the impression from my class that the South deserved every bad thing it got, and then some. But when I talked to my family, some of whom, the great aunts and uncles, actually remembered the hardships of Reconstruction, I got a contrary impression that the Radical Republicans had gone too far, creating a white backlash that, as far as the South was concerned, was still lashing back today. Even though they were black and the Yankees conquerors were supposedly on their side, all they talked about was how corrupt the Yankees were. I learned about carpetbaggers, Yankee outsiders who moved south after the Civil War to suck the blood of the ruins, and scalawags, who were southern-born greedy turncoats who tried to cash in on Yankee spoils.

In my spare time I spent countless hours at the Coatesville public library poring over American and southern history books. There was quite a big collection, but there was so much dust that it looked as if I were the first person to open these books for decades. I guess because the North had won the Civil War, they were able to walk away from it in a way that the southerners couldn't. The people of Dixie were apparently obsessed with the war and all the "might have beens" that could have secured their victory. Strangely enough, I never saw a black in the Coatesville library, and it wasn't because we were excluded from it, like the YMCA. I wanted to tell my friends to "come on down," as what I was finding out was very, very interesting, but again, I kept that mouth shut. They might have questioned why *I* was so interested, and that was a line of inquiry to be avoided at all costs. Still, I developed a new insight into the aphorism "knowledge is power." All those books I read did indeed make me feel far more secure in a world where everything else was so uncertain.

One thing that especially struck me in my readings about the South was the fate of those other outsiders, the Jews, who had initially prospered mightily in the South, and the terrible scorn that was heaped upon them after the Civil War. A lot of the Yankee peddlers who came south to sell their wares happened to be Jewish and were hated for the extortionate prices they charged to a captive audience. On the other end of the spectrum were the old-guard southern Jews, like the Moses family. One beloved Moses had been governor of South Carolina before the Civil War; his son Franklin Moses used his father's fine image to become the scalawag governor right afterward. The same man who was a brilliant orator for secession and who physically helped tear down the Union flag from Fort Sumter after its capture, young Moses now sang a totally different tune—the Yankee aria written by Stevens and Sumner.

Moses was a very bad seed who took bribes from anyone and basically turned the governor's mansion in Columbia into the House of the Rising Sun, a bordello where anything went. It was known in South Carolina as the Chateau de Plunderville. With his imported French champagnes, Russian caviar, and the fine silks in which he draped his girlfriends, Moses was one of the only men in South Carolina who maintained the old plantation lifestyle, living even higher after the Civil War than he had before it. Moses also openly maintained, at taxpayers' expense, half a dozen black mistresses. This did not endear him to white southerners. Eventually, Moses proved too much even for his Yankee patrons. Hounded out of office and out of South Carolina, he became a con man in Boston, using his southern pedigree to swindle New England aristocrats. He did a six-month term in the Boston House of Correction, and afterward committed suicide in a bleak rooming house.

Because of egregious examples like Moses and the high profile of Jewish merchants, Jewish people came to be perceived by white southerners as both Christ killers and South killers. It seems that these southerners had become increasingly fundamentalist in their religion after the war, looking to God to heal their wounds, and Jews became one of the main scapegoats for the trials of the South. My relatives also seemed to buy this party line and regarded the Jews, who themselves had been slaves in Egypt and were also "different" from the Anglo-Saxon majority, not as their natural allies but as enemies of the South. Despite the years of subjugation, southern blacks still maintained the loyalty of birth. Prejudice is unfair wherever it comes from.

The net result of Radical Reconstruction was one step forward, ten steps back—and ultimately the exodus to the North that saw much of my Edgefield kin relocate in Pennsylvania. In the 1870s, once the white backlash kicked in, the key concepts that arose in the white southern view of the new class of freedmen, as the former slaves were known, were what I called the three I's: impudence, insolence, and inferiority. Any black who asserted his new post–Civil War rights, the rights that hundreds of thousands of Americans, including President Lincoln, had died for, was considered pushy, rude, and way, way out of line. Blacks were expected by southern whites to "know their place," and that place was basically back in abject, bowing, and scraping servitude.

If southern whites didn't want blacks on the streetcars with them, imagine how they felt seeing them elected as representatives in their state houses and in Washington. The cornerstone to white arrogance and prejudice was a deep-seated weirdly scientific conviction that black people were genetically of a lower order than whites. And despite that distinguished-looking first group of black representatives, there weren't many examples of accomplished blacks in the 1870s to rebut that presumption. After all, when you've been held in bondage for 200 years, it's a little difficult to generate those artistic and scientific accomplishments that would make white people respect you.

The chief instrumentality of white southern rebellion against Radical Reconstruction was the Ku Klux Klan. The white southerners may have blamed the Yankees for their troubles, but they took this hatred out on southern blacks. It was a lot easier to scare and bully penniless and defenseless ex-slaves than it was to intimidate the armed and uniformed occupying federal troops that had already conquered the South and burned and pillaged much of it. I could understand southern resentment of their victors, but I couldn't understand why they were so cruel in taking out their anger on the poor freedmen. That seemed to me the most cowardly part of all. However, the South was always known as "The Rebels," and this new rebellion against the Yankee occupation proved to be enormously effective and enormously damaging to the cause of civil rights, which was set back nearly a century in the process.

The Klan, which began as a polite secret society for high-born Confederate junior officers, devolved after the war into a bloodthirsty cult, populated by southerners we now know as rednecks, a reference to how their necks would get burned from their backbreaking toil in the cotton and tobacco fields. (Proper southerners never went into the fields and remained lily white. Their slaves did their work for them.) The Klansmen's white robes and pointed hoods made them look like ghosts. This image may have been their most potent weapon, as the freed blacks tended to be both very religious (only God could have seen them through the tribulations of slavery) and very superstitious. With their towering bonfires, their bloodcurdling rebel yells, and the surprise thunder of their horses' hooves in the middle of the night, the

Klan seemed to blacks like the emissaries of Satan himself. The legend, my relatives told me, still fearful, was that these were the ghosts of confederate soldiers, risen from the dead and straight out of hell. Their message to the freedmen: Don't vote, don't aid the Yankees, and, above all, never touch, or never look at, a white woman.

The fear of black rape seems to have been the preeminent goad to organizing the rise of the Klan and its leadership of this new southern insurrection. "They sure thought our men had something *special*," one of my great-aunts, Aunt Calliope, told me with a wink. "I still don't know what it might be. I'm still waitin' to see what it is. The men I've known . . ." Then she broke out in a naughty laugh. She was almost ninety and had grown up as a slave and a freedwoman, with the Civil War and Reconstruction and the Southern Redemption, as the whites called kicking the Yankees out and the blacks back into "their place." She had seen it all and liked to talk about it. "You're the only one who ever asks me, Essie Mae," she said. Calliope had gotten her name from her slave masters, the Butler family, who had a great passion for classical antiquity. They liked having a house slave named after a Greek goddess, the muse of poetry. "Fetch me a mint julep, Calliope," I could imagine them ordering her.

Calliope was tiny and fragile, all dressed in black. In appearance, she reminded me of one of the witches in *Macbeth*, but she was sweet and loving and oh so wise. When she told stories, she waved her hands expressively and emphatically. She was so frail, I worried that she might pass out, or worse, from all the motion, but she seemed to derive energy from our conversations. Calliope lived in a tiny room in a rooming house in The Spruces, which she kept immaculately but lit with candles rather than electric lights. She said she somehow never could get used to modern power. She lived in the past, and I was thrilled to go on time travels with her.

Getting back to the Klan, Calliope told me how the old Democratic ruling aristocrats, like her former owners, the Butlers, got everyone worked up with the fear of black sexual assaults. "Once we had the vote, once we had the education, the next thing they thought we was gonna take their women," she said.

"That was the worst thing that could ever happen to them. They were afraid once the white women got with the black men, they wouldn't have no use for the white men no more. If a black man so much as tipped his cap to a white lady, he'd get strung up, just like that, ain't nobody gonna stop them."

Lynching was the embodiment of "southern justice." I used to think lynching meant hanging, but I found out it originally meant any kind of frontier justice, meted out by a mob. The term derived from the Lynch brothers, who lived in Virginia during the Revolutionary War and founded the town of Lynchburg. There were no courts during that insurgent time, so the Lynches called themselves "judges" and sent their minions out to punish, by torture, hanging, burning, whatever was handy, all enemies of the new state, from British sympathizers to horse thieves. By Reconstruction, lynching, which could mean either hanging or burning, became the punishment for black men who were a perceived threat to the sexual color line. I found it ironic that the biggest song of the last year had been a jazzy number by the Andrews Sisters called "Beat Me, Daddy, Eight to the Bar." When I thought about my brutalized ancestors in the South, I couldn't conceive of whipping as an appropriate subject for public amusement.

"They might have lynched me," I thought. "Me and my mother."

"No, they never mess with the women, only the men. They didn't lynch women. We got our own punishments." So Aunt Calliope explained the bizarre double standard of interracial sexuality in the Old South, which continued in the New. Calliope knew about my father, my real white father—everybody in my family did. Only I had been in the dark. Yes, it was an enormous secret, but most of my mother's family was far away here in Pennsylvania to be out of gossip range and the ones in Edgefield looked like they'd seen enough Klan intimidation and "know your place" conditioning to never open their mouths about anything. The fine white women of the South were all supposed to be pure virgins until marriage, and after that eternally faithful to their white husbands. Any sexual relationship between a white woman and a black man was immediately presumed to be rape of the most brutal kind. But white men, on the other hand, were entitled, by nearly divine right, to have the run of the henhouse, or slave quarters. "The massas all looked after their children, no matter who birthed them. That was part of what it meant to be a gentleman," Calliope said.

Calliope told me one story about the richest cotton planter in Edgefield, James Henry Hammond, who had open sexual relationships with two of his slaves who happened to be mother and daughter. "That's what they did back then. The wives all knew, but that was the way it was. Massa was king," Calliope said. Hammond, reveling in his sexual freedom, also had children with both mother and daughter. And if father was king, his son was a prince, for he, too, had sexual relations with his father's slave lovers.

It was incredibly risqué, if not for those times, certainly for mine. I was growing up in the time of the Hays Code in Hollywood. You couldn't see stories like this in the movies. *The Little Foxes,* with Bette Davis, which centers on a corrupt southern family, was the wildest thing I saw in 1941. But there was no sex, and nothing like the tales my aunt was telling me.

Waving those hands now with agitation, Calliope described how John Henry Hammond agonized over what to do with his illegitimate children. He decided that it would be cruelty to them to free them and send them north, even with money. He believed they would live far better as his protected slaves in the South than as footloose free people in the North. He did, however, arrange in his will that his slave children were not allowed to be sold outside the Hammond family. While he was having his affairs with his slaves, Calliope continued, Hammond was also "stepping out with the swells." He was accused of having seduced four of his own nieces by his sister and her husband Wade Hampton II, who was supposedly the richest man in the entire South before the Civil War. Again, it was a kingly thing to do, and despite the rumors of incest, Hammond was still elected to the U.S. Senate.

After the Civil War, despite the kings having been deposed, the kingly style continued. Calliope recounted the tale of the noble Francis Pickens family, the one who was ambassador to Russia and whose daughter was South Carolina's Joan of Arc, a poster child of racism. At the same time Joan was conducting her crusade against blacks and Yankees, the widow of the ambassador had a brother and a best friend who came to live with her on the old plantation, not far from Old Buncombe. Each young man took a former slave as a common-law wife and had children with her. These mixed-race offspring all grew up in the great house, accepted as part of one happy family. "Pickens and pickaninnies," Calliope joked.

What Strom Thurmond was doing with me, then, was part of a long Edgefield tradition. Another aunt told me that Judge Thurmond was supporting my mother; that was why she didn't have to work. I didn't ask her about the arrangements. Money, I had been taught, was none of my business. I also heard that Carrie took trips down to South Carolina to see the judge, but if money was none of my business, love life was even less. I was still fairly shy with Carrie. We were still in the getting-to-know-each-other phase. Moreover, I had barely seen her after our trip to Edgefield together. There had been a few daily visits on weekends, when we were never alone but were with other relatives. I yearned to sleep in the bed with her again, to *feel* like a daughter.

I also dreamed of getting a letter from my father. If he were a true southern gentleman, how could he just forget me like this? How could he be that cold and distant? He had seemed so interested in me. Was he only being polite? The only person who could answer the question was Carrie, and I needed to be alone to ask. If I tried to ask Mary, I worried that she might have been hurt. Obviously, she and Carrie had agreed that Mary would be my full-time mother. If I asked too much about my "other parents," I might be jeopardizing the ties to the one I had. I didn't want to be left with no one at all. Despite having what seemed to be more parents than any girl could handle, my biggest fear was ending up an orphan.

I was listening to the hit song "Deep in the Heart of Texas" when I heard about Pearl Harbor that December. Everyone's world immediately was turned upside down. War was all around us, but none of my friends thought we as Americans would go to war. Now we had been attacked, and we had no choice. We were all scared—scared of Hitler on one side and the Japanese on the other. Many of the boys in the high school immediately began enlisting. I knew I might never see many of them again. Worrying about my parentage took a distant second place to survival, but it still would have been reassuring to share my fears with someone who truly cared about me, and I wasn't sure who that was.

"He's volunteered," Carrie told me, taking me aside when she came for a Christmas visit.

"Isn't he too old?" I knew the judge was now around forty.

"Yes, but he's a lieutenant in the reserves," she said, knowing everything about him. Judges are exempt, but he's very patriotic, and he knows the right people. He's an Edgefield man," she said proudly. "They need to fight. It's in their blood. His grandfather was right beside Robert E. Lee when he surrendered. War runs in the family."

But is it really *our* family? I wanted to ask her. Talk about being the poor relations. We were the invisible relations. What bothered me the most was that my mother never told me that my father said goodbye to me as he was going off to war. As it turned out, he didn't go overseas for over a year, but I didn't know that at the time. Maybe he did love my mother, or maybe he used her—but where I was concerned, my father didn't seem to care.

As Coatesville hunkered down for war, I tried my hardest to put Strom Thurmond out of my mind. Yet like a moth to a flame, I couldn't stop reading about South Carolina and the *Gone with the Wind* world that was at least half my birthright, but was a birthright I could not claim. I wanted to find out the worst about this forbidden family, so that I could hate them and want nothing to do with them. After all, did they not formerly own slaves? And was not Will Thurmond the genius who put the pitchfork in the hands of the Ben Tillman, so that he could wield it against black people? And what was my father up to? What kind of justice to blacks did he dispense?

Back at her rooming house, Aunt Calliope told me more about slavery. She was never whipped or chained or abused in any way, she said. She worked in the house, not in the fields, but even there she recalled no brutality. "One day we were workin' for rich people, and the next we were workin' for poor people," was how she described the upheaval the Civil War brought. Most slaves stayed with their old masters. Because the Yankees confiscated whatever wealth the masters had, the freedmen worked for nothing except food and lodging, or as sharecroppers. "Nothing changed much for us. We prayed a lot before and we prayed a lot after."

As far as politics was concerned, Calliope barely remembered the brief period during Radical Reconstruction when newly enfranchised blacks dominated the state legislature and went to Congress. "The Yankees ran that show," she recalled. She could barely remember having the vote. "We had it, and then they took it away. It was like a school play, having our people in the state house. But then they canceled that play, and they took our vote away. They called it civil rights, but there wasn't nothin' civil about it." The strange part was that the people who took away the civil rights that the Civil War had been fought for were the former slave owners, the "massas" Calliope and her people had been so loyal to. In essence, my white family had gone to war against my black family.

This war of "Redemption," to rescue the Old South from the blacks and their "Yankee puppeteers," was led by a coalition of the Confederate aristocracy that included both the Butlers and the Thurmonds. In fact, Edgefield was the nerve center of South Carolina's "freedom fight" against Reconstruction and the Northern occupation. The key man here was General Matthew Calbraith Butler, who lost a foot in a Civil War battle but returned to fight in the next, mounted on his white steed. Butler was the cousin of Preston Brooks, the bold assailant of Charles Sumner.

In the small town of Edgefield, "everyone was kin," as Calliope said. This was certainly true among the ruling class, who were equally united in their desire to reclaim the power they had always enjoyed. General Butler's partner in redemption was another Edgefield fighting man, General Martin Witherspoon Gary, a Harvard Law School graduate known as the Bald Eagle of the Confederacy. Gary not only used his legal skills in defending Klan leaders accused of fomenting violence but also his military skills to foment it himself. Gary and Butler were the masterminds of the "rifle clubs" that sprung up to cloak mob violence in the respectability of polite gentlemen's sporting societies.

The showdown between the Old Guard and the New occurred in 1876 in a town near Edgefield called Hamburg. The largely black state militia had its authority challenged by a Butler-led confederacy of rifle clubs, including the Sweetwater Sabre Club, which was headed by the pre-pitchfork Ben Tillman. The united clubs wore makeshift uniforms that consisted of a chemise died blood red with berry juice. From this, the rebels became known as the Redshirts. Outnumbered by the swaggering Redshirts, the black militiamen tried to defend themselves, and shot and killed one white man. One was all it took to incite what became known as the Hamburg massacre. The Redshirts attacked the militiamen, seizing forty prisoners. One by one, they would bring a captive out into Main Street and shoot him in the head. Then, in true sporting fox-hunt style, they released the other captives and chased them down, shooting them as they caught them. It reminded me of the Coatesville burning of Zack Walker, though the evils were multiplied.

Despite Republican control of the legal apparatus of the state, the Redshirts were not punished in any way. Butler, getting on his aristocratic high horse, flatly denied he or his clubmen had any responsibility for the carnage. Instead, he blamed a faceless mob of "poor white trash," local Irish immigrant factory workers, for going on a drunken spree. No witnesses were bold enough to step forward to contradict the formidable general. A few months later, Ben Tillman led another massacre at nearby Ellenton. Forty more blacks were executed in a swamp. The bodies remained on the ground for days, for no one dared come out to bury their friends for fear of joining them in the hereafter. Again, no witnesses came forward, and no punishment was meted out.

In the gubernatorial elections of that year the Redshirts terrorized the polls and prevented enough blacks from voting to elect one of their own, the patrician General Wade Hampton III. An enormous mountain of a man, Hampton, in his leisure time, liked to play the mountain man, hunting bear with his bare hands and a huge knife. Before the Civil War he was the largest slave owner in the whole South, possessing at one time over 3,000 slaves. After the War he was forced to declare bankruptcy, selling his once-priceless English antiques on the Columbia courthouse steps for the less than princely sum of barely 100 dollars. The scalawag Governor Franklin Moses having been banished, there was no other market in the postwar South for the finer things. With no money, the former U.S. Senator Hampton had no choice but to return to politics.

The Redshirts fastened onto Hampton as a powerful symbol of What Used to Be. They paraded him around to campaign rallies in a Roman-style chariot, like a gladiator, wearing a laurel wreath around his head. Aunt Calliope described the political rallies as "a kind of medicine show." On the dais where Hampton was to speak sat a black sack tied up in chains and labeled "South Carolina." The moment Hampton ascended to speak, a beautiful blond all dressed in white robes would emerge from the sack. The band would play "Dixie" and the crowd would go wild.

Because blacks still had the vote, and even the most shameless intimidation tactics weren't foolproof, Hampton went after it. Many of his 3,000 former chattels were trotted out to offer testimonials to his benevolence. Among black voters, his biggest campaign asset was his "Mauma" Nelly, who had raised him. "That clinched it for him," Calliope remembered. "Wade Hampton wasn't a bad man. It was the ones behind him who were up to no good."

Armed with this support, Hampton won a photo-finish election. Just as tight was the 1876 Presidential race between Hayes and Tilden. By this year enough Old Southern Democrats had gotten themselves pardoned and reelected to Congress to politick against the Radical Republicans. Hayes was Republican, but not Radical, and was willing to play ball. Thus, the Southern Democrats cut a deal with him, throwing their support to Hayes in return for his promise to end Reconstruction and take the federal troops out of the South. It was Yankee Go Home, and it worked. Ben Tillman and the Redshirts were never prosecuted, and Matthew C. Gary went to Washington as South Carolina's new senator. The South was about to rise again.

The new messiah here was Ben Tillman, and his Svengali was my grandfather, Will Thurmond. It didn't make me feel very good that Tillman was arguably the meanest man in the history of American politics, and my grandfather was the man he turned to for meanness. To try to defend Tillman was to try to defend my family, and in 1941 I was trying to do precisely the opposite. The more I learned, the more I wanted to wash those white people right out of my black, non-cheerleader hair. But a lot of white people thought The Pitchfork was a great man, and I kept on reading to try to understand why.

In his own way, Tillman was what we might call a progressive. Southern admirers called him the "Agricultural Moses," leading the farmers toward a Promised Land that never fully bore fruit. He was the champion of the small farmer, not the big planter, and instituted many reforms that benefited the common man, as long as he was white. He founded the new agricultural college at Clemson, where my father eventually graduated. He was a great friend of public education and inspired my father to become a teacher and an expert in agriculture. Not that Tillman was a farmer himself. He came from a distinguished, slave-owning Edgefield family and was highly educated. He loved writing poetry and quoting the classics, almost as much as denouncing "the Negro." He used his upper-crust connections to drive the Yankees out of South Carolina, then he used his populist charisma to drive the aristocrats into oblivion, much on the advice of Will Thurmond.

"Nobody spoke as good as he did," Calliope reminisced about Tillman. Again, she spoke without rancor, which confused me.

"But he hated you," I said.

"He didn't hate *me*," she replied. "When you live as long as I have, you best think about love, not hate."

The genius of Ben Tillman, and thus the genius of Will Thurmond behind him, was to give his beloved small farmers someone above them to resent and someone below them to take it out on. After generations of being scorned by the planter elite as the lowest caste of society (blacks as slaves were outside society, and hence didn't count), it empowered the poor whites to feel superior to someone, now that blacks had entered the calculus of American life. "Before, they'd only looked up. Now they could look down," Calliope explained. The "Negro crisis," invented by Tillman and Thurmond, gave the poor whites a crisis to respond to, as well as an opportunity to "save" their civilization. Nobody had ever called the piney woods of these dirt farmers civilization.

Tillman thus gave them pride, and they gave him their votes. Elected governor in 1890, he went to the U.S. Senate in 1894, succeeding his ally Matthew C. Butler, and remained there until his death in 1918.

Tillman's mission was to put "uppity niggers" in their place. Despite the Klan, despite the Redshirts, despite a million obstacles, blacks in the South had made progress in the two decades following the Civil War. The threat to whites was that this progress had only just begun. Tillman was presented as the man to stop it, the terminator of black advancement. The first stop was the ballot box. Once blacks had achieved political equality, social equality would inevitably follow. They could vote themselves into white schools, white trains, white parks, white neighborhoods. Voting, the key to civil rights guaranteed by the Fourteenth and Fifteenth Amendments, the Civil War's constitutional legacy, had to be abridged. Violence wasn't enough to stem the oncoming tide.

Originally, right after the war, the argument was made that freed slaves, because of their lack of education, were too ignorant to vote and would simply be the tools of unscrupulous Yankee political profiteers or scalawags like Franklin Moses. But now, two decades later, blacks were getting some education, separate and hardly equal, but it was an education nonetheless. This knowledge was power—a power that had to be snuffed out. There were clever legal ways to do this, ways dreamed up by the brilliant mind of Will Thurmond, hitting the Negro where it hurt, with literacy requirements, poll taxes, and residence rules.

"They asked me how old Christ was when he was born," Calliope recalled, giving me an example of the kind of tests voter registrars put blacks through. She had no clue and was denied. Later, she moved to another county and somehow passed, because the registrar knew she had been a loyal servant of the Butlers and would vote the Democratic line.

"Ben Tillman was good to his people," she said, meaning his slaves. She told me how he built a mausoleum for his main manservant, his best friend in the world. "He just wanted to get elected," she said, dismissing his lynch advocacy as mere campaign rhetoric. Once Calliope got her vote, she cast it for The

Pitchfork. She was a sucker for Wade Hampton's "Mauma," for Ben Tillman's valet. "He was a good man," she maintained to the end, "just doing his job."

Tillman's "job" was taking away everything black people had gained from the war and leaving them in constant fear of the white mob. As another uncle said to me, "I don't think the Jews in Germany are in any more fear of Hitler than the blacks in South Carolina were of Tillman." I read a speech Tillman gave in which he advocated lynching as an acceptable form of justice for blacks—and exhorted the mob to "Kill! Kill! Kill!" the Negro rapist, which is what he reduced all black men to be. Tillman styled himself the great defender of white, southern female purity, if not chastity. I wonder what he would have thought of his wizard's son, my father?

What follows is my understanding of the racial philosophy of Ben Tillman, as at least partially conceived by Will Thurmond, and ostensibly espoused by my father Strom Thurmond. It became the southern racial orthodoxy, and, as such, made me feel like the worst blot my proud, white family could conceivably have. During his five decades of influence on the national political stage, Ben Tillman carried this philosophy around the country, North and South, East and West, and apparently found millions of adherents. The rest of the country didn't have quite the issue with "the Negro" as Tillman did in the South, but as I learned in Coatesville, crossing the Mason-Dixon Line did not make the race problem disappear. Tillman was a brilliant and charismatic orator, and he drew huge, admiring crowds, just like the crowds that burned Zachariah Walker in 1911 at the pinnacle of Tillman's popularity. What I called the "Tillman Solution"—a plan to totally subjugate the black race—was not that far removed from the "Final Solution" espoused by our war enemy Hitler.

What Tillman believed in was something he called "race antagonism," a kind of racial Darwinism in which each race wanted to dominate all others. In his mind the "master race" was the white Anglo-Saxon race, which he called "the flower of humanity" and gave credit for most of civilization as he knew it. Blacks, in his view, were "barbarian Africans," an inferior and savage race, marked only for toil and hard, menial, thoughtless labor. Any progress the blacks had made Tillman attributed to the benefits of slavery. White slave owners had "civilized" and "Christianized" their savage chattels, proof of which was how loyal many blacks were to their masters during the Civil War and in the early years of emancipation.

During Radical Reconstruction, the venal Yankee occupiers of the South gave the freedmen what Tillman called "a taste of blood." The "virus of equality" infected the race with the dire result of an unquenchable desire for equality, political and social. They wanted the state house, then they wanted the white house, not only the one in Washington, but the little one on Elm Street. In short, the "New Negro" would be satisfied with nothing less than to marry a white woman. When that did not happen, the Negroes reverted to their savage jungle natures: taking out their animalistic anger by raping white women. That, above all, was what white America had to rally to protect itself from. This visceral threat to hearth and home cut to the quick and galvanized a nation into race hatred.

When Tillman was asked about white men raping black women, he dismissed the question as one of extremely poor taste, as if no white man could be so debased as to desire a black woman. What would he have thought about Strom Thurmond and my mother? Probably that my father was in severe need of counseling. He didn't give white men a free pass with black women, because he couldn't seem to imagine a civilized white man ever coveting one. And if "civilized" white men acted like savages in lynching blacks, it was justified as protection of the race, if not chivalry. Tillman advocated mass search parties to hunt down and shoot young, black men, men like Zack Walker, whom he equated with jungle animals: "We must hunt these creatures with the same terrified vigor . . . that we would look for tigers and bears."

Tillman was a maestro at orchestrating white rage. When Booker T. Washington became the first black invited to dine at the White House by Theodore Roosevelt, Tillman turned it into a national scandal, proof of all his crackpot theories. The only corrective to Roosevelt's "entertaining that nigger," he raged, was "our killing a thousand niggers in the South before they will learn their place again."

But how did Tillman explain the brilliance of Booker T. Washington? "By the proportion of white blood in his veins," Tillman said. Like me, Washington was a person of mixed race, whom Tillman described as "the frustrated and no doubt futureless class of mulattoes." Mulattoes, Tillman stated, may be smarter than "pure-blooded" blacks, and even "the lower types of whites," but such exceptions to Tillman's law of the jungle were destined to become nothing more than oddities in racial science. Thanks, Grandfather Thurmond, was all I could think when I read these theories.

My great-grandfather, George Washington Thurmond, had slaves of his own, but in the dozens, not hundreds. He was a cotton farmer, not a lordly planter. The Thurmonds were not exactly aristocrats, unlike the Pinckneys and Rutledges of Charleston and the great rice plantations, who had signed the Constitution, or the Hammonds and Butlers of Edgefield, whose vast cotton fields enabled them to live like English lords. The Thurmonds had achieved a modern white-collar prominence through their legal and professional skills. They were nonetheless extremely influential, and the fact of their deep intimacy with Tillman made me think of them as savages themselves. I was glad, then, that Strom Thurmond had disappeared from my life as quickly as he had entered it. For a moment, I had begun to think of myself as white, or at least partly white. If the Tillman–Thurmond axis was the source of my whiteness, I didn't want a drop of it. Black could not have seemed more beautiful.

CHAPTER FOUR

Life with Father

THE WAR YEARS were my high school years, and it was hard to study the past when the present was so dramatic. One benefit of the war was that it completely took my mind off my personal past, not that that past was coming back to haunt me in any way. I never got a letter, a call, a word from Strom Thurmond, and I barely saw my mother. I heard she was doing volunteer work in Philadelphia. I went back to Mary and James as my parents, and I committed myself to being the same plain teenager I always was before all these surprises about my birth came popping out of the closet. I reembraced my original home and my black roots, and wrote off Strom Thurmond as a secret footnote to my personal history. I assumed I'd never see him again, and if I did, it would have no effect on me. It was much easier being my old self.

Of course I was growing up. I was still a virgin and never thought I'd be anything else until I got married. Marriage was an unlikely prospect, with all the boys going off to war the minute they graduated. Still, I liked to flirt; I liked to learn the new dances like the jitterbug and the Lindy Hop. My friend May and I would go to the fancy Jewish dress shops, the Parisian and Cohen Brothers, where her mother had an account. Thanks to that account, we'd finally get to try on clothes, pretending how we'd go to New York City one day and wear them in the Easter parade, and then to some fancy restaurant or nightclub, like we saw in the Fred Astaire or *Thin Man* movies. We still loved the movies, even if half of them seemed to be about the war we got so much about in the papers and the radio. The best one was *Casablanca,* though I have to admit I felt closer to Ingrid Bergman than Dooley Wilson, the black pianist who played "As Time Goes By."

I began identifying with black successes in public life. In the movies I became a fan of Lena Horne in *Panama Hattie*. I longed to see Paul Robeson on Broadway. I bought Nat King Cole's first smash "Straighten Up and Fly Right" and played it until it wore out. I must admit, though, that, like any bobby-soxer of any color, my heart belonged to the adorable Frank Sinatra, who was creating riots at the Paramount Theater in New York. I hated boxing, but I followed Joe Louis, the "Brown Bomber." I noticed when black soldiers did something heroic, when they became officers, when the Navy's first black captain took command of the U.S.S. *Booker T. Washington*. Blacks started raising two hands with what we called the "Double V," victory abroad, and victory at home. Having had a taste of the South, even here in the North, I felt it would be a long time coming, and I thought a great deal about the hypocrisy of black soldiers giving their lives fighting a racist for a country that was still treating them in such a racist way. But patriotism quickly vanquished all negative thoughts, especially when the radio played some song like "This is My Country" or anything from the new hit *Oklahoma,* which made us all feel like pioneers with nothing but a wonderful, new frontier ahead of us. When I saw that the WACs were finally accepting black women, I thought about joining once I graduated, if this awful war was still going on.

Everything was rationed—meat, milk, coffee, shoes, socks. The fancy Golden Dawn hosiery shop had nothing to sell, and the halls of Kresge's and the shelves of the A&P were half empty. Luckily, my family had a lot of good cooks who could make a little go a long way and taste great. Over dinners we talked about the war and cried about people we knew who had died in it, but we also tried to enjoy life. We'd play records—big band stuff, anything by Duke Ellington or Glenn Miller's "I've Got a Gal in Kalamazoo." We'd have fun going on about Hollywood romances, little Mickey Rooney and big Ava Gardner. We gossiped about the marriage of Cary Grant, on whom we all had crushes, to million-dollar-baby Woolworth heiress Barbara Hutton. Life was so unfair that a rich girl who seemed so boring to us could get this heartthrob. Movies, even more than baseball at the time, were the American pastime, because this was before Jackie Robinson broke the color line and gave blacks sports heroes with whom they could identify. Somehow, movies were different. Even up in the balcony, we never felt excluded from the projected fantasies.

One day the call came. It was late 1944, after D day had turned the tide in Europe, and things for the allies were finally looking good. Mary, my mother once again, picked up the phone, and it was Strom Thurmond. He was on leave in Philadelphia and wanted to see me, he said. He asked Mary if she would bring me to town. Why he called at all mystified me. It was like winning a lottery I didn't want. And why he didn't call Carrie, whom I had only heard from on the phone and hadn't seen all year, mystified me as well. Although I was ambivalent in my response, Mary didn't allow me any choice in the matter. I *had* to go see him. And as I thought about my true emotions, I felt unable to resist his siren call, despite the fact that, like Ulysses, it could result in my crashing on the rocks.

I wanted to belong to someone, even if this particular someone might not want me to get too close. Every girl wants her daddy, and I wanted mine, however unlikely a parent he might be. I also wanted to ask him, as in the Bible, "Why hast thou forsaken me?" But now he was here, and he wasn't forsaking me any more. Yes, I was weak in saying yes to seeing him, but how could I truly say no? All the hatred, all the resentment I had built up as a defense against his rejection of me, now had to go on hold. Nonetheless, I assured myself that I was ready to pull it out if I needed it.

We took the train to Philadelphia. We didn't stop at Chester. According to Mary, Carrie was busy with her war efforts. Too busy to meet the man she loved? I wondered but held back the thought. Carrie, for whatever reason, had abdicated her motherhood of me to her sister, affirming the decision made when I was born. I would have liked her to be a part of this homecoming, but it was not to be. We took a cab from the train to a large, anonymous businessman's hotel. I would have thought a man as distinguished as my father would have stayed at a luxury palace like the Bellevue Stratford on Rittenhouse Square, not at this semi-fleabag. Maybe he didn't want anyone to see him, but, if so, why was he bothering at all? It wasn't as if we had a deep relationship. Mary called him from the lobby, and he asked us to come up. It would have been nice if he had taken us out for a meal, but, then again, given his family's deep beliefs, the sight of him in public with two black ladies was probably more than he wanted to handle.

We went to the balcony, not to a bedroom but to a dayroom that traveling salesmen would hire to show their wares. When Strom Thurmond opened the door, I was bowled over by how handsome he was. This was my father? Wow! He was all dressed up in his khaki uniform, his chest gleaming with medals which were exceeded in their brilliance only by his piercing blue eyes. Most of what little sandy hair he had three years ago was now gone, either through age or the army barber, but he was tan and ruddy and stood amazingly erect. War had agreed with him. "Hello," he said awkwardly. He had not met Mary before. He shook her hand, then turned to me and looked me up and down, as he had when we first met. "How are you, Essie Mae?" Before I could answer, he shook my hand in that powerful vise of his. I must have grimaced with pain. "Are you feeling all right, young lady?"

"I'm just fine, sir."

"It sure is nice to see you both. It is so nice to be back in the United States." He showed us into the small room and had us sit down at what looked like a card table. The room was Spartan, although there was a nice view of what looked like Constitution Hall in the distance. He offered us each a glass of water, nothing else. "Essie Mae, I hope you've been drinking water, like I told you."

I was amazed he remembered.

"It's the only thing that's not rationed," Mary said, and Judge Thurmond chuckled.

"The best things in life are free." He sized me up again for a long time. "I hope you've been watching your diet," he said, as if he were accusing me that I hadn't. "Try to avoid the fried foods," he admonished both of us. "I know you all love them; try to think how bad they are for you before you eat them. And no pot likker," he continued his health lecture, referring to the mix of fatback and vegetable juice from cooking the greens with pork shreds. "Just steam them. Vegetables are delicious by themselves. Let God do the cooking."

"Well. You sure do look good for a man who's been to war, Mister Strom," Mary said.

"I haven't seen a vegetable for so long, I'm homesick. I miss that barbecue. I can't wait to get home to Mama." A home I'll never be invited into, I thought.

My father told us all about his wartime experiences. It sounded a little like a lecture he might have given to the Rotary Club back in Edgefield, but I didn't take that personally. That was his style, a little bombastic, like that of a schoolteacher, which he had been. He liked to hold forth and go on and on, though not for the sake of hearing himself talk. He kept those blue eyes trained on Mary and me, to make sure we were listening and learning. Nor was he a braggart. Despite all the medals on his chest, he spent a lot of time explaining how dull his first two years in the service had been, chained to a desk. "They thought I was too old to shoot anybody but myself," he said self-deprecatingly.

He told us how hard he had to pull strings to give up his exemption from service because he was a judge. Despite the nobility and rightness of the Allied cause, a lot of people were pulling strings to stay out of battle, not get in. He bragged to us how fit he was and showed off by making us feel the muscles in his arms. They were as hard as rocks, as firm as his handshake. He seemed a little silly, like a boy and not a judge, yet he had the medals right there to prove his valor.

He entered the service as a captain at a military police battalion in Albany, New York, then rose to major at Governors Island in New York City where he was stationed for over a year, doing personnel work and lobbying to get sent into battle overseas. I couldn't help but wonder why he didn't arrange to see me like he was doing now on one of his leaves. Finally, in 1943, he got his wish, and, by now a lieutenant colonel, was sent to England. "I loved those cathedrals," he went on and on about how beautiful places like Westminster Abbey and Salisbury and Wells were, and how barbaric the Nazis were to be bombing these sacred monuments to Christian civilization. "Savages," he called the Germans, somewhat ironically, I thought, for weren't they the master race of Aryans that Ben Tillman so admired? And wouldn't Ben Tillman have called blacks—like Mary and me—"savages"? And yet here we all were together.

The judge made D day come alive for us. He flew over the English Channel in a glider, as part of an airborne convoy of over a hundred such motorless planes towed in the air by normal aircraft, then released to soar on their own over Utah Beach, where the battle was raging. Neither Mary nor I had ever been in a plane. It sounded amazing and terrifying, to fly without power, like a bird, with Germans shooting all around you. It was like a movie, but real, and the man bringing it all to life was my real father, which was still surreal in itself.

The judge's glider crashed on French soil, and he was badly injured. As with his muscles, he showed off the scar on his knee by pulling up his trousers. That, I guess, was a badge of courage that he wore as proudly as his medals. He described the whole area as littered with crashed gliders, and how, under heavy fire and with blood pouring from his wounds, he helped unload a jeep from inside the glider and drive around the battlefield rescuing other soldiers, all under heavy Nazi fire and bombs exploding all around him. After D day, he fought in the Battle of the Bulge and helped liberate many towns in France and Belgium. He went through an inventory of the decorations on his chest, which included a Purple Heart for being wounded, a Bronze Star for combat bravery, a French croix de guerre, and a Belgian Order of the Crown.

"Did you kill anybody?" was all I could ask him.

"The opportunity did not arise," was his answer.

His role in liberating the concentration camp at Buchenwald in Germany made a huge impression on him, he said. "Savage" was the word he kept using. He told us how when he entered the camp he saw a huge pile of bodies piled up like logs. Then one of the bodies moved, and he felt as though he were in some kind of horror movie in which the dead came back to life. As it turned out, most of the bodies were alive. The Nazis had stacked them up to starve to death. They were too weak to walk, and they were just laid out in the rain and cold to die. My father called medics, and he and his troops disassembled this mountain of death and tried to save these poor people. "The vast majority of them ultimately did not survive," my father said, always using big legal-type words like "majority" and "ultimately" instead of saying "Most of them died." I suppose that's how judges were supposed to talk—an occupational hazard.

My father mentioned other Nazi tortures he saw: skinning the Jews and using the skin as lampshades, smashing the heads of Jews with massive hammers. "Savage," he repeated. "We never had a problem with Jews," he commented. There was a note of ruling-class superiority in his tone that made me uncomfortable. He was passing judgment on the Jews, declaring them "okay." But who was he to judge? Yes, he *was* a judge, but this wasn't a court. I reflected on the Jewish shops in the Edgefield square, and I thought about the "problem Jew" of South Carolina, Franklin Moses. Then I censored my thoughts of racial supremacy, Nazi tortures, and southern lynchings. They were natural thoughts for the times we were in, but they were not right for me. Here was my father, a war hero, making our world safe again, and I was blaming him for the wrongs of his father and of the South. They weren't his fault. After all, here he was with me. How bad could he be?

He went on about the generals he had seen—Eisenhower, Patton, Omar Bradley—about how cold Europe was, about those English cathedrals and Notre Dame in Paris.

"The place with the hunchback?" I interjected.

"You must go to a good school," he complimented me, surprised perhaps that I would have any knowledge of literature. Again, I veered myself away from unfair thoughts. "What do they have you read?"

"*Great Expectations, Silas Marner, Moby Dick.*"

He seemed even more surprised. "That's very good, Essie. What about Shakespeare? Any Shakespeare yet?"

Somehow, I felt it was my turn to show off. "Tomorrow and tomorrow and tomorrow, creep in this petty pace from day to day, till the last syllable of recorded time. And all our yesterdays have lighted fools the way to dusty death. Out, out brief candle . . ." I couldn't believe the look on Mary's face. She had never once sat down with me to talk about my studies. She had no idea what I was learning.

"Well, I declare, Essie. That's fine work. You keep studying like that, there's no telling what you can do. Fine work," my father repeated. I'm not sure if he was proud of me or simply shocked. For a while, nonetheless, I basked in his approval.

My less charitable thoughts returned when it was time for us to go. Judge Thurmond never once asked about Carrie, never said "I'd love to take you to see those cathedrals," never said "I'd love to show you around Edgefield." He didn't say when he might see me again. All he did was to advise me to eat a lot of carrots, which were good for my eyes. He had noticed my new glasses and I had told him the story of my music teacher. That struck a health chord with him, one of his favorite subjects, and expounded about carrots and vitamin A. "I would tell you to eat liver, but I don't care for it myself," he said. "But stick to carrots and spinach and leafy vegetables. And don't forget to drink plenty of water." He did not offer to buy us a new lamp or take us out for a healthy meal. He just handed Mary a large envelope. "Here's something to help you out."

"Thank you, Mister Strom," she said.

Then he crushed our hands one last time and saw us out the door. There were no kisses or hugs. He didn't ride down to the lobby in the elevator.

"Is he ashamed of me?" I asked Mary when we were out in the street.

"Ashamed?" She opened the envelope and counted 200 dollars in twenties, just as before. "Do you call this ashamed?"

Two hundred dollars was indeed a lot of money, but spread out over three years, it wasn't *that* much. Wasn't a daughter worth more than that? "That doesn't mean he cares about me," I said.

"It does to me. It does indeed," Mary said.

Again, my meeting with my father soon felt like it had been a dream. I didn't hear from him or about him at all. He had told us he was going to the Philippines. I prayed that nothing awful would happen to him in the Pacific theater. I worried when I didn't hear from him that it had. But he had been out of touch in New York, and then Europe, and now he was out of touch in Asia. What difference did it make? I still held on to an insane, unrealistic hope that he would come home and one day, some way, somehow, we might be a real father and daughter.

It was back to my job at Coatesville Hospital and back to school for the twelfth grade. Nineteen forty-five was the year we won the war, and an unforgettable one in many ways. I wept when Roosevelt died of a stroke in April down in Georgia. He had looked so tired in the newsreels, the nurse in me said something was wrong, and it was. I knew America would never get a leader like that again. He seemed so compassionate, despite being so rich and patrician and different from poor people. He was the patron saint of poor people; he led us out of the depression, out of the war. What would America do without him? I didn't have a lot of confidence in his successor, Vice President Truman. With his Missouri twang, he seemed like a farmer, like someone from Edgefield, and not a statesman. Yet he would prove us all wrong.

Mussolini and his mistress Clara Petacci were hanged in Milan. The attention to the mistresses of the worst two men on earth brought that term unpleasantly into my consciousness. I hated to think of my mother as someone's mistress, but that's what she was, and it was a miserable position, even at the top. After Hitler committed suicide, the diaries of his mistress Eva Braun were made public. She wrote about how badly, how indifferently he treated her, all the lies and broken promises. She said she wished she had a dog instead. That made me think about my mother as well. What was she getting out of her "romance," if that was what it was with the judge? Envelopes of twenty-dollar bills? That wasn't romantic to me, not enough to put up with the hopelessness of it all. Maybe he was better to her than to me. I was only a daughter, an accident, but she was a goddess. Maybe he was seeing her. Maybe she was getting the love I was not. I never saw her, either, so I couldn't know. I kept having these conflicting emotions, caroming between pride at my ancestry and regret that these two people had ever crossed the path of my awareness.

As a senior in high school, I was forced to make some career decisions. I had always privately hoped I would attend college. That seemed to be the passport to a better life. Since I had very good grades, I think I could have gotten into a good college. However, in those days, blacks, especially black women, rarely got a higher education. That was a luxury we couldn't afford. Scholarships were rare, plus our families needed all the income an able-bodied child could bring in. And so most of us went to work, rather than staying in school. My nursing apprenticeship provided me with what seemed a logical compromise: I would go to nursing school. As a little girl, my career dream had been to become a nurse. Even if college couldn't happen, at least another dream could come true. My five summers at Coatesville Hospital were the perfect resume item. I was well-qualified to go to a nursing school as part of a big city hospital. Tuition was free, plus I would earn an income as well while I was working toward my nursing degree. Earn while I learn. It seemed the right thing to do, if not the only thing.

The three best nursing programs for black women were at Mercy-Douglas Hospital in Philadelphia; Freedman's Hospital in Washington, D.C.; and Harlem Hospital in New York City. These were all basically black hospitals, with mostly black patients, although each had a number of white doctors on staff. It didn't occur to me to apply to a program for one of the great university hospitals like Columbia Presbyterian or Massachusetts General or Johns Hopkins, though I might have been qualified to get in. I guess I "knew my place," my white father notwithstanding. There were talented blacks at all these institutions, but I was too locked into the self-perception of race limitation to try to test the color lines. I was shy and self-effacing and had never really been away from home other than that one trip to the South and a few visits to Philadelphia. So going away at all was a big deal. I was much more comfortable staying with my own people. Penetrating the white universe was far too intimidating a prospect. If my own white father didn't want me, why would anyone else?

I chose Harlem Hospital mainly because my "half-brother" Calvin Burton was now living in Harlem and working for the post office. He would look after me. The idea of having family in the big city was reassuring. Furthermore, I had always wanted to live in New York, especially after all those Fred Astaire and *Thin Man* black-and-white odes to art deco, skyscrapers, cocktails, tuxedos, jazzy foxtrots, and fast-talking sophisticates. It was the most glamorous place on earth and the total opposite of everything I had known up to this point in my life. I was more than ready to "Take the A Train."

Calvin embodied all the glamour I associated with New York. He looked like a movie star (at least, like a movie star such as Billy Dee Williams later on: There were no black, male movie stars when I first landed in New York). He dressed in dashing clothes, natty suits, ascots. Whenever he came home to Coatesville, he'd tell us tall tales of Harlem nights, about the clubs, the music, the restaurants, the people from all over the world who came up there to swing. It sounded like the American version of Paris's Bohemian Left Bank, except that it wasn't occupied by Hitler and it was black.

After Calvin graduated from high school, he had gone into the Civilian Conservation Corps, one of Roosevelt's new deal programs. After Pearl Harbor, he volunteered and enlisted, but he was soon discharged when the army doctors discovered he had a heart problem that he didn't know about. He then went to work at Worth Steel in Delaware and met and married a New York City girl who brought him to Harlem and changed his life. I hoped Harlem would change mine as well.

I said a fairly unemotional farewell to Mary and my stepfather. It wasn't like I was going overseas, or at least that's what I told myself to keep from crying. I had never lived away from home before, and I was a little scared and a lot excited. Carrying a big suitcase with the nicest clothes I had to wear on those Fred Astaire nights, I took the Pennsylvania Railroad by myself to New York, passing Philadelphia and wondering what how my mother was doing. We had talked on the phone, and she seemed very excited about my big move, praising me for being accepted by all those prestigious programs. I hoped to have time to go and visit with her, or, better yet, have her come to visit me in Manhattan, where my fantasy was to show her the town and go to a Broadway play together and watch all the fancy gentlemen in the audience get knocked out by her lovely looks. I was a little sad to be on the train all alone, but the anticipation of my new adventure made me forget the lonely thoughts.

I myself was knocked out by the sight from the train of the skyscrapers across the Hudson River. I had seen them in the magazines and in the newsreels, but here they were, looking even taller than I imagined. I could make out the Empire State Building, the tallest in the world, and my heart started racing. The train disappeared into a long tunnel. When I emerged at Pennsylvania Station, it was like I had left small-town life behind and entered, via a space capsule, a whole new world. The station was an immense Roman temple with thousands of people passing through and bright lights advertising everything from Camels to Coke to Chevrolets. There were lots of men in military uniforms and lots of others in the corporate uniform of dark suits, carrying *Wall Street Journals*. I could feel the surge of big business all around, the energy of the metropolis.

Thank goodness Calvin appeared to greet me, as I was overwhelmed by all the bustle. He had on a tweed jacket and a silk tie and seemed very sophisticated. We shared a big hug. We stood in a taxi line and got a cab uptown. New York cab drivers were famous for being big talkers, but ours didn't say a word, only to grunt with annoyance when Calvin gave him the address in Harlem. I got a sore neck from craning my head out the window looking at the skyscrapers. How in the world did they build them so tall? We drove up Eighth Avenue, and Calvin pointed out Times Square and the great theaters. I saw the marquees for *Carousel*, and *On the Town.* I knew the music from the radio and excitedly hummed it to myself. Here I was, for real. "New York, New York. A wonderful town. The Bronx is up and the Battery's down."

"Why wasn't Harlem in the song?" I asked Calvin.

"We've got our own music," he said with a warm smile.

The cab entered Central Park, and suddenly the city became the country, with horse-drawn carriages and endless greenery. It was September and the leaves were turning brilliant colors, and it was magic. Through the trees I caught glimpses of more skyscrapers. Calvin told me they were apartment houses on Fifth Avenue and Central Park West.

"Who lives there?" I asked him, full of questions.

"Rich people. This is a money town. Oh boy."

As we drove out of the park, the buildings resumed. They were apartment houses, five and six stories, much lower than the skyscrapers that were everywhere else in New York. Some had fancy striped awnings on the windows, but most looked run-down. Lots of men, black men, were just standing on the sidewalk, as they had been in the South. "Welcome to Harlem," Calvin said.

As we kept heading north, a lot of the buildings looked bombed out or burned up. This wasn't the Harlem of my imagination. I guess I expected a Cotton Club on every corner, fancy stores that sold the natty clothes Calvin was wearing. Instead, I got a war zone.

"We had a big riot here two years ago," Calvin explained. "Because of the war there's been no money to rebuild."

"A riot over what?"

"Black and white," he said. "What else?" He told me how a black MP had stood up for a black woman whom a white policeman, an Irishman—all the cops here were Irish, Calvin said—was arresting for being drunk. The cop shot the MP, and all Harlem went wild. "We're in Europe and Asia fighting and dying for America, but in Harlem we're still second-class citizens," Calvin summed up. The "pot had been boiling" for quite a while, Calvin said, ever since the New York police commissioner had declared Harlem off-limits to all white servicemen. The commissioner blamed the staggering rate of venereal disease in the military on Harlem's prostitutes and began the biggest vice campaign in the city's history. "We don't like our ladies' honor impugned," Calvin said, with a sad smile.

In the riot, hundreds of people were injured, hundreds of buildings and stores burned and looted. "White-owned," Calvin pointed out. "We know who our friends are."

Calvin lived with his wife and a young daughter in an apartment house on 118th Street off Eighth Avenue. The stoop was filled with loitering men, sleeping and reeking of liquor. The building looked as if it had once been grand, with columns and ornate brick design and stained glass, but those were better days. Inside, the halls were dirty and reeked of leaking gas. Calvin said it was full of "hotbed" apartments, which meant the landlady would rent a room to two separate lodgers, one by day and the other by night. Calvin's own apartment was small but very clean, with a lovely view of the steep, lush landscape of Morningside Park, topped by the great rotunda and classical academic halls of Columbia University. Calvin called Columbia the "American Acropolis" because of all the famous scholars who taught there. It was a school, he said, for "white geniuses." Where, I wondered, did black geniuses go?

A lot of black geniuses were associated with my new home, Harlem Hospital, on Lenox Avenue and 136th Street. After meeting his wife and child, I was taken directly to my new home by Calvin, who gave me a lovely sweater as a welcoming present, plus a little keychain that was a miniature stethoscope. "Good luck, doc," Calvin said, hugging me as he dropped me off. "I'm so proud of you, little sister," he said. That remark provided a universe of security to a highly insecure young girl, and it gave me the strength to face my intimidating new world.

I was assigned to a nurses' dormitory with a young lady named Corinna from New Jersey. In my class of forty, there were women from all over the country, as well as from Africa and the Caribbean. All the girls seemed very worldly and confident, unlike myself. All of them were black, or at least shades of black. By contrast, about a quarter of the doctors at Harlem Hospital, a grand Georgian complex surrounded by trees and covered with ivy and looking like a university, were white. Apparently, for a doctor, especially a surgeon, there was no better training than here. The violence in Harlem provided a unique and unmatched catalog of injuries and wounds on which to operate.

"This place is to stab wounds what MIT is to physics," my new roommate said. Assault trauma was the technical word. "You get more violence in Harlem than any place in the country, and all that violence ends up here as medical case studies. You got diseases here—tropical diseases, malaria, beriberi—that you don't find elsewhere, not downtown for sure, and doctors eat that up." With immigrants from all over Africa and the Southern Hemisphere, Harlem was one big medical laboratory, and Harlem Hospital was the heart of it.

Harlem Hospital started out as white as Harlem had, a fancy "uptown" for rich Manhattanites who wanted to live in the country. By 1904 the subway was opened as far as 145th Street and Seventh Avenue, so the country was only a token away. In the 1920s, however, after World War I, black people from the South began streaming into the North and needed somewhere to live. Realtors, who had overestimated the original demand for Harlem, began renting to blacks to fill their empty apartments. The old, black neighborhood in the West sixties, which was known as San Juan Hill, in honor of Theodore Roosevelt's black Rough Riders who fought in Cuba beside him, gave way to this new one. And the whites who occupied these fine buildings made an exodus of their own, to the Upper West Side of West End Avenue and Riverside Drive. It was another meaning of the phrase "the Harlem shuffle."

The people from the South thus went from sharecropper cabins to luxury flats, originally rented to upwardly mobile immigrant Jews, with steam heat, electricity, private toilets, and elevators. It must have seemed like the space age to them. For all this luxury, though, the new blacks in Harlem couldn't get decent medical care. Harlem Hospital, if it treated blacks at all, did so in a similar way to Coatesville Hospital, putting them in the poverty ward, or, far worse, using them as medical guinea pigs, testing medicines and therapies on them without their knowledge or consent. Up until 1920, there was not a single black doctor on the staff to stand up for his people. It became known in Harlem as a place "to go and die." In the 1920s, a great uproar arose over this heinous practice, and black doctors began to be recruited.

The leader of Harlem Hospital's transformation, and the director at the time I arrived, was Dr. Louis Wright, probably the most famous black physician in America. Born in Georgia, the son of a doctor, Wright had graduated from Harvard Medical School in 1915. Despite this, he could still not secure an internship at a white hospital. He thus went to the Freedmen's Hospital in Washington, D.C., which was affiliated with Howard University Medical School. After heroic service in World War I in France, where he nearly died from being gassed on the battlefield, he went home to Atlanta to begin his practice. The racism there, which he had tasted at Harvard and in his early medical days, inspired him to go north where he might both do better and do more good than he could in Georgia.

Like many educated blacks, Dr. Wright blamed many of America's current racial woes on President Woodrow Wilson. Despite his international idealism and wartime success in making good on his motto to "make the world safe for democracy," Wilson was a Virginian whose condescending attitudes toward blacks were a product of his upbringing. Wilson was very much a "separate but equal" man. He believed in segregation in government jobs, which was a major step backward for black, federal employees. It was also a symbolic retrenchment that emboldened racists throughout the country. The Ku Klux Klan, quiet for decades, held a 40,000-man march on Washington. Southern senators were able to block the first antilynching bill that had been brewing since the "red summer" (of blood) of 1918, when a huge wave of lynchings had swept the South. Blacks left the South to make a living, but they also left to save their lives.

One of these refugees, Dr. Wright came to New York and became a leader of the NAACP. Because of his Harvard credentials, a lot of northern black physicians, mostly educated at Howard, resented Dr. Wright and felt he looked down on them. It was well known in Harlem that wealthy and famous blacks invariably chose white, downtown doctors, and black doctors were understandably insecure. Dr. Wright was not. His mission was to create a black medical corps that was equal to, if not better than, the twin towers of medicine in Manhattan—Columbia-Presbyterian and Cornell-New York hospitals. I was profoundly honored to be on Dr. Wright's team.

Perhaps because everyone was trying harder to make Dr. Wright's point, Harlem Hospital seemed like a boot camp to me. I didn't think humans could work that hard. I'm sure the slaves in the cotton fields didn't have any worse hours than we nurses did. Another part of the reason for our endless hours was the recent appointment of Mrs. Alida Dailey as superintendant of nursing. Mrs. Dailey was the hospital's first black appointee. Even though all the nurses had been black since Dr. Wright's upheavals in the 1920s, the "supers" continued to remain white women. As the first of her race on the job, Mrs. Dailey must have felt she had to be a drill sergeant, and she was.

I had to wear a strict and dowdily old-fashioned uniform of a long blue dress, black stockings, and black shoes. My first autopsy nearly killed me. The late patient had had lung cancer, and when they cut him open, his lungs were as black as tar. I never even thought about having a cigarette after that. Somehow, it didn't bother the other girls in my class, who just smoked away. They told me I was "too sensitive."

I was learning a lot about medicine, but I was too fatigued to take stock of any of it. The regimen was endless. We'd get up at dawn to prepare for surgery and observe and sometimes assist at operations. Then we'd work on the wards, changing catheters, drawing blood, dressing wounds, assisting with X-rays, and, worst by far, preparing corpses for the mortuaries. Whenever we weren't on the wards, we were in class, learning all about medical tests and procedures and memorizing laboratory ranges and evaluating symptoms.

I must have come down with at least five fatal diseases in my first month, so mighty was the power of suggestion in learning about all these exotic maladies. What turned out not to be hypochondria were the constant colds I would get. No, they weren't lung cancer or tuberculosis, as so many of us students thought, but we still felt rotten, and were susceptible to a lot of contagious maladies due to our low resistance. I rarely got more than four hours of sleep a night, and sometimes, if I saw an empty room, I'd flop down on the bed and fall into the deepest sleep before the screams down the hall would inevitably wake me up. It was definitely a test of our stamina. I suppose the idea was to teach us a kind of professional grace under pressure, but to me it seemed like they were pushing us beyond human endurance.

I was too fatigued and overworked to take advantage of the magnificent city I was in. I could see the skyscrapers downtown from the hospital windows, but I could never find any time to get into the subway, which for a nickel could have been my magic carpet to endless adventures, and take Manhattan the way I had dreamed of doing. It was more like being in prison. I understood why they put prisons in the country. Being in sight of all the big buildings and bright lights turned temptation into punishment. Despite its prestige, despite the honor of the medical calling, I began to wonder whether I had "the right stuff" to become a nurse.

My only recreation those first few months was to go on long Sunday walks on nearby Seventh Avenue. If Broadway was the Great White Way, then Seventh was the Great Black Way, the main drag of Harlem. The shopping may have been on 125th Street, but Seventh Avenue was where the action was. With a tree-and flower-filled median, it was a wide, majestic boulevard. It was the path for both parades and the grand funeral processions where people were dispatched to heaven in style, often to a jazz band's accompaniment. There were movie palaces along the way, the Alhambra, the Lafayette, where from a plush orchestra seat I watched Joan Crawford in *Mildred Pierce*. It was the first time I hadn't been exiled to the colored balcony, the "nigger heaven," as it was called after the title of a famous Harlem Renaissance book by Carl Van Vechten. To me, it was heaven to be able to sit wherever I chose. It was a celestial escape from the infernal duties at the hospital, which at my most exhausted moments seemed less a cathedral of healing than a medieval torture chamber, full of screams and blood and dead bodies.

I passed the famed nightclub Small's Paradise and despaired of ever having a date who would take me dancing. I wandered into the lobby of the Hotel Theresa at 125th and Seventh. This was the Waldorf Astoria of Harlem. Joe Louis stayed there, and Eddie "Rochester" Anderson and Hattie McDaniel, and all the African and Haitian diplomats whose color precluded lodging at the Waldorf. I found it hard to believe that, until 1940, the Theresa, like Harlem Hospital, had been whites-only. Where had the stars stayed then?

I saw where they lived. The two grandest neighborhoods in Harlem were Strivers Row and Sugar Hill. The former, the blocks of 138th and 139th Streets off Seventh, were elegant town houses built in the 1890s for rich whites, designed by the famed architect Stanford White, whose firm designed Columbia University and Madison Square Garden, where I also longed to go. Powerful lawyers and judges and businessmen and ministers and professors lived here now. Dr. Louis Wright lived in one of these mansions.

Such high achievers constituted Harlem "society," which apparently was as stratified and snobbish as that of Park Avenue. All the people I saw coming out of those houses were all quite light-skinned, such pallor being a badge of class. Did that mean I could be part of the Harlem elite? Or if they heard my connection to Pitchfork Ben Tillman, would these swells slam the door in my face? I was working so hard, I was certain the issue would never arise. Darker-skinned entertainers lived here, too: comic Stepin Fetchit, composer Eubie Blake, boxer Harry Wills. Harlem was proud of its native sons, and everyone lived vicariously through them. Walking on Strivers Row was our equivalent of going to Beverly Hills and taking a bus tour of the homes of the stars.

The other great address was Sugar Hill, way north of 145th street above the Polo Grounds, where the Giants played. The preeminent address in all of Harlem was 409 Edgecombe Avenue, a fourteen-story luxury apartment house that had once been all Jewish. Now the Jews came as guests, people like George Gershwin, Felix Frankfurter, George S. Kaufman, and Dorothy Parker. Their hosts were the new black aristocracy, people like lawyer Thurgood Marshall, genius scholar W. E. B. Du Bois, artist Aaron Douglas, folksinger Josh White, and, in the penthouse, Walter White, head of the NAACP.

A potent symbol of black power, 409 was a palace on a hill, yet it seemed completely out of reach to me. I felt a greater kinship with the people on the ground, the poor men on the stoops, the kids playing in the gutters, the desperate folks lining up at the pawnshops. That was the real Harlem, not the Harlem of chauffeurs and liveried doormen and Cadillacs and minks. Yes, these trappings of wealth were proof that blacks could "make it" in America, but the people in the street were a greater proof of how far we had to go. Given my secret white heritage and my inclusion in this exclusive nursing school, I guess I qualified for what Professor Du Bois had categorized as the "Talented Tenth," that top percentage of blacks he believed would lead the race to glory. Nevertheless, in reality, I could barely keep my head above water. Alone in Harlem, I couldn't have felt more marginal.

I found shelter from this storm of loneliness and alienation at the Abyssinian Baptist Church on 138th Street between Seventh and Lenox Avenues. This grand marble edifice was the most legendary congregation in Harlem, if not America, thanks to its charismatic minister, the Reverend Adam Clayton Powell, Jr., who in 1943 had been elected as New York's first black congressman. While the dashing Powell was religious aristocracy (his father, Powell, Sr., had founded the church), he was by no means a stuffed-shirt. He had shocked church elders by marrying a beautiful "high yaller" showgirl from the Cotton Club, Isabel Washington, and was as likely to be seen in the nightclubs as he was at the pulpit. Whatever his personal habits, Reverend Powell was a terrific speaker and a sassy symbol of hope. He hated discrimination, and he railed against it both in church and in Congress. Powell was so light-skinned that it was always said that he could have "passed for white." Perhaps the most inspiring thing about him was that he didn't *want* to.

A lot of girls, the light-skinned ones, frequently talked about passing, marrying into the white world, preferably the rich, white world, and living on Easy Street—Park Avenue, not Lenox. Here I was, *born* into the rich, white world, the plantation world, and yet where was I? It could have been easy to be resentful, because I was "it" or at least half of "it," yet it was doing me no good aside from two envelopes of money. I was grateful to have a church to turn to, to count my blessings and pray for more, and to watch this great "white" preacher embrace his blackness. If he could be happy with it, so could anyone else.

In his sermons, Reverend Powell often invoked Marcus Garvey, the famed separatist leader whose Black Freedom Hall stood right next door to Abyssinian Baptist. The Reverend got me so interested in Garvey, I went to the Harlem branch of the New York Public Library to read about him. Having thought the Coatesville library was an august cathedral of learning, I was totally knocked out by the grandeur of the New York libraries, never more so than when I visited the main branch at Forty-second and Fifth Avenue, with its lion statues outside and soaring ceilings within, and its endless books on everything you ever wanted to know. It was being inside this library that first inspired me to think about becoming a teacher. Maybe it was the shafts of sunlight, streaming in from the heavens over the fine wood tables, and the countless readers from every nation on earth wrapped up in their books and studies as if they were at prayer. In any event, it was a religious experience for me that ultimately would become a conversion.

My goal in going to the library was to learn more about Garvey and the notion of black pride and awareness, and I was glad I did, because it made me prouder in the process. Marcus Garvey was a Jamaican who came to New York and founded the Universal Negro Improvement Association, which swelled to millions of members at its height after World War I, when lynchings were at *their* height. He set up his own Black United States, serving as the president with his own black army with black generals, his own Black Cross with black nurses, his own religion with a black God. Black Pride seems to have originated with Garvey, who was known as the Black Moses because of his desire to lead his people out of their figurative current slavery back to the Promised Land of Africa.

Not all blacks embraced Garvey, who, in the picture books I paged through at the library was big and fat and wore plumed hats and flashy uniforms. He appalled the intellectual elite, such as W. E. B. Du Bois, with his doctrine of racial purity. Garvey even supported the Ku Klux Klan, because he concurred with their bloody mission to separate the races. I'm not sure what he would have thought of me. In any case, the southern-accented federal government of Woodrow Wilson was about as comfortable with Garvey as they were with leprosy. They were able to crucify him for mail fraud in connection with the sale of stock in his Black Star Line, on which he was planning to ship his disciples back to Africa. He was imprisoned and then deported as an undesirable alien. He died in complete obscurity in London in 1940, but Reverend Powell wouldn't let us forget his former neighbor's proud mission. Powell, like Garvey, was often accused of being a charlatan, albeit a tonier one. I guess that's what happens when you make the white power elite as nervous as these two black leaders did.

In the hallowed halls of the New York Public Library, I also read a famous novel called *Passing*, by Nella Larsen, and I learned that she was one of the key writers in what was known as the "Harlem Renaissance," a flowering of the black arts which took place in the late 1920s and early 1930s. A lot of the girls in my nursing class, especially the ones from outside the New York area, were reading it. It was a kind of *Sex and the Single Girl* for biracial women of the time, except with a very bleak ending. Many of my classmates, despite the nature of our supposedly selfless, nunlike career, had fantasies of coming to Manhattan, meeting a rich man at the hospital, and settling down to the good life.

Passing was just such a story about two young and beautiful light-skinned childhood friends who meet in their late twenties after having not been in touch since their teens. One girl has married a prominent black doctor associated with Harlem Hospital and lives on Strivers Row, where she is active in black charities and Harlem "society." (I immediately thought of Dr. Louis Wright, but this was supposedly fiction.) The other girl, who is blond and blue-eyed but still half-black, has "passed" for white and married a powerful Park Avenue banker who is also a hard-core racist. His pet name for his olive-skinned wife is "Nig." He had no clue about her mixed blood. In the book, the two friends reconnect, and each decides the other has the better life. The doctor's wife wishes she had "passed" and escaped from Harlem, while the banker's wife is sorry about the tense charade she is living and yearns to go back to Harlem. In the end, the white banker discovers his wife's deception, and he catches her at a glamorous black party in a Sugar Hill luxury apartment modeled on 409 Edgecombe. The book wasn't clear whether she is pushed or jumps out the window, but the message was clear: Passing was a bad idea.

Nella Larsen herself was biracial, the daughter of a Danish mother and a West Indian father from the Virgin Islands. Like me, she had become a nurse, training at Lincoln Hospital in New York. She worked for a time in Tuskegee, Alabama, at Booker T. Washington's Tuskegee Institute, but she hated the South and came back to New York and worked as a nurse at Lincoln hospital and then the city's health department. However, she found nursing very unsatisfying and quit the profession to become a children's librarian. She worked at none other than the New York Public Library at Forty-second Street and Fifth Avenue. There she was inspired to become a writer.

Larsen's first book, *Quicksand,* which featured a cultured and urbane mixed-race heroine who marries a backwoods preacher, won her many awards. Her second, *Passing*, was acclaimed as one of the best novels ever written by a black woman. Larsen became the first black woman to win a Guggenheim Fellowship to research her next book in Europe. And then her world fell apart. Like Marcus Garvey, she seemed to have been railroaded on questionable charges, here that she had plagiarized a short story from an obscure white woman writer. She never wrote again. Nor could she even get her librarian's job back. Instead, she was forced to go back to nursing. I heard she was working in a small, black hospital in Brooklyn. I would have liked to have met her, but I doubted that she was receiving many fans at that point.

Larsen's sad ending didn't make me dissatisfied with being black in any way, but it did underscore my own dissatisfactions with the nursing profession. That someone could leave it had never occurred to me before. I had seen the career choice of curing the sick as an irrevocable one. That Nella Larsen could abandon it for becoming a librarian and a writer somehow made it seem okay to think about doing something else to help others, though her bad luck in the process stirred up all my superstitious instincts.

Still, I was seriously reevaluating my decision. The nursing program was beating me down. It wasn't so much the endless hours or even the mundane tasks that took up a lot of my time, such as mopping floors and emptying bedpans, which seemed more appropriate to janitorial training than nursing. The real problem for me was the sick people. Yes, it was going to be my job to help them get well. But the vast majority of cases that came to Harlem Hospital seemed to be caused not by acts of God, but by acts of man—the savage police beatings, the shootings and stabbings over women and money and thwarted crime, the rickets and scurvy of children too poor and uncared for to eat a decent diet, the old people abandoned and left alone to die. The doctors may have thrived on these "case studies," as they saw them, but I didn't. I was both horrified and outraged at the poor care these black people were receiving daily—the preventive measures that would have helped to keep them *out* of Harlem Hospital.

I decided I wasn't cut out to become a Florence Nightingale, always responding to emergencies like a fireman. It occurred to me that I wanted to help people through education. That, I saw, was what most of the patients lacked, that and a fair chance in life. If knowledge was power, schooling seemed the best way to give black people a fair chance in America, and that's where I wanted to put my energies. The fact that my father had been a schoolteacher and was so proud of it may have lurked in the back of my head. One tends to want to follow in a father's footsteps, especially if those footsteps led to the kind of distinguished career he was having. Somehow, even if it were wishful thinking, I seemed to sense him looking over my shoulder. I felt in my heart that he would approve of my change of plans, wherever in the world he might be.

The difficulty here, though, was that I knew that if I wanted to become a schoolteacher, I would have to go to college. Money was a big issue, in that my family didn't have any to speak of. I had my scholarship to nursing school, but it wasn't transferable. It really was less a grant than a work-study sort of program; in effect, I was working my way through nursing school, and was I ever working! College would be different. These were the days before college scholarships were as prevalent as they are now. Back then, they were highly unusual.

Despite all of this, I made the hard choice of dropping out of the nursing program. I didn't really discuss the matter with anyone besides Calvin. "Now who's gonna look after my bad heart?" he teased me, but he was totally supportive. "You follow your heart, little sister," he told me. "You gotta love what you do, or it'll do you in." I didn't consult with the family in Coatesville. I didn't want to disappoint them.

Of course, at the beginning I felt badly about leaving. I wasn't helped by Mrs. Dailey, the superintendent of nursing, who took my decision to drop out as a personal affront. "We're investing a lot of resources and a lot of energy on you, Miss Washington," she told me with an impatient scowl on her already stern face. "Do you realize how many young ladies we had to disappoint when we chose you for the program?"

"I'm sorry, Mrs. Dailey," I sputtered. "I don't want to seem ungrateful."

"You don't seem. You *are*."

"What else can I do?"

"You can stay right where you are. Get back to work like a real nurse. We don't have time for whining and wailing."

I hated being treated like a malingerer. "I don't want to waste any more of the hospital's time, and your time, if this isn't right for me."

"Miss Washington, can you sincerely say you can do more good in some classroom somewhere than you can on our front line saving lives?"

"I believe so. Yes ma'am. I want to try."

"Once you go, don't expect to come back. Your place will be taken."

"Yes, ma'am," was all I could say.

"And it will look awful on your resume, to be a dropout. It raises a lot of questions. Schools don't like those questions. Neither do employers."

"Yes, ma'am." I felt as if I were being interrogated for some heinous crime.

"What will your parents say? Have you discussed this with them?"

"Yes, ma'am," I lied. If she only knew who my parents were, she might have been a little more sympathetic.

So I moved in with Calvin, who was very hospitable to find space for me in his already crowded flat. I slept on the couch in his living room, enjoyed waking up to the spectacular view, and felt excited about getting to know the world below 110th Street. To that end, I planned to enroll for some classes in education and psychology at New York University in Greenwich Village. To pay my tuition, I needed a job, and jobs in 1945 were hard to come by, for blacks or for whites. My first position was as a front desk clerk in a dry cleaners in Harlem. I lasted two months. After the excitement, heartbreak, and despair of Harlem Hospital, the cleaners was a very dull place, just a lot of middle-class people, or people who aspired to become middle class, bringing in their nice suits and dresses.

At the cleaners, a fellow clerk found an opportunity downtown, and we both leapt at it. A ritzy ladies shop off Fifth Avenue called Jane Engels needed two stock girls. We weren't to wait on the customers; fancy, white women who seemed like debutantes in those Fred Astaire movies had that task. Our job was to fold up the clothes after the customers tried them on, wrap boxes, and do an infinite amount of dusting. The owner was fanatic about dust. She dressed us in gray-and-white maid's uniforms that she said came from Paris and insisted they weren't for domestic maids, but for *couture* maids, as if I understood the difference. She claimed the maids at Christian Dior wore the same outfits, and that was supposed to give us a sense of pride and dignity. I think we made ten dollars a day, but I worked six days a week, and it was a living. Besides, I was now in Manhattan, the real Manhattan, at last.

In the six months I worked for Jane Engels, I never once saw a black customer, although one of the clerks did mention that both Hazel Scott and Ethel Waters had bought clothes there, and Billy Eckstine had gotten something for one of his girlfriends. I did see movie stars, which was a total thrill. The first was Claudette Colbert, a regular customer. I was amazed at how tiny she was. She had seemed so big on the screen. I wanted to tell her how funny she was in *The Palm Beach Story*, but I didn't dare, for fear of losing my job. Other stars who came in were Rosalind Russell and Kitty Carlisle. Then there were the wives of famous men, like Phyllis Cerf, whose husband Bennett ran Random House. These ladies, whom I overheard planning lunches at the Colony, evenings of Toscanini at Carnegie Hall, and dancing at El Morocco, were so elegant and talked in that fancy New York "theahtah" style. They made me feel like a sharecropper in Edgefield, a complete hayseed country girl. The salesgirls looked and sounded as sophisticated as the customers; they had to make the sale and earn the commissions they lived on. In reality, most of them were poor, Jewish girls from the Bronx and Brooklyn, and they were incredibly nice to me and the other stock girls. We were all together in this sisterhood of style.

After work I would take the subway to Greenwich Village to go to my classes. Just as I had never seen anything like Harlem, I had likewise never seen anything like New York's answer to Paris's Left Bank, its avant-garde Bohemia. There were lots of little coffee shops, or cafes, as they were called here, where people seemed to be sitting outside smoking at all hours, especially those when everyone else was at work. There were many small theaters, known as Off Broadway, and the men all had long, straggly hair; goatees; and mustaches. What struck me most were the large number of interracial couples, all of them black men with white women, many of whom looked like artists wearing gypsy-style clothes and lots of exotic jangly jewelry. I guessed being a true artist meant having a black boyfriend, most of whom seemed to wear berets and sport goatees, and may have been artists themselves. These women were definitely not Jane Engels's customers. I didn't see one white man with a black woman, however, though I'm sure it must have happened in this atmosphere of anything goes. I had visions of Judge Thurmond and my mother walking arm in arm down Bleecker Street and holding hands in a cafe and nobody noticing them at all.

I must have seemed like a complete square. Wearing my French maid's uniform and carrying my school books, I'd get out of the subway at Sheridan Square and walk over to Washington Square to my NYU classes. I worried that people would think I was dressed for Halloween, but the nice thing about New York was that nobody noticed anything. I found NYU to be a factory school. The classes were huge, the teachers were impersonal lecturers, the students were in a big hurry to get out of class and go somewhere else. I didn't form any close attachments. There were a few other black students in my classes, but they paid no more attention to me than the white ones. Maybe it was the maid's uniform. Maybe it was just New York.

A boyfriend might have been the answer in this busy, lonely town, but I wasn't meeting anyone. Nor was I actually looking. One boy from high school in Coatesville called on me when he got out of the service. I took him strolling on Seventh Avenue, and we went to Small's Paradise, one of the few surviving nightclubs that had made Harlem so famous as America's Partyland during Prohibition. The more famous Cotton Club, which never admitted blacks in its heyday, had by now moved to midtown. They used to have "battles of the bands" here—Count Basie versus Duke Ellington—in which hundreds of revelers would be up dancing, doing the Charleston, but now things were relatively sedate, and riots had scared the white Park Avenue crowd from coming uptown to "go slumming." In any event, no sparks flew between this nice boy and me, though I sensed he wouldn't have minded. I was too serious about my studies to think about romance, lovely as that might have been. Furthermore, I had never had a serious boyfriend up to that time, so I didn't actually know what I was missing.

Another man who came to call on me generated a more enthusiastic response. Sometime late in 1945 or early in 1946, after beginning my classes at NYU, I got a call at Calvin's from Strom Thurmond. He had tracked me down through Mary. He said he was in New York on business and wanted to see me. He had called me at Harlem Hospital and was worried when they told him I had left the program. I told him that I had decided to go into teaching instead of nursing and was taking classes. "You know how I feel about teachers," he said, and invited me to meet him the next day. I had never been more excited. It was as if Santa Claus had come to town to see me. I tried to control my emotions, because I had seen this man come and go like the wind. I wanted to protect myself from great expectations and their attendant letdowns, but I couldn't quell my feelings. The call of one's father is nearly impossible to resist.

Oddly, this time my father asked me where we could meet. I assumed we would connect at his hotel, but for some reason he seemed uncomfortable with that idea. Maybe he was with other people—people who would be watching him. I had another idea and asked him to call me back to see if I could work it out. I could and I did.

"Harlem?" he exclaimed when I suggested he come uptown to meet me. He couldn't have been more surprised if I had suggested Peacock Alley at the Waldorf-Astoria. "You want me to come up to Harlem?" The German fortifications he had just stormed during the war couldn't have seemed more daunting to him. "Harlem?" he repeated.

I explained to him that a friend of mine, an older nurse from Harlem Hospital, had a nice apartment on Sugar Hill that she would lend to me for the afternoon. I had called her and told her I had a friend in from out of town whom I wanted to entertain. She was very kind. She didn't ask who or why, though she knew it was hardly some torrid, clandestine affair. I gave my father the address, and he reluctantly agreed to come uptown.

I must have changed clothes five times that morning. I called in sick from work. I tried to brush out my hair so it would be straighter, "bouncier" hair like they wanted for the cheerleaders in Coatesville, but it was not destined to be. So I made my way to the subway, the Seventh Avenue IRT, to go up to

Sugar Hill and meet the most important man in my life. I wished he felt the same about me. Maybe he did. As far as I knew, I was his only child, unless my mother was keeping more secrets from me. And here he was, coming to New York to see me. He had to care or he wouldn't be here. This was the first time I would be all alone with him, just he and I. I was totally nervous about how to handle myself. I stopped at a bakery and bought some pastries, which I later realized this healthy eater would never touch. I stopped at another grocery and looked for some bottled water, but they didn't sell any. Those were the days before Evian was everywhere, so I bought some ginger ale and hoped that was healthy enough for the man.

The doorman at the Edgecombe Avenue apartment building, down the block from the famed 409, let me into my friend's apartment, filled with nice paintings and antique furniture. It was much nicer to meet here than in some hotel, as we had done in Philadelphia. I stood at the window for an eternity looking down at the street, waiting for my father to come. I expected a cab. I didn't think he would be taking the A Train. Instead, he arrived on foot.

"Yankees!" my father exclaimed as he came though the door in a frazzle. "Yankees!" Apparently, he wasn't able to find a taxi and tried the subway and took the wrong line up to Washington Heights. Coming to Harlem was as big a challenge to him as D day. He apologized for being late. I offered him some ginger ale. He asked for water. He looked around the apartment as he caught his breath. "Very lovely place, Essie Mae," he complimented me.

"My friend has good taste," I said. "I wish I could live here someday."

"I didn't realize how nice . . ." he let his voice trail off.

I looked at my father as hard as he looked at me. His medals were gone. He was wearing a nice business suit and a tie. I wasn't sure what to say to him without the assistance of one of my two mothers.

"Have you been eating right, Essie Mae?" was his first question. I immediately felt fat again, but tried not to be too defensive about it.

"Now that rationing's over I may have been overdoing it," I said.

"All they eat up here is meat," he noted. "New Yorkers, all they know is steak, roast beef, corned beef, pastrami, hot dogs. Their idea of a vegetable is a fried potato. I hope you get some home-cooked meals."

Oh, what I'd have given for a big steak. "I eat out all the time, sir. I'm either working or at school, so it's hard to do much cooking. How are you, sir? How was Asia?"

He told me about his tour of duty in the Philippines, how dangerous it was even after Japan surrendered. Renegade Japanese soldiers would hide in caves just to ambush and murder American soldiers. He was convinced that both Japan and Germany would want to go to war again. It was just a matter of time, decades maybe, but in our lifetime. "We have to disarm them. We have to occupy them. We can't trust them. We already tried that once," he said.

Again he didn't ask about my mother, as if he already knew. He just asked about me, why I had left nursing school. It was like being with Mrs. Adair all over again. "That sounded like a fine program," he said with a look of concern. "Are you sure you gave it long enough? I didn't care for Clemson when I started, but I grew to love it."

"I think I've done nursing long enough now, sir, to know it's not for me." I explained my many summers at Coatesville Hospital, of which he was unaware.

"That does it then," he said, like the judge he was, deciding my case. Not guilty. "What shall we do next?"

It was the first time he had ever used "we" with me. I was flattered.

"I want to go to college," I said.

"What subjects do you like?"

"English. History. Social studies. No math."

He chuckled. "What is it about ladies and math? Considering how you all love to shop, you'd think you'd be wonderful in math."

"In stores, maybe, not in school," I begged off. He chuckled again.

"Where would you like to go to college? Do you like this NYU?"

"No, sir," I said. "It's too big."

"What about Columbia University? That's a fine school."

"I'm not sure about New York City, sir."

"What about Harvard University? Or Wellesley?"

"Pardon me, sir." I had no idea what Wellesley was.

"A fine school." Every school he mentioned was a "fine" school. "It's a college for ladies outside of Boston. You could get a fine education there. Or at Harvard. I know people up there."

I knew what Harvard was, America's oldest, most famous university. President Roosevelt had gone there. And the other President Roosevelt. And W. E. B. Du Bois. And Dr. Louis Wright. Was my father crazy? What right did I have to consider such a grand place as that? And who was going to pay for it? He probably didn't know I was a maid in a dress shop, trying to pay for two nondegree extension courses at NYU. Now he was talking about Harvard. A lady wasn't supposed to talk about finances, a black lady never. Was he offering to get me in and to pay for it? And if he were, was he doing it to get rid of me, to send me so far north that he'd never have to see me again?

What he said next made me ashamed for having such insecure thoughts, though I certainly was entitled to them. "What about coming down to South Carolina? We have a fine college right in Orangeburg."

"That could be nice," I leapt at the opportunity. I had no idea what or where Orangeburg was, but if the choice was going to Harvard without my father, or going to Orangeburg with him, I would have taken Orangeburg in a flash. "Nice" was not necessarily the appropriate word to use in planning an education, but it was the only word I had at my disposal at the time.

"What is Orangeburg?"

"It's our state college," he said. Suddenly my heart sank, as I realized what he meant was "our Negro college." What other college in South Carolina would accept black students? He didn't have the heart to say the word. In fact, he had never spoken the word in my presence. He couldn't bring himself to do it, but there it was. My father saw me as a *Negro.* I may have been half black and half white, but the rule in the courts was a drop of blood made you black. I don't know what else I was expecting. I had lived my whole life as a Negro, but to hear it from my white father, and a judge at that, made it a brutal ruling, and one with no appeal. I could either go to a "Yankee" college or a "Negro" college, but I couldn't go to a "Southern" college, because that meant a white college, and, despite my white father, I couldn't be white.

"They're doing a lot at Orangeburg. The state's spending a lot of money there. It's going to be a fine school. It's only an hour or so from Edgefield. It would be right nice to have you there. I'm going to get you some information on it, a catalog. I think it might just suit you, Essie Mae."

"Maybe I should think about Harvard, if you know someone up there," I said boldly, spurred by the resentment of being "classified."

"The more I think about it, why go all the way up there? If you want to be a teacher, Orangeburg is as good as any. Besides, the price is right."

"The tuition isn't high?" I violated the female interdiction against discussions of cost.

"Not like Harvard. Don't worry, Essie Mae. It will all be taken care of. If that's where you'd like to go, that's where you will go," he assured me. Then he went on about how much he had enjoyed teaching. "I taught vocational agriculture," he said, "at a high school near Edgefield. It wasn't Shakespeare, but it was to my boys, because Shakespeare wasn't going to put food on their tables."

"What is vocational agriculture, sir?'

"It's how to run a farm. The boys took 'voc ag,' and the girls took 'home ec.' "

Harvard was sounding better and better. I hadn't particularly liked South Carolina, and I had no interest in farm life. Here I was in Manhattan, the progressive capital of the world, surrounded with radical ideas like interracial marriage and passing for white and homosexuality and Communism, and my father was suggesting I come back down to rural, racist, reactionary South Carolina and study agriculture. I preferred Shakespeare. I didn't wish to insult him, though. His intentions were good. I promised him I'd look over the catalog when I got it.

"We've got to get you out of this city, Essie Mae," he said to me. "It's no place for a girl like you to live. It's a rat race. I've seen the whole world now, and there's nothing in it like South Carolina. I can honestly say that it's God's country."

As we began our good-byes, he handed me one of those thick envelopes, the money envelope. "I hope this will help," he said.

"Thank you, sir," I said, putting it into my purse.

"I'll be in touch with you," he promised and gave me his powerful, painful handshake. Again, no hugs, no kisses. I wished we could have gone out and had an unhealthy pastrami sandwich together. I didn't want the Colony or the Stork Club. A hot dog cart or the counter of Chock Full O' Nuts would have done. Nobody would notice us. That was the great part of New York, the anonymity. But he obviously didn't think that way. He was a judge. Judges had to be above reproach.

I saw my father to the door. I offered to go down with him to help him find a cab. He refused. "I can do it," he assured me, as if he were bravely off on some mission impossible. Or perhaps he didn't want to be seen in the street with me. How would that look, a southern judge and a young, black woman leaving a Harlem apartment building? He shook my hand again and was gone.

I treated myself to a ginger ale and some of the uneaten sweets and luxuriated in my friend's apartment. For a moment I felt rich, and even richer when I opened the envelope. This time it was 500 dollars, which seemed like winning the lottery. I went shopping at Macy's and bought myself a dress. I felt I had earned it. Maybe I would wear it to my Harvard interview.

CHAPTER FIVE

The Governor's Daughter

IN THE END, it all came down to money. I was sorry my father put the idea of Harvard into my head. I sent off for an application and was immediately intimidated by the catalog. Harvard's sister school, Radcliffe College, had photos of women who all looked like Katharine Hepburn standing in front of ivy-covered Georgian buildings, seemingly deep in brainy discussions or doing things like lawn bowling or croquet. There were no black faces, though there was a picture of an Indian girl in a sari, who must have been related to Gandhi or someone extremely important. Adding to the intimidation were all these pictures of famous Harvard graduates, the Roosevelts, the Adamses, the Lodges, Emerson, Thoreau, Robert Frost, T. S. Eliot. Again, no black men, not even the great Du Bois.

The application was endless and overwhelming. I hadn't taken many of the courses required to enter, especially in math and science, where my high school had been weak, and which I didn't care for anyway. And the tuition was far beyond my means. No wonder the girls all looked like Katharine Hepburn. They were rich, society girls, daughters of successful Harvard men, no doubt. They had to be. No one else could afford this. It was one thing if Judge Thurmond was sponsoring me in some way. But after dangling the Harvard bait at me, he switched to Orangeburg. I wasn't about to write him asking for help at Harvard. That would have been totally presumptuous. I threw the application away. It made no sense for me. I read about Wellesley, too. Their idea of a "person of color" seemed to be a daughter of a Chinese emperor. I didn't bother to apply.

The Columbia application was just as hopeless. There were the Roosevelts again, who had gone to law school here, and Alexander Hamilton and De Witt Clinton and all the big names in New York's illustrious history, and Rogers and Hammerstein and Hart of Broadway and Lou Gehrig, the Pride of the Yankees. There was a token dark face, like in the Harvard book, an African chief in tribal robes. Barnard College, the women's branch, seemed like a finishing school for brainy debutantes. And the tuition was out of reach.

I thought about City College, which was up in Harlem, and I thought about NYU, and keeping my Jane Engels job and working my way toward a degree in five or six years instead of the normal four. However, while I was thinking, my half-brother Calvin decided to move out of the city to Long Island. There went my free lodging, and there went New York. Rather than look into black schools in Pennsylvania, where tuition would continue to be an issue, I followed the path of least resistance. I decided I had no better option than to accept my father's "scholarship" to Orangeburg, whose official name, according to its small and modest catalog, was The Colored Normal, Industrial, Agricultural, and Mechanical College of South Carolina. Nothing on the educational earth could have seemed farther from Harvard. That my father could speak of them in the same breath was a comment on either his intense South Carolina chauvinism or an equally intense racial myopia. As long as black students weren't darkening the door of his beloved Clemson or the majestic University of South Carolina, any school they went to was just "fine" with him.

According to the catalog, which had no pictures at all, much less of famous alumni, the school had been founded under the Morrill Land Grant Act in 1890 "for the best education of the hand, head, and heart of South Carolina's young manhood and womanhood of the Negro race." There wasn't much Shakespeare, much history or social studies. It was an "ag," or agricultural, school, for an agricultural state, and hence dear to my father's heart. My initial, more cynical view was that it was an institution designed to put the children and grandchildren of slaves back into the fields, albeit at a higher level. Yet, the more I studied the catalog, I saw that amidst all the vocational training were some liberal arts courses, some humanities, enough to get an education, enough to be able to become a teacher and do some good. Besides, as the judge said, the price was right.

I tried to enjoy my remaining months in New York until I entered college in the fall of 1946. I felt a little like a soldier on his last shore leave before shipping out for the front. Even though I was going far away to Dixie, and Calvin was only going to suburban Long Island, we both felt the same way, "to get it while we could." He was extremely kind to me. We went to the Apollo Theater and the Savoy Ballroom and heard Cab Calloway. Calvin took me to the Polo Grounds, not to see the Giants, but to see the Cuban Giants of the Negro League. We also went once to Yankee Stadium across the Harlem River in the Bronx to see the Yankees get beaten by the Boston Red Sox. Ted Williams hit a home run in that game.

I went to all the movies I could, both in Harlem and on Forty-second Street, where the idea of the segregated balcony had gone the way of the back of the bus. My favorite film was the tearjerker *Brief Encounter,* about a tragic wartime affair. It reminded me of my mother; that made me cry even more. Even though the film was set in wartime London, and was about stiff-upper-lip British people, half the audience I saw it with was black women, crying their eyes out. Movies were truly a color-blind phenomenon. Calvin and I went to see Ethel Merman belt out the great numbers in *Annie Get Your Gun,* the biggest show on Broadway. The whole city was humming those songs. My favorites were "I've Got the Sun in the Morning and the Moon at Night," and "There's No Business like Show Business." We went to Broadway another time to see Pearl Bailey in *St. Louis Woman,* a play written by two famous black writers, Arna Bontemps and Countee Cullen. To see a black play on Broadway seemed a big deal. Most of the audience was white, and they loved it. To think I was leaving this oasis of tolerance for the land of lynching sent me into a bit of a tailspin. I was afraid of the wilderness I was about to enter.

I was having second thoughts about going south when Calvin came in with the *New York Times* one spring morning. "You may be a governor's daughter," he said with a big grin. Then he showed me the paper. Judge Thurmond, my father, was running for the governorship of South Carolina. I read it three times to make sure they were talking about the right man. Yes, indeed, they were. He had resigned his judgeship in May and declared his candidacy. There were eleven other candidates, including the incumbent Governor Ransome Williams, whom the *Times* implied was the odds-on favorite. My father's main issue was his attack on something called the "Barnwell Ring," a cabal dominated by a powerful Jewish politician named Sol Blatt from the small town of Barnwell, which my father was accusing of running the state for its private, selfish interests. My father, the paper said, labeled Governor Williams as a tool of the Ring.

I had no idea my father was particularly interested in politics at all. I had even less an idea that he was such a firebrand. I knew nothing about South Carolina politics, or any politics for that matter, but I was so proud that my father had thrown his hat in the ring, and with such gusto. My next thought was that I wouldn't be coming to Orangeburg, after all, and the choice wouldn't be mine. Why would this gubernatorial candidate want to risk having a secret half-black daughter in his own backyard? I kept checking the mail, fully expecting a letter of some sorts instructing me to withdraw my application. Nothing came. I called Mary in Coatesville, who knew nothing about the election. She had never voted in South Carolina and had no idea about the situation there. "He's got all the connections," she noted, reminding me, "His father elected The Pitchfork. Don't forget that."

Completely up in the air about my future, I went down on the train one June Sunday to Chester to see my mother. My half-brother Willie was now in high school and was away with friends. I had my mother all to myself, which was rare. I hadn't seen her for a long while. She kissed me and held me, but she trembled and felt weak. She looked older, tired. She was thirty-six now and still had her beautiful figure, perhaps a bit skinnier, and she still walked with that swing, but I sensed a fatigue in her. She insisted she was feeling well, continuously steering the subject back to me, asking me all about New York and hanging on every word. I had long harbored this fantasy of my mother and I hitting the town together, and it hadn't happened. Now I was planning to leave, and I worried about seeing her even less. I told her I had seen my father and about Orangeburg.

"I know all about it," she said.

"Did you see him?" I couldn't stop myself from asking.

"From time to time."

"Where?" I was hurt by the possibility she might have come up to New York to meet him and had not called me.

"In Philadelphia," she calmed me, sensing my possessiveness, in this most unpossessable situation. "The trains run everyday, you know, darling."

"Did you know about this governor thing?" I asked.

She seemed very sad at the question. "He never talks about politics with me, darling."

"Did you vote?"

"Not down there. None of us did. No point, really."

I asked her about Sol Blatt and the Barnwell Ring.

"Barnwell's just a speck on the map. Makes Edgefield look like New York," she said.

"So how can they have all this power?"

Carrie rubbed her fingers together in a "money" gesture. "That's a white man's game, Essie. We can't play. We can't even vote." She did tell me that Sol Blatt was my father's archenemy. Blatt was the Speaker of the House of the South Carolina legislature. Back in 1940, he had tried to block my father's election as circuit judge, an election by the legislature, or General Assembly, not the general public. Blatt had his own man, the powerful state highway commissioner George Timmerman, who had been my grandfather Will Thurmond's law partner. "Everybody knows everybody there at the top," Carrie said. But my father had outflanked Blatt, lobbying every member of the Assembly until he had the votes to win. "That man can turn on the charm," my mother said, "to men *and* women." Having been bested in the judge contest, Blatt was out to get even in the gubernatorial election.

Carrie also told me that before he had become a judge, my father had been elected a state senator. Before the Senate, he had campaigned for Edgefield County Schools' superintendent. He had won that as well. I had no idea he was such a successful politician. "He knows how to win. That's the sportsman in him. Win, win, win. He has to win, and he does. He is a highly motivated man," my mother described him.

"Will he win this time?" I asked.

"Honey, I don't know. It's not up to me. I expect Sol Blatt and his boys will do all they can to stop him. They hold grudges, you know."

"But what about me? I can't go there now."

"Where did you get that idea, child?"

"I don't want to spoil anything."

Carrie laughed wearily. "You're not going to the newspapers. Your father's expecting you. He told me. It's a fine opportunity. Get that degree. He wants you to go. So do I."

Maybe, I thought, my mother had asked the judge to take care of my education. Maybe that's why he was doing it, for her.

"He cares about you, honey. He really does. Believe me." My mother must have been reading my troubled mind. "Don't let go of him. That man is going places," she said wistfully, as if she had already lost him herself.

My mother told me how Strom Thurmond, even as a young man, the young man who fathered me, talked about his political aspirations. "It was in his blood," she said. Young Strom wanted to give his family the honor of being governor, or senator, an honor his father should have bestowed were it not for his hot temper and the scandal of having killed a man. "He was going to make it up to them. That was his mission." She recalled how he idolized Pitchfork Ben Tillman, treasuring autographed books Tillman had given him, quoting long passages from his eloquent speeches. I assumed he'd left out the references to "killing Negroes" when orating this political "poetry" to the woman he loved.

"How did you feel about that?" I asked.

"I was proud of him, proud that he cared for me." She told me that once he started getting elected to things, he could never stop, and that she knew the juggernaut he was on would ultimately displace their relationship. "He couldn't rightly take me to Columbia," she said, without bitterness, but with barely concealed regret. "It's nice how he keeps seeing me whenever he can. During the war was nice. It was like he was a free man. Nobody knew him up here." I got the impression they had seen quite a bit of each other when he was stationed in New York. Perhaps that's why I saw so little of my mother during that time. I didn't begrudge it to her. But where could it lead?

"You think he'll stop?"

"I don't know."

"If he won't see you, why would he see me?" I wondered and worried.

"It's different, Essie," she answered cryptically. "The man said he'd look after you—he will. He's proud of his word. I know that."

It was a sad good-bye with my mother. I didn't like crying in front of her, but I couldn't help myself. I just had this deep feeling that she loved my father so much, and that he loved her, that they had happy times in Philadelphia, romantic times. I had heard the expression "law is a jealous mistress." I gathered politics was even more jealous. I know my father was a brave and patriotic man, but I suspected that one of the reasons he joined the army when he could have easily gotten out at his age was to be able to come north and see my mother. In the South most men were married by the time they were twenty-one, often a lot younger. Here was my father, unmarried at forty-four, which was like Methuseleh back then. It was unheard of to be a bachelor that late in life. I think it was because he had a special woman in his life. A man, I thought, could love only one woman, and that woman for Strom Thurmond could have been my mother.

The tragedy here was the hypocrisy and the secrecy. A bigger tragedy given my father's apparently unquenchable ambitions, was that he was being forced to choose between love and career, and career was clearly going to prevail. Yet, he couldn't seem to let go of her. Was having me near him some sort of consolation prize for himself? It may have been, and the consolation for my mother was that her daughter's education, if not future, was being assured. Romantically, however, there was no such thing as second place, and I could see it in my mother's stricken expression as she said one last farewell and wished me "miracles" in what lay ahead.

I followed the South Carolina election as best as I could by reading the New York papers, which covered a little of it, and more so by going over to Times Square, where they had papers from all over the country, often only a day behind. The paper from Columbia, South Carolina, *The State,* would have a headline about my father seemingly every day, often accompanied by his photo, speaking or shaking hands. Now I understood where that killer handshake came from. The news vendors were nice enough to let me browse.

The most surprising thing I learned was that my father was described as a "progressive," and a "disciple of Roosevelt." Those were sweet words to a black person, sweeter to a black daughter. I had assumed all southern politicians were cut out of the exact same archconservative racist cloth, but here was my father following in the beloved Roosevelt's footsteps. I knew about campaign promises being taken with less than a grain of salt, but what my father was promising was music to my ears just the same. He was advocating lots of Rooseveltian public welfare, helping the poor, the aged, children, farm and factory workers, and, believe it or not, "Negroes," which is what everyone called us then, without any repercussions of political incorrectness. We didn't have enough clout to change the language.

Whatever the name, Judge Thurmond seemed to be on "our" side, especially in educational reforms. He talked about the state's shameful illiteracy rate, and that by elevating the status of the Negro, he was elevating the status of the state. Whenever he gave a speech about black education, I felt that he was speaking to me. "Come down here, Essie Mae, and see how well I'm going to take care of you." When I got my admission letter in the mail from Orangeburg, it was if my father had sent it himself. From being ill at ease about this major shift in my life, from North to South, I was now excited about what struck me as a potentially great adventure, a new frontier. Imagine moving to a state where your father was so powerful. How thrilling would that be?

The fantasy quickly became a reality. By August, my father had won the primary election, defeating the incumbent governor. He faced a runoff election with his runner-up, a doctor from Florence, whom my father attacked as not having supported President Roosevelt in past elections. He kept going after Sol Blatt and the Barnwell Ring, implying that every politician in the state, except for himself, was under the Ring's powerful thumb. When I finally saw a picture of the Ring leaders, Blatt and his henchman Senator Edgar Brown, I realized my father could not lose. He was a media wizard. Blatt and Brown looked like identical twin villains, both bald with shaven heads, thick glasses, matching black suits, and narrow ties. They reminded me of the evil Lex Luthor in the *Superman* comics, or a sinister version of the hairless Shmoos in *Lil Abner.* Even though my father didn't have much hair left, he looked like a youthful Adonis compared to Blatt and Brown. All a voter had to do was compare the photos, and my father would win.

And he did. In the early September runoff, Strom Thurmond easily defeated the doctor and became governor of South Carolina, the tenth from Edgefield. The last one had been Pitchfork Ben Tillman. Despite my grandfather's instrumentality in that racist reign, I was confident that my father, a Roosevelt man, would atone for my grandfather's racial atrocities. He was starting where it mattered, with his daughter, by having me come to Orangeburg. Thus, I went to Penn Station and got on the train heading south, not with a heavy heart but rather a buoyant spirit of new possibilities.

That spirit deflated no sooner than I changed trains in Washington, D.C., and boarded the segregated coach, which seemed exactly like the same stifling car I had taken on my first journey south five years ago. Again, I saw the same bedraggled men loitering in the stations, the same tobacco and cotton fields, the same sharecropper cabins, unfit to live in. After an eternity of clickety-clack and cigarette smoke, I got off the train at the Union Depot in Columbia. Same White and Colored waiting rooms, water fountains, rest rooms.

Why I thought the world war might have changed things I'll never know. I guess I felt that if our black soldiers could fight for America, America could fight for them, but that was not to be. Not now.

I spent two long hours in the back of a bus to Orangeburg, which was a fairly large town compared to Edgefield. I saw a sign stating the population was 15,000 (the same as Coatesville), compared to the 2,500 in Edgefield. Columbia then had 80,000 people. There were big cotton mills and other factories on the outskirts of the city. The smokestacks were nowhere as tall as the ones in Coatesville, but they symbolized industry. I took it as a sign of progress, that the South wasn't all sharecroppers in the hot, hard fields.

It was September and brutally hot and humid, so hot that no one was out in the main square where the bus let me off, carrying my two heavy suitcases. I was sorry I had brought my winter clothes with me. I couldn't imagine it ever being cold here. The first thing I noticed at the square was the towering monument of a Confederate soldier with a rifle and slouch hat. The sign read: "IN DEFENSE OF OUR RIGHTS, OUR HONOR, OUR HOMES." Large pools with goldfish swimming in them reflected the monument. Big Confederate flags flew from nearby banks and public office buildings, as well as from the imposing First Baptist Church anchoring a corner of the square.

I had no idea where the college was. I wandered up and down the main drag of Russell Street. There was a tall hotel, the Hotel Eutaw, maybe ten stories, which was a skyscraper down here. Nattily dressed black bellmen stood outside, and Cadillacs pulled up, driven by white men in seersucker suits and straw hats. Evidently, there was some money in the area. Reinforcing this notion was the array of stores on Russell Street. There was a big McClellan's Five and Ten, a McCrory's, a Kresge, an Efird's Department Store, several big movie theaters, appliance stores, jewelry stores, and a large number of fancy dress shops and men's stores with more of those seersucker suits in the windows. All the clothing stores had Jewish names over the doorways. This was like it had been in Edgefield, but on a much larger scale. That was the most reassuring thing about Orangeburg—those Jewish names. If these outsiders could make it in this very alien place, there might be hope for me.

I saw two nice-looking restaurants, the Sanitary Café and Ferris's Restaurant. I was starving. My first instinct was to go in and have a bite. Then I looked in the windows and saw no black patrons. I remembered where I was and tried to ignore the delicious smell of the hot grease that fried the chicken and shrimp. The five-and-tens all had lunch counters. I peered in and saw them full of white people enjoying grilled cheese sandwiches and milkshakes. There were a few black people in the stores, shopping but not eating. I didn't dare attempt to get food, even to go. I had heard about southern hospitality, but I knew where the line was drawn. I went back to the Hotel Eutaw and asked one of the black bellmen where the college was. He told me it was about a mile away. He found me a taxi with a black driver, who took me to the campus.

Sweaty and ready to drop, I finally reached the school known to everyone as "State." It was on the edge of town, far away from the business district, very green and filled with trees, with attractive brick buildings adorned with those classical white columns that are the hallmark of southern architecture. Some call it Jeffersonian, after the president's famed home Monticello. Some call it Palladian, after the Italian architect who inspired Jefferson. I call it "plantation." In any event, the college looked impressive, substantial, and quite collegiate, much more like Columbia, though nowhere as grand, than like the factory buildings of NYU. There was, however, one very disturbing feature: a tall wire fence that encircled the entire perimeter of the large campus. It reminded me of nothing other than a prison.

The campus was bustling with arriving students. My first impression was how proper everyone looked, all the young men in coats and ties, all the young women in nice formal dresses. There were no jeans, no T-shirts, no shorts. The hot weather called for comfort, but the school obviously called for decorum. I felt sloppy. I wanted to find my room, bathe, and change. A second, bigger impression was that *everyone* was black. Harlem wasn't this uniformly black. I hadn't been in an all-black environment since my one year of segregated junior high. It felt unnatural, as bizarre as that tall prison fence around the campus. And everyone was so serious, so dignified, so proper. These were people in their late teens, early twenties, some older, who I suppose were coming back to school after the war. But they all seemed much more grown-up, like businesspeople more than students. No one was throwing balls or clowning around or having any fun. I quickly surmised that college, at least this college, was going to be a very serious enterprise.

I went to the administration building, presented my papers, and was given my assignment in the women's dormitory. The registration process was very efficient, very somber. Everyone was polite, no one effusive. I guess I again was expecting that southern hospitality that wasn't forthcoming from blacks or whites. I liked the dorm, which had big rooms and high ceilings and fans that provided the breath of fresh air that nature herself was withholding. There was a housemother who happened to be the college president's aunt. She assigned us our rooms, which were homey, in contrast to the stiff reception.

I had two roommates who slept in bunk beds. They were kind enough to give me the single bed, which I thought was very gracious. They said it was because I had come the longest distance. One roommate was a nice girl from Columbia whose schoolteacher mother had been a graduate of State, making her second generation and "high class" in the social scheme here. She had very light skin. I wondered who *her* father might be. The other was a pretty girl from Jacksonville, Florida. Her father had an exterminating business, which must have done well, as she wore fancy clothes. She was also quite fair. In fact, there were many light-skinned women, seemingly half the campus. There were lots of middle-class girls from all over South Carolina, as well as from Georgia and Tennessee. They were all talking about their fathers—doctors, lawyers, businessmen. No one mentioned janitors or porters, and certainly not sharecroppers.

I was frankly surprised that so many black families in the South were doing well enough to send their children to college, which I thought was a fairly unreachable holy grail. Seeing these girls in their fancy dresses, setting out their silver-framed photos of their attractive families on their dressers, comparing notes on summer holidays in the Blue Ridge or on the Outer Banks, I was astonished at the prosperity around me. It made me proud, if not a little insecure. State was not exactly a black finishing school, as there were plenty of poor students there as well, as I would find, but it was far more affluent than I was, or than I would have guessed. With all the family comparisons, I was tempted to brag about my father. "You think your daddy's so special? Well, you know who my daddy is? He's the governor of this fair state. He is Mister Palmetto himself," I would have loved to say. "In your face" is the expression today. But the temptation quickly passed. I wasn't crazy. And I was very grateful to my father for making it possible for me to come here to State. I couldn't afford to lose the opportunity in front of me. For me, it was a state of grace.

The girls were very curious about me, and especially about why I had come all the way down here from Pennsylvania. Why didn't I go to Howard or Lincoln? The idea was for blacks to *leave* the South, not come here. I told them I had relatives in Edgefield, that I was a South Carolina girl at heart. I wanted to come home to my roots. I'm not so sure they bought it. A lot of them seemed to be intrigued by the idea of going north themselves, of getting out of the South, despite their families' having done well here. The North was still the "Promised Land" to them, and why someone would voluntarily leave heaven and go back down South, if not to hell, then somewhere short of paradise, was confusing to my classmates. When I told them I had lived in Harlem and started out in nursing school there, they were all the more impressed and mystified that I would trade the Cotton Club for the cotton fields. Luckily for me, there were no other girls from Edgefield who might have known more about my past or be privy to rumors that may have emanated from Old Buncombe. While there was clearly a lot of white blood in these girls' veins, I didn't want *my* white blood to become an issue that might interfere with my education.

Directly adjacent to State was another all-black institution, the private Claflin College. It, too, had tall, impressive buildings and lots of serious students, as well as a high fence. State had 1,000 students, Claflin 600, making

Orangeburg the center of black higher education in the state, sort of a black college-town version of Cambridge, Massachusetts, or Cambridge, England, for that matter. Claflin, I learned, had been founded right after the Civil War by a Yankee philanthropist who was committed to educating the children of slavery. This man, Lee Claflin, also founded Boston University. State was founded in the 1890s when the federal government required each state with a large Negro population to establish a land-grant, or "trade," school that was "separate but equal" to the white public trade colleges that would not admit them. Clemson, my father's alma mater, was such a white land-grant college, founded under the governorship of Pitchfork Ben Tillman, who convinced an heir of his idol John C. Calhoun to donate the Calhoun plantation as Clemson's campus.

At our first convocation in the school's large auditorium, President M. F. Whitaker, a distinguished educator in the W. E. B. Du Bois mode, made it clear what a tight ship he was running. The discipline seemed more suited to West Point or Annapolis than a regular college. That fence was there for a reason, to keep us on campus. The fence and the gates, which were never locked at night, seemed to be there for symbolic value, to comfort the uneasy white residents of Orangeburg about all the young, black people in their midst. State students were invariably so well behaved there was no need for locks or for white anxiety. We were allowed to leave the school grounds only on Mondays, Wednesdays, and Fridays, and had to be back by 5 P.M. in time for dinner. On Tuesdays and Thursdays, we were allowed off campus to go to the local movie theaters. We were admonished to always sit in the balconies. But at least we had the movies. That was a relief.

On Saturdays, we could have dances, parties, and so forth, but always on campus. We were grounded to avoid any "incidents" when all the white farmers (and potential Ku Klux Klan types) would come to town for their big night out. On Sunday, we were to go to church to pray. Orangeburg was full of churches, and we were advised to avail ourselves of them. There were also required Friday chapel services, to put the fear of God in us about the weekend ahead. From what I could see of the impeccably mannered, polite students, the fear had long ago been instilled. There was absolutely no need for that fence, despite what our white neighbors must have dreaded.

Aside from geometry, I loved all my classes, especially literature and history. I knew I was getting a "higher education." The classes were small, and the professors who had master's degrees from Harvard, Columbia, and the University of Chicago took the curse off of "black education." I can't imagine white education being any better. Unlike at NYU, where you would never speak to a professor without an appointment set weeks in advance, I got to know all my teachers, who'd have us to their homes and give us all the time we needed.

Of course, this being South Carolina, and this being a state-supported school, there was no such thing as "black studies." Yes, we took pride in black successes, from Hannibal of Carthage to Booker T. Washington of Tuskegee, but, for example, we were never asked to read and analyze *Uncle Tom's Cabin*. The Civil War was not portrayed as a battle over slavery but rather one of economics, of agriculture versus industry. I was eager to take the more advanced courses. Furthermore, the school was anything but a hotbed of politics. There was no chapter of the NAACP, nor any other political organizations, unlike in New York, where somebody was always protesting something. I very much doubted that Reverend Adam Clayton Powell would be invited to speak to us.

The students didn't seem interested in changing the world, only in improving *their* private worlds. The main focus was on career and marriage. Most of the students were taking practical vocational courses, bookkeeping, accounting, industrial efficiency, engineering. I saw lots of courses in crop science and the like that I'm sure my father would have been thrilled to see me enroll in, but I much preferred reading Dickens and Balzac and Faulkner, and learning about the pharoahs of Egypt and the Caesars of ancient Rome, Charlemagne and the Magna Carta, Leonardo da Vinci and Rembrandt, to learning the optimal way to can peaches or the science of hothouse tomatoes. I did take education courses and practical things like typing and shorthand. Whatever I took, the education I was getting continually excited me about the education I was going to be giving one day.

In my spare time I naturally went to the movies, not caring much where I sat whenever the screen lit up with the likes of Gary Cooper, Cary Grant, and Ingrid Bergman. The most popular film was also the naughtiest, *The Postman Always Rings Twice* with Lana Turner. I was surprised they even showed it there in the Bible Belt, but both whites and blacks lined up. There were three student cafes near the campus that served only blacks; they became our hangouts, to drink Cokes and malteds (liquor was strictly prohibited, on and off campus), eat hot dogs and burgers, and listen to the jukeboxes, and sometimes dance to singles like "Zip-a-Dee-Doo-Dah" or "Hey! Ba-Ba-Re-Bop," or "Come Rain or Come Shine." There were black singers and white singers, and Bing Crosby was just as popular as Louis Armstrong. The State students weren't "Uncle Toms," however—they simply weren't politicized at this point.

With our curfews and fences, we lived in an all-black universe, but our eyes, and hope, were always on the white one down the road. We all loved our outings downtown, to go shopping, or more accurately, window shopping at all the stores, pretending we were rich and could get any of this finery we wanted. Maybe, we hoped, this education would pay off one day. The white storekeepers were generally very kind to us, never running us off or shooing us away or even giving us dirty looks. And the white customers generally paid us no mind and went about their own business. Of course, State students were famous for their good behavior, so I guess the Orangeburg whites approved of us as "a credit to our race" and were deeply relieved that we weren't on some savage rampage that Ben Tillman might have predicted.

Everything was going very well at school. It was football season, late October when the weather had cooled down a bit and the leaves were starting to turn. Saturdays were football days. When we played at home against another all-black school like North Carolina A&T (Agricultural and Technical) or Tennessee A&I (Agricultural and Industrial), the campus was like a carnival. We had marching bands before the game, bonfires afterward, and great dances when the bands would take off their uniforms and put on suits and play jazz and bebop. The big men on campus were the football players, and the top girls were the cheerleaders, who were always the girls with the fairest complexions. In those days, the closer you were to white, the "classier" and more beautiful you were considered. I never considered going out for cheerleading, my fair complexion notwithstanding. I just wasn't a cheerleader type; I was too introspective. I would never be bubbly enough.

This weekend, the team was playing away, in Georgia somewhere, and we weren't allowed to follow. Not even the cheerleaders could go. The home team advantage held even greater significance in those restrictive days. As lively as State was on home-game weekends, that's how dead it was on away games. I was surprised when I was called to the administration building, to President Whitaker's office, on that sleepy Saturday. Had I done something wrong? Was someone in my family sick? Thoughts of disaster ran through my mind as I raced across campus to Lowman Hall. I climbed the long staircase and went to the president's office. I was surprised he was around on Saturdays. This must be awful, I shuddered. A secretary in the outer office greeted me and showed me into the inner sanctum. There with the president of State was the governor-elect of the state.

"Hello, Essie Mae," Strom Thurmond said, standing up and crushing my hand with that magic grip that had gotten him elected.

"Hello, er . . . Judge . . ."

"We're already calling him Governor," President Whitaker said.

I wasn't sure what to say. I was in a panic. What did the president know? My father seemed totally relaxed, so whatever it was couldn't be bad.

"I hear you're doing very well here at State, Essie Mae," my father said.

"I like it very much, sir."

"I knew you would," he said, turning to President Whitaker. "She could've gone to Harvard, but I talked her into this."

"We appreciate that, Governor. I believe it's better to be a big fish in a small pond rather than the other way around." The president addressed me. "I hope we're keeping you busy."

"Yes, sir," I declared. "I'm learning a lot."

"That's what we're here for," President Whitaker said. "Listen, Governor, I'll leave you alone. I'm sure you have lots of catching up." The president exited his big office. My father and I were alone. He gave me a big smile.

"What does he think?"

"He thinks you're an excellent student," my father said.

"No, not about me. About . . . you know, sir," I simply couldn't say it. The fact of his being my father made me uncomfortable beyond belief.

"I told him that you're a dear family friend from Edgefield. That your family helped my family for a long time. That we're really all one family. Which is true, isn't it?" Strom Thurmond grinned at me. I wasn't sure if it was a conspiratorial grin, or a loophole grin, or a happy-to-see-you grin.

"You never told me you were going to be governor."

"I had no idea when I last saw you. It just happened."

"Congratulations. It's wonderful. I can't believe it."

"Thank you, Essie Mae. Neither can I. I'm in the army being shot at one day, and in the mansion the next. Life can change just like that."

"It's a nice change."

"Yes, it is. And I'm happy for you to be here. Now you stick it out, you hear?"

"Yes, sir."

"I've got big plans for this school. I'm going to do all I can for it," he promised. "How's the food?"

"They serve us lots of vegetables, sir. All homegrown," I said, knowing he would be pleased.

He was. "Are you getting exercise?"

"I walk to town, sir, every couple of days."

"Walk every chance you get. Stay off the buses."

Who wants to ride in the back anyway? I wanted to say, but didn't.

He told me that he expected to accomplish a great deal in office, because his chief nemesis was stepping down as Speaker of the State House.

"Sol Blatt?"

"How do you know that, Essie Mae?"

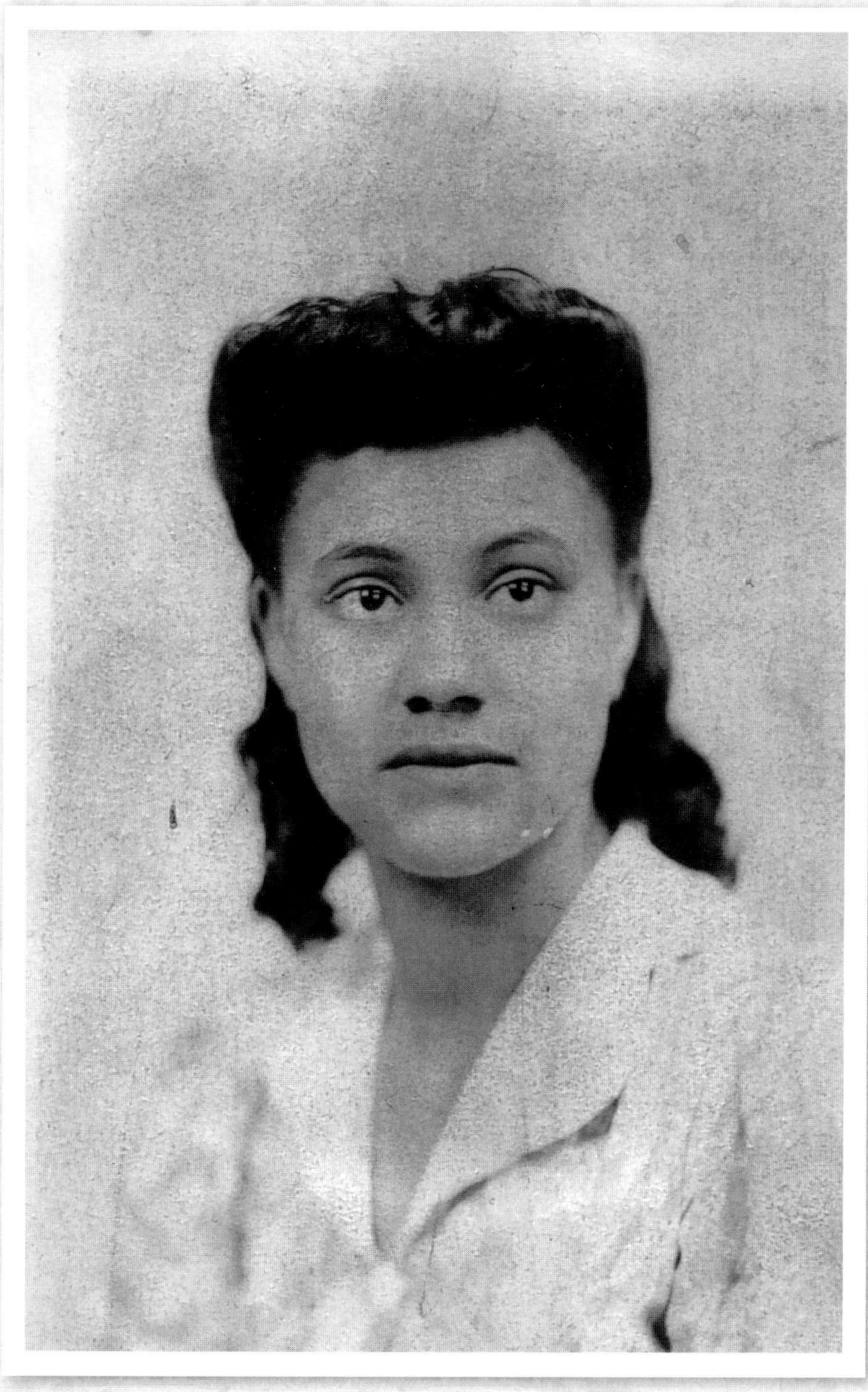

AGE SEVENTEEN, JUST MONTHS AFTER
I MET MY FATHER FOR THE FIRST TIME.

PLAYING WITH MY COUSIN CHRISTINE, CALVIN'S DAUGHTER.

MY COUSIN CALVIN IN HIS WORLD WAR II UNIFORM.

MY CHILDHOOD HOME IN COATESVILLE. THAT'S MY UNCLE BOWMAN'S CAR PARKED OUT FRONT.

MY HALF-BROTHER WILLIE CLARK PLAYING FOOTBALL WITH A NEIGHBOR. WE MAINTAINED A CLOSE RELATIONSHIP THROUGHOUT OUR LIVES.

AT A NEW YORK NIGHTCLUB WITH CALVIN'S WIFE LENORA (LEFT) AND HER GREAT-UNCLE AND GREAT-AUNT.

MY FATHER AS PRESIDENT OF CLEMSON COLLEGE'S LITERARY SOCIETY, 1923.
HE WAS TWENTY YEARS OLD AT THE TIME.

ALPHA PHI ALPHA—JULIUS'S FRATERNITY AT STATE. THAT'S HIM IN THE MIDDLE OF THE TOP ROW. JESSE OWENS IS SEATED LEFT OF CENTER.

MY FATHER CHECKS THE POLL RESULTS DURING HIS RUN FOR PRESIDENT IN 1948.

MY FATHER CARRYING HIS YOUNG BRIDE ACROSS THE THRESHOLD.

I LOVED MOTHERHOOD RIGHT FROM THE START. HERE, I AM AT HOME WITH JULIUS, MONICA, AND WANDA.

MY FATHER WITH HIS SECOND WIFE, NANCY, AND THEIR FIRST CHILD.

OUR SON RONALD

JULIUS, JR., AS HANDSOME AS HIS FATHER

WANDA AT HER HIGH SCHOOL GRADUATION

MY FATHER AND HIS FAMILY AT THE SENATE.

MY DAUGHTER MONICA WITH HER HUSBAND GERALD AND MY GRANDDAUGHTERS MARIA (STANDING), ALISHA (RIGHT), AND MARCEE (SEATED).

A FAMILY PORTRAIT

WANDA AND I VISIT WITH MY FATHER'S SISTER MARY TOMPKINS AT HER HOME IN EDGEFIELD, SOUTH CAROLINA.

MY RETIREMENT FROM TEACHING IN 1997

"I read the newspaper, sir. The Barnwell Ring. You beat them."

"I sure did. I declare! You know about Sol Blatt."

"Why was he so bad?"

"He cared more about his cronies than he cared about this state. He's what you call a real politician. I'm just an amateur."

"How did a Jew get so high up in this state, especially after Governor Franklin Moses?"

"You know everything," my father marveled.

"I like history."

"If you know your history, you won't repeat its mistakes," he said. "You're a real South Carolinian, Essie Mae. As far as Franklin Moses, he came from one of our finest families. I think the Yankees brainwashed him. That was a crazy period, where people, even the finest people, got turned upside down. As far as Jewish people, South Carolina has always welcomed the Jews. Look at the other Moseses, Judah P. Benjamin; some of our greatest leaders have been Jews. Sol Blatt, I wish he was *more* of a Jew. He married a Gentile woman, eats all the pork he can if it means a vote. If you're a good person and a talented person, in this state you can write your own ticket."

But not if you're a good and talented *black* person, I mused. But it was a bad thought. Here I was in South Carolina, getting my dream of a college education. Who was I to be greedy, to be ungrateful? Rome wasn't built in a day, was it?

"I'm proud of you, Essie Mae, knowing about all this," the governor-elect said to me.

But not proud enough to protect my vote, I thought but again suppressed the heresy. I was thrilled he had come to see me. That took courage. More important, it proved to me, once and for all, that he cared.

He didn't stop caring. He came to visit one more time before the end of the year, also on a quiet Saturday. President Whitaker again let us use his office. I gathered that my father had business with Whitaker, formulating his "big plans" for the college; he didn't want to leave without seeing me. It was all very proper, very polite, handshakes, not hugs, no talk of family. Whatever our cover story, it was justified by the formality of our interaction, talk of courses, history, and politics. He reminisced about his own education at Clemson, where the only choice he had as a major was agriculture, engineering, or textiles. He had no choice, he said, and waxed eloquent about his teachers and his starring days on the track team. He described how he once ran eighteen miles in new shoes that caused him to lose all his toenails. He was so proud of this because of the pain he endured and the record he set. "It's a shame women don't run," he said. "The best exercise there is, and you can do it anywhere. All you need is a road." He also told me how Clemson was a military school when he went there, and about the virtues of the military discipline he learned. Pain and discipline could have been my father's middle names.

Yet it all added up to one big lecture, no true love or true confessions, which was what I would have savored. Diet was as personal as it got, and not just for my benefit. I once heard my father expound on the virtues of turnips to President Whitaker, how many vitamins the turnip greens had, how they should be serving them in the cafeteria. He didn't give me any envelopes of money on these college visits. As my room and board were paid for, there was no need for any. I don't think he wanted the president see him passing me cash. That might have implied a different relationship, and my father, lawyer, judge, now governor, had to be above reproach. Yet I did find it rather bold for a man of his position to risk all kinds of scandal by coming to see me. It was so gallant. It was chivalrous. It was daring. I loved it. What woman wouldn't respond to a great man taking such great risks for her.

My connection to my father was hardly fatherly, however. It remained as distant as when I had visited him with my two mothers. Our surface dealings were precisely that, all superficial and completely unemotional, despite my inner turmoil. The governor-elect was a very cool character. He never showed his hand. I could see how he had done so well in battle. Nothing rattled him, and he was always in charge of the situation. That's what leaders, I supposed, were made of.

I was impressed at how discreet the college president was, not that he thought the governor and I had anything to hide. Still, a visit with a mere student by the governor-elect was grounds for major gossip, and given the president's aunt's role as our housemother, the likelihood of a rumor starting was high. Nevertheless, I never heard a word. On the other hand, my classmates were so ladylike and well mannered that I doubt they would have done anything to make me feel uncomfortable, even if they had known the facts.

In early January 1947, I was chosen by President Whitaker to go with a group of State students to Columbia to see the gubernatorial inauguration. By now it was actually cold, colder than I ever imagined South Carolina could be, perhaps in the high thirties, and I was glad I had brought my Yankee clothes. My father gave a wonderful speech, a liberal speech, in which he spoke of a "New Era" of reforms that would help working people and poor people. He actually sounded like Franklin Roosevelt, or Roosevelt with a southern accent, talking about New Deal–style measures.

Education was a big issue, particularly black education, which I'm sure is why Whitaker took us to hear Strom Thurmond. He also railed against the evils of the poll tax, which was a way to keep poor people who couldn't afford the tax, from voting. Everything he said rang of hope. Here was a friend of poor people, of black people, who wanted to get rid of the power politics of the Barnwell Ring. Here was someone who wanted to replace the racist "good ol' boys" with something fair and just.

A lot of my female classmates talked about how young and handsome the new governor was. I was careful not to brag myself, but I had to agree with them. Despite his lack of hair, he was tall and fit, and, for forty-four, quite a striking and vibrant man, masculine and powerful, every inch the soldier, now the statesman. Imagine. There was my *father* up there on the steps of this magnificent state house, being sworn in as chief of this state. Next to him was his mother, my grandmother, whom I had never met, and whom I might never meet. She looked old and very skinny, like someone from another era.

I had seen ancient photographs of the Old South, and Eleanor Gertrude

Strom Thurmond resembled those hardscrabble farmers' wives, tough and flinty and without a smile. She was the antithesis of the Scarlett O'Hara plantation goddess. But that was the movies, and this was real life. If my father seemed a bit formal and stiff, I could see where he had gotten it. Gertrude was scary, formidable. I would have bet my life she didn't have a clue about my mother. She looked as if she would have killed her son if she had. Small wonder he found comfort in the arms of my mother, who was nothing like his own.

Thus, on one hand, I felt special on this crisp Inauguration Day, yet on the other, I felt completely, as it were, out in the cold. The rest of my father's family, *my* family, was standing behind him, his two tall brothers and his three sisters. I had seen only one before, the lady who had brought the envelope of money to us in Old Buncombe. I saw she had a twin. One was Mary and one was Martha, but who could tell. There was another sister, Gertrude, who was a spinster and a schoolteacher. And both brothers, John William II and Allen George, the two gynecologists. Maybe their mother was so forbidding that they chose this specialty as their only way to find out about women. That my father, his older brother, and his sister were *all* unmarried was a bizarre statistic in the South, where marriage was the bedrock of the social order.

I just kept staring at my grandmother. She was the key to all these mysteries, mysteries I was afraid I would never solve. I wanted to be up there on the podium with them. This was my family, but I didn't know them and they didn't know me. In time, in time, I prayed to myself. If my father could change this state, with its Confederate flags flying and its Confederate soldiers standing vigil atop their obelisks, I had reason to hope he could change his own house. I flattered myself by thinking that my own existence might have something to do with his progressive stance. As we black students filed into our all-black bus on our way back to our all-black school, and my white father and his white family and friends prepared to celebrate his taking office, I had reason to hope that the fence that separated my world from his was on the verge of coming down.

I got a chance to test my father's values in action right away. Soon after the inauguration, South Carolina showed its old and true colors by having a lynching. In February 1947, a twenty-five-year-old black man named Willie Earle was arrested in Greenville for assaulting and robbing a white cab driver. When the cab driver later died, a mob of thirty-five white men, most of them fellow cabbies, all armed with shotguns and knives, broke into the jail where Willie Earle, who was an epileptic, was being held. They dragged Earle out of the jail, just as the mob had dragged Zachariah Walker out of Coatesville Hospital in 1911. Earle was shot in the head multiple times, and his body was eviscerated by the long knives of the white mob.

I was horrified. Lynchings were a symbol of the South, and here it was. The fact that I had been privy to them in Coatesville didn't dilute their impact. There, they were the exception; here, the rule. I read in the paper what the jailer said when he surrendered Earle to the mob: "They had shotguns and I danced to their music." It wasn't all that clear that Earle was guilty of killing the cabbie. Earle's mother said he had come home drunk. His jacket had blood stains on it. He carried a Boy Scout knife. But that was all the proof they had. Whatever, this poor epileptic was entitled to a trial, not medieval torture.

My father expressed his outrage. He called the lynching "a blot on the state of South Carolina." I was surprised to learn that it had been the Palmetto State's first lynching in twenty years. Referring to his wartime service, my father invoked the Nazis in denouncing mob rule as "against every principle for which we have so recently sacrificed so much." The governor wanted to bring industry to the state. He wanted to attract the top professors to its colleges. He wanted respect around the country. How could he get any of it with such barbarism?

The governor worked hand in hand with J. Edgar Hoover and the FBI to round up Willie Earle's lynchers. President Truman was proving to be a far stauncher advocate of civil rights than his predecessor Roosevelt. Armed with this federal mandate, the authorities indicted thirty-one of the killers and identified the ringleader and trigger man as a taxi dispatcher named Roosevelt Hurd. It seemed like an open and shut case that would do a great deal to rehabilitate South Carolina's reputation as a hotbed of racism, to expunge the curse of Pitchfork Ben Tillman.

I was quickly disheartened to see the tide begin to turn in favor of the white mob. Many of the white businesses in Greenville contributed to a fund-raising campaign for the accused murderers; thousands of dollars were donated. Then the all-powerful Columbia newspaper *The State* commenced its own campaign. First, it denounced FBI interference with southern justice. Ever since Reconstruction, the South detested any federal or "outside" interference with its internal affairs. The sight of Yankee investigators was a provocative red flag to southern bulls. Furthermore, *The State* declared Willie Earle guilty without a trial. The paper simply presumed he was the murderer and would have been executed anyhow. All the mob did was save South Carolina the cost of a public execution.

My father was steadfast in expressing his commitment to justice, a sentiment echoed by the NAACP, which had taken a strong interest in the case. The whole nation was watching, and I found it invigorating to witness my father on the same side as the NAACP. The trial began in Greenville that May and was the largest lynching trial up to that date in American history. The testimony was grisly: Witnesses described how Willie Earle had been dragged, pistol-whipped, stabbed, shot, and cut to pieces. Still, none of the defendants would confess to anything. They admitted "hearing" the torture and shooting and slicing, but none admitted "seeing" any of it. And not one witness would come forward to finger a single suspect.

The trial was a legal circus that galvanized the country like the O. J. Simpson trial, minus the celebrities and the television. As it went on, the white people of South Carolina got more and more protective of their own. Sympathy mounted for cab drivers forced to pick up "dangerous Negroes" to earn a living in these depressed postwar years. Most of the accused cabbies had been World War II veterans, and *this* was the thanks they were getting for defending their nation. Defense lawyers attacked the northern press for sensationalizing the issue to sell papers. They attacked the FBI agents as troublemakers and meddlers, the "outside agitators" label that would later be pinned on civil rights activists in the 1960s. They attacked President Truman for trumping up the case to pander to prejudiced Yankee voters. It was North versus South all over again, the first time I would see an issue reduced to regional animosities, but hardly the last.

In the end, the South won, as it would time after time, in its effort to restage the Civil War over civil rights. The all-white jury of Greenvillians convened for only a few hours before returning with a mass acquittal. Bands played "Dixie." People danced in the streets. They lit celebratory bonfires in Orangeburg that chilled me with the images of the burning of Zachariah Walker. The college administration warned us to stay away from town, even on our free days.

I was scared for a while, but it passed. What scared me even more was the apathy of most of my fellow students. Not that I was a firebrand. I was as meek as the rest. But there were no protests, no marches, no petitions, no real interest. At least I was desperate to *talk* about what was going on. The others just let it slide. They didn't discuss the horror of the lynching. They didn't express relief that they had a governor, my father, who was standing up for black rights. The collective trauma of the event seemed to dissipate at the State gates. Like most of white South Carolina, the State students tended to assume Willie Earle was a drunk, a bad seed, who had committed a crime he shouldn't have and paid the price. It was a southern price, but he lived here and should have known better. This wouldn't happen to a State student. We were too smart. We were too good. We were destined for success. We were black, but we were *different*.

My father held his line. Disappointed in the verdict, he asserted that the fact there had been a trial at all would deter future lynchings, and he was right. He was praised by all the Yankee papers, particularly by the *New York Times,* which was considered by southerners the house organ of the spirit of Radical Reconstruction.

Throughout the months of the state's wrenching legal ordeal, my father continued to visit me on campus, if only for a half hour or so. His favorite question, which he asked whenever he saw me, was "How does it feel to be the daughter of the governor?" My answer was always the same: "It doesn't bother me at all." I was trying to joke with him, but he took it with a stone face. To him, I suppose our deep secret wasn't a joking matter. Still, this was the first time he himself had verbally acknowledged that I was his child. He used the D-word, which he had not done in our previous meetings. It didn't get closer than that, but to me it was a breakthrough. The other breakthrough was that at the same meeting when he used the D-word, he actually hugged me good-bye. These small gestures of affection meant the world to me. It was the first time he had embraced me or given me anything more than those iron handshakes. Yes, it was behind closed doors, away from prying eyes, but, given my father's previous straight-arrow aversion to any public, or private, display of affection, it seemed like a miracle to me. Being the governor's daughter felt good indeed. Just knowing I had a father felt good. The title was icing, fancy icing, on an increasingly good cake.

My father barely mentioned the Willie Earle case, as if he were ashamed to bring it up on this black campus, notwithstanding his being on the right side. In fact, he never mentioned anything about *my* being black. I think he was confused. Because I was his, whether he wanted to "claim" me or not, in his eyes I wasn't really, fully a "Negro." The whole issue seemed to make him uncomfortable, and so, smooth political statesman that he was, he didn't address it. We talked briefly about the Willie Earle matter, but not once did he refer to race, only to justice, about a man who was denied a fair trial, and about a mob who unlawfully hijacked justice to their own malevolent ends. It wasn't black and white; it was crime and punishment.

To the rest of America, it was black and white, North and South. When I returned to Coatesville for the summer of 1948, that's all the people there wanted to talk about. My family and friends had been worried about me, though the family who were aware about my father knew that there was nothing to worry about. Who could have been in better hands? Even though I lived in a fairly black world in Coatesville, it was nowhere as black as my world in Orangeburg. The sense of separation of the races wasn't the same. The tension, which existed before the Willie Earle case and was accentuated by it, wasn't here. We may have "known our place" in Coatesville, but we weren't forced into it by the barrel of a shotgun.

I went to Chester to visit my mother Carrie that summer. She didn't look well at all. She had been having kidney problems, she said, and seemed puffy and older, haggard. The sexiness in her step was diminished, although she was now living with a man, a black man named George, who was rarely around when I was there. Carrie didn't seem to want to talk about him, other than to say it was good to have a man around for Willie, who was going through his teenage phase.

She confided that she hadn't heard from my father once during the entire year I had been at Orangeburg. "I think he's forgotten me," she concluded dejectedly.

"If he's remembering me, how can he forget you?"

"You're his girl. He's a gentleman, always a gentleman. He keeps up with his duties."

"Doesn't he have one to you?"

"Only to look after you, baby," Carrie said, as drained of hope as I had seen her. I tried to pep her up by telling her about State, about the inauguration, about my own growing up, and she expressed lots of love but little verve. It was more like relief that at least something was working out. I could tell she still was carrying a torch for my father, but now that he was on the national stage, the opportunities to continue their secret and forbidden romance had been extinguished. If they could lynch Willie Earle, I shuddered at what South Carolina could do to my father, and to me, if it came out that he had a decades-long love affair with his black maid. Not only would it have instantly destroyed his political career, but I sincerely believed it would put me, as well as my father, in physical jeopardy.

That the state's standard-bearer could fall from grace in such a way could precipitate the worst sort of reprisals. Sex and miscegenation were powder-keg topics in the South. Once that fuse was lit, the explosion could be fatal. I had seen the irrationality of race hatred. The dragon's fire-breath of the Klan was as palpable in South Carolina as the scent of magnolias. I could see the anger, the suppressed rebel violence on the faces of the poor white farmers, the factory workers, the unemployed, always looking for a scapegoat for their misfortunes and dislocations. No, the Civil War was far from over. I didn't want to be caught in the crossfire. But above all, above my personal fears, I felt awful for Carrie. Love had made her happy, and now the loss of that love was making her physically sick. It made me cautious about love myself. I hadn't fallen yet, and given my secret background, I wasn't sure I'd ever be able to let go and take the plunge.

CHAPTER SIX
Heart of Dixie

WHEN I RETURNED to Orangeburg in September 1947, the Willie Earle issue had helped to polarize the nation and send the whites of South Carolina back to their barricades. President Truman was more than infuriated by the farce of southern justice. He said so when he addressed the NAACP in Washington that summer and he devoted his energies to his President's Committee on Civil Rights, which issued a scathing and revolutionary report that fall entitled "To Secure These Rights." It declared Truman's war on discrimination. But below the Mason-Dixon Line, it was the South that felt that war had been declared on all that it held dear. Truman was demanding that Congress enact sweeping legislation protecting black people at the polls, in schools, at work, in their travels, and in the military. As I rode that awful hot and muggy Seaboard Railways segregated coach down to Columbia, I had a feeling I would be traveling in air-conditioned comfort and plush seats in the not-too-distant future.

Again, at State, it was college as usual. I was rushed for a sorority, which is where most of the social life took place for sophomores and older. The two top "Greeks" as we called them, were Alpha Kappa Alpha and Delta Sigma Theta. I was honored that both came courting me, especially since good grades and college achievement were even more important in these black sororities than looks and style. They wanted "leaders," as the Greeks were active in lots of charity work and tutoring in the community, not merely giving parties. I chose the Deltas, who were known for maintaining the highest grade average on campus. The initiation was anything but brainy. I would have to walk to class a certain way around campus for a week, two steps forward, one step back. The "Delta Walk" looked spastic; that was the point. Then my new "sisters" fed me what they said were slithery, slimy, and nasty worms. This test of my loyalty and sisterhood, not to mention constitution, was in truth cold spaghetti. Once the hijinks were over, I got back to my studies. I took more American history. We were entering dramatic times, I sensed, and I wanted to be armed with knowledge.

I also discovered men. Or they discovered me. Being in the sorority gave me a new confidence, a sense of belonging that being the governor's daughter did not. The sorority was all positive reinforcement, and it made me sure of myself. Furthermore, to earn extra spending money, I took a series of clerical jobs on campus. On Sundays, my friends and I attended the local Presbyterian church because the preacher there gave the best sermons. I was busy all the time, and that served to enhance my self-esteem.

The first person at Orangeburg I began dating was a man in every sense of the word. At twenty-five, Matthew Perry was five years older than I was. He was what you would call a Big Man on Campus. I met him through a girl in my sorority one day outside the temporary barracks, military-style Quonset huts, that had been put up to house the male students. There was a glut of students after the war and nowhere for them to sleep. The school graciously gave the nice, old dorms to the women, while the men basically camped out or slept on cots in the gym. The girl was a beauty, and no sooner than we started talking together, she ran off and Matthew ran after her, leaving me all alone. Some time later he tracked me down at the library. I didn't want to speak to him, but he persisted, explaining that the girl was an epileptic, like poor Willie Earle, and when she ran off, Matthew was worried she was about to have a seizure and went to her aid.

Matthew and I joked about the inauspicious way we met, and we quickly hit it off. Matthew was just back from the service and seemed very mature. What attracted me most about him was his voice, a mellow, soothing baritone. He often spoke at student assemblies, and he mesmerized me, just like the Presbyterian minister. I have a weakness for voices, and Matthew had the best. He was from Columbia, and planning to be a lawyer, which was a good career choice for a man with a voice that could surely sway juries.

Matthew was also the first politicized man I had met at school. He was a member of the NAACP, which had an office somewhere in the black part of Orangeburg, far away from campus. The college itself never would have permitted it, for fear of losing its state funding. The NAACP in southern white eyes was more than just black. It was subversive, Yankee, Communist, any bad thing the whites could throw at it. They reacted to the NAACP the way we blacks reacted to the Ku Klux Klan. Matthew hardly seemed like a firebrand. He was cool and authoritative, and he was seeking justice, just as I felt my father was. I never, ever mentioned to Matthew or anyone else my genealogy, though I'm sure it would have given us endless things to talk about. In any event, he was positive about Governor Thurmond as "the best we could hope for" in the state we were in.

Matthew might have been the man of my dreams, or any girl's dreams. He would go on to become the first black federal judge and one of the preeminent jurists in the country. However, I met another man, whom I fell head over heels for: Julius Williams from Savannah. He was in the top fraternity, Alpha Phi Alpha. He was also extremely handsome, tall, with olive skin and wavy hair. He once had flirted with me outside the library. He often sat on a bench outside, smiling at the ladies as they went to study. They all liked him and smiled back, but not I. I didn't want to be like all the others. One day Julius said to me, "Hey, stuck-up." I think I glared at him. I finally got to know him at an Alpha dance, where I had a date with one of his fraternity brothers. Julius pulled rank on him, and the other Alpha inexplicably took ill and left me to Julius, in whose arms every girl at the party wanted to be.

Julius was twenty-eight, a war hero who had just come back from the Marine Corps in the Pacific. He had thrilling stories about Iwo Jima, Leyte Gulf, Corregidor, and other battles. Unlike other students at State, Julius was completely self made. His father had a trucking business; his mother was blind.

He had come to Orangeburg as a pre-med student, with plans to go to Harvard Medical School. He would be my own Dr. Louis Wright. I had all this nursing experience we could talk about, but he seemed to find interest in whatever I had to say. We were both serious students and loved studying in the library, then going for walks to discuss what we each had learned. It was a true campus romance, and it was the happiest I had ever been.

My father came to visit me that fall when I returned to campus. It was a very short stay. We continued to meet in the president's office, with his chauffeured black convertible parked outside the administration building. He wanted to know if I had had a good summer. He did not ask about my mother, which I found unusual if not rude. I wanted to tell him how badly he was hurting her by not being in touch, but I didn't. I had no idea what might have gone wrong between them, aside from the obvious futility of the relationship. He was a grand and busy leader; who was I to pester him about affairs of the heart when he had affairs of state to attend to? He never asked about my social life. That was too personal for him. "I believe you've been eating better, Essie Mae," he noted. "You look thinner." Not "you look lovely," but "you look thinner," which meant that before, as I suspected, he thought I was fat. I was relieved that boys were noticing me now. If they weren't, I might have been devastated. The governor wished me a good school year and gave me a hug, which I couldn't help but treasure. Then he left and the big car rolled away. There was nobody around to observe us, or so I thought.

This time, unlike the last school year, the rumors began. Governor Thurmond had come to visit a girl on campus. The girl was his daughter. Who was that girl? That was the big campus guessing game that fall. Luckily, my name never came up as one of the candidates. The one who did was a sorority sister of mine named Lizzie Mae Thompson, who happened to be the whitest girl on campus. Poor Lizzie Mae. Everybody knew it had to be her, and it drove her crazy that no one would believe her disclaimers. I would have liked to come to her rescue, but all I could do was play the part of the Sphinx and keep the riddle all to myself. I focused on my classes and on my newfound romantic life.

Then another romance almost derailed my own. My father, I found out, had fallen in love. It came with a photo in *The State* of my father with a stunning, very young lady at an October football game between Furman College and the University of South Carolina. The headline read "Governor to Wed." Wed whom? I was puzzled. Then I realized that this homecoming queen on his arm was to be my stepmother. Her name, according to the paper, was Jean Crouch, and she was indeed a beauty queen, having served as last April's Azalea Festival "Miss South Carolina" in Charleston. She was twenty-one years old, less than a year older than I was, and she had just graduated from Winthrop College, an all-women's school in Rock Hill. She was currently working as the governor's assistant.

Today, it would be sexual harassment. In 1947, it was still very scandalous, a forty-six-year-old governor and his twenty-one-year-old aide. I was appalled. Appalled that he had abandoned my mother for this child, appalled that she wasn't that different from me. It made me feel creepy, having sat and been so close with a man, my father, who was now marrying a woman my age. There were endless photos of Jean Crouch in the papers in the weeks ahead. She was from Barnwell County, home of the Barnwell Ring my father hated so much. An honor student, Jean had won the Sol Blatt Medal for her academic prowess. At Winthrop College, she was preparing to become a teacher, just like me. She was active in church, just like me. The main difference was that she was white, or at least whiter than I was. But not that much. Yes, she was pretty, in a fresh, girl-next-door way, but there was no way she was as beautiful, as radiant as my mother. I prayed the news didn't get to Philadelphia; it would destroy my mother to see this, just as it was destroying me.

I took it out on Julius. I wanted so badly to share my pain with him. I wanted even worse to tell the whole world and derail this marriage, which I easily could have done, as long as I was willing to pay the price of ruining my own life. In those days they didn't have student psychiatrists, certainly not at State. I surely could have used one, though I would have probably been too paranoid about divulging my secret to tell a doctor, patient privilege notwithstanding.

Luckily for me, Julius was very understanding and didn't demand an explanation for my change in behavior. He didn't press me, but he was always standing by. When the lovebirds married in early November, barely weeks after the engagement bombshell announcement, it seemed like a shotgun wedding. I was beside myself with pain. I couldn't believe my father hadn't called on me, or at least called me, to tell me what he was doing. I didn't expect him to ask my permission, but as his daughter, I felt he owed me—and my mother—an explanation. Obviously, he was too ashamed. I resigned myself to never seeing him again.

The wedding was at the Elko Baptist Church in the Barnwell hamlet where the Crouches lived. The press pictures showed my father looking resplendent in a tuxedo, his bachelor brother by his side as best man. The bride looked perfect in her white satin gown. I read that there were twenty-six relatives at the private ceremony. Too bad the groom's daughter couldn't have been one of them. It didn't matter. That was one invitation that I would have refused.

The newlyweds were off to Miami and Havana for their honeymoon. Before they left, *Life* magazine did something to help me get even with my father. They took his picture, standing on his head, wearing nothing but white boxer shorts, black socks, and wing-tip shoes. Behind him beamed his bride, in a sweater and shorts, sitting on a bicycle. It looked like he had pulled off his pants to show off to the photographer. The caption read "Virile Governor." It was as undignified a shot as one could imagine, a politician's worst nightmare, especially one like my father, who had been widely called the "Southern Roosevelt," who always insisted on being above reproach. Here was the man who wouldn't be seen in a hotel lobby with me, standing on his head in his underpants.

Rather than retreating into the shadows until this storm of ridicule blew over, my father came out swinging. Adding to his list of wrongs in my book, Strom Thurmond now became a white supremacist. Just a year before, he was improving our schools, giving us the vote, prosecuting our tormentors, looking out for us. Suddenly, after his marriage, Governor Thurmond began a political about-face. He became an outright racist, cloaked in the ancient doctrine of states' rights. There was nothing Rooseveltian at all about this. He had said Franklin Moses had been brainwashed by the Yankees during Reconstruction. Now it appeared that Strom Thurmond had been brainwashed—if not by the Ku Klux Klan, then by the ghost of Pitchfork Ben Tillman.

He would have laid the blame on President Truman, who, in Strom Thurmond's mind, might have experienced some mind alteration himself. The good old farmboy from Missouri had somehow become a "lefty." Strom Thurmond, as if to show off for his young wife once again, took it upon his athletic shoulders to stand up for the honor of the South, just as the Confederates had done at Fort Sumter a century before. In the process, he lost sight of all the hope he had given to black people, all the good he had promised to do.

Strom Thurmond's "conversion" came at the Southern Governors Conference in Tallahassee, Florida, in February 1948. The main issue of the meeting was supposed to be the improvement of black university education in the region, but Harry Truman had created an emergency that had to be responded to. The president had given an address to Congress on civil rights, the first of its kind in American history. He called for a permanent Congressional Commission on Civil Rights and a Civil Rights Division in the Department of Justice. Truman was standing up for blacks like no one since Abraham Lincoln, and actually far more than the Great Emancipator.

Southern whites responded by bombarding the White House with hate mail. Be the southerner that you are, they exhorted him. Be a man. You wouldn't want your lovely daughter Margaret stuck in a Pullman car with a dirty, smelly, savage, angry Negro, would you, Mister President? Such was the tone of the letters cited in the papers. And the southern governors went as wild as their constituents. Strom Thurmond declared that South Carolina, for one, was "ready to fight." Because this year, 1948, was an election year, and the Republican front runner, Governor Thomas Dewey of New York, was emerging as the favorite, Truman needed all the help from the Democratic "Solid South" that he could get. Now, standing on principle over civil rights, it appeared that Truman had permanently alienated the South and slit his own throat politically.

At the Governors Conference, my father put a gun to Harry Truman's head. He sponsored a motion giving the President forty days to rethink his position and back off from it. He denounced Truman's proposed civil rights measures as "anti-American" and, by implication, denounced the black population Harry Truman was out to protect. The South Carolina NAACP issued a statement as to how disappointed they were with their Governor. My father responded by publicly removing President Truman's photograph from his office wall. "Truman stabbed the South in the back," he told reporters. In Washington, D.C., at a Democratic fund-raising dinner, the senator from South Carolina, Olin Johnston, led a boycott when they found out that black leaders would be seated at their table. The behavior of these powerful politicians was both childish and sinister at the same time.

When Truman did not cower under the Thurmond ultimatum, my father's response was to up the ante of his racist rhetoric. He helped organize a "states' rights" convention in Mississippi, which, as the press described it, was more akin to a Klan rally. With the big band playing "Dixie" after every speaker, my father called for a total repudiation of the Truman wing of the Democrats and the recognition and respect due to the South by the great party of Thomas Jefferson of Virginia, slave owner–intellectual. The governor dredged up the wrongs of Reconstruction, denouncing the freed slaves as a "millstone" around the neck of the South. Echoing The Pitchfork, my father said the only progress "Negroes" had made was because of the generosity and tolerance of their former masters.

Strom Thurmond defended segregation laws as "essential to the racial protection and purity of the white and Negro races alike." I wasn't sure if this was my father talking or the ghost of Adolf Hitler. With his perfect-looking wife always at his side in photographs and newsreels, I kept thinking of Eva Braun, who was far less a public accessory than Jean Crouch Thurmond. What was my stepmother thinking? Of course, she was one of them, the white southerners that my father was playing to, so she probably was not as appalled as I was or, I'm sure, my mother would have been. If the South had been stabbed in the back by Harry Truman, my mother and I, and the blacks of South Carolina, had been stabbed in the back by Strom Thurmond. In keeping with their traditional political apathy, the students at State didn't seem to feel at all betrayed by the bizarre regression of their supposedly progressive governor. Perhaps they expected nothing of any white southern politician, and hence were not surprised or, at least, not as surprised as I was. For all my father's racist histrionics, there was virtually no discussion of it on campus.

I didn't go home that summer vacation. I couldn't face either of my mothers with the news of my father's transformation into The Pitchfork of the twentieth century. Perhaps I might have brought them some comfort by being there to commiserate with them about how he had betrayed us, but I wasn't sure how much good that would do. I was hoping they weren't aware of his change. This was before every home had television (theirs didn't), and there was some chance Strom Thurmond's antics weren't on the northern radar. After all, when I lived in New York, the only way I could find out about South Carolina was to go to the out-of-state newsstand at Times Square. Pennsylvania was far less likely to follow this carnival show in Dixie. Besides, I had too much rage to seek company for my misery. I wanted to forget.

So I got married. Julius Williams had been steadily pursuing me, and I finally got over my distrust of all men and realized this man was special. But we had to keep it a secret. Neither of us had any money, and we needed to continue living in the college dormitories, which married students obviously couldn't do. It was one more secret I had to keep, and for years I continued to keep Strom Thurmond a secret from Julius. Although my father had never once ordered me to keep my mouth shut about him, I was simply *conditioned* to be discreet. I was worried that if Julius knew, it could somehow be held against him, that the Ku Klux Klan might hurt him, or something dreadful like that. So I kept my history, and my anger, to myself.

That summer we gave ourselves an extended honeymoon by finding jobs at a ritzy, white resort in Hendersonville, North Carolina, in the cool and lovely Blue Ridge Mountains. We actually got married there and shared a room. We assumed the resort would never report us to State College. This was before computers and other background checks. Besides, we were just menials. Julius worked as a waiter in the fancy dining room. All the waiters at these resorts were black. That was the southern style. I guess it reminded the guests of the Good Old Days before the Civil War. As the song went, "Old times there are not forgotten."

I worked as a babysitter for assorted families, so they could go dancing at night. I spent a lot of time taking care of the young son of the two alcoholic owners of the resort. He was a wise guy who would always stop me when I tried to tell him a fairy tale or some bedtime story. "I heard that one before. That's not the way it goes." And then he'd tell it his way. We got along well and became good friends. It made me wonder at what stage in life southern whites, if not many others, started thinking of blacks as "other."

It was a romantic summer. Julius and I would hike in the woods, swim in mountain streams, live the outdoor healthy life. My father would have been proud of me, but I didn't care what he thought any more. We'd watch Jackie Robinson, the first black major leaguer, play for the Dodgers, or we'd laugh at "Uncle" Milton Berle on one of the resort's several televison sets, which were still quite the luxury at the time. One day, off we went into Hendersonville and sat in the balcony to watch *Key Largo*. Everyone was talking about the romance of Humphrey Bogart, who was, like my father, well over two decades older than his wife, Lauren Bacall. Nobody seemed to mind about them; they were *the* fabulous screen couple of the time. Likewise, nobody seemed to mind about Strom Thurmond and his very young wife. They, too, were considered the dream couple of politics, certainly in the South. Here he could do no wrong, not among white people.

My father never ceased to amaze me. At the resort Julius liked to watch the news on the television. It was there that I nearly fell out of my chair to learn that Governor Thurmond was now running to become President Thurmond. His endless attacks on President Truman had made him so popular below the Mason-Dixon Line that a new party, the States' Rights Party, had been formed by disaffected Democratic leaders. They became known as the Dixiecrats.

They had a raucous convention in Birmingham, Alabama, where the delegates chanted "nigger," waved Confederate flags, and burned Truman in effigy. They held up pictures of Robert E. Lee and Jefferson Davis next to pictures of my father. They wore the dreaded "red shirts" that the southerners wore when they drove the Reconstruction troops out in a reign of terror and lynching.

Then they nominated as their standard-bearer my father, who was considered the Great White Hope of the South at that time. The stations played, over and over, a televised speech he had given, angrily shaking his fist and pointing his finger, declaiming, almost screaming, "On the question of social intermingling of the races, our people draw the line. All the laws of Washington and all the bayonets of the army cannot force the Negro race into our theaters, our swimming pools, our schools, our churches, our homes."

"I don't like that man," my new husband said, turning off the set in disgust. "I fought Hitler to end up with *that*? What's the difference?" I could see the pain and venom in Julius's eyes. I prayed he couldn't see the fear and shame in mine. I didn't want to keep any secrets from my new husband, but this one was way outside the normal secret category. My father was coming across as an enemy of the people, my people, my husband's people. Julius was sensitive about a lot of things, not the least of which was human rights, civil rights, and civil wrongs. I know he wouldn't have expected me to be my father's keeper, yet by the same token he might not have wanted me to keep Strom Thurmond in my life, which was now *our* life. He might have expected me to denounce this white supremacist, if not expose him. I wasn't sure, but I was terrified of taking the chance of having to choose between my father and my husband. I sensed that there was a good chance that if Julius had suspected I had that man's blood in my veins, he might have mooted the whole issue by leaving me right then and there. So I did what I had always done. I kept my mouth shut, hoping against all reality that the issue would somehow miraculously disappear and I could go on and enjoy the new happiness of married life.

It would hardly go away. Strom Thurmond was soon on the cover of *Time*. I was shocked that he would be dignified by that prestigious magazine. Not only was the nation taking him seriously; newspapers and radio and television commentators were saying that the Dixiecrats had a *chance* to win the election.

The logic went like this: Harry Truman could not win the presidency without the South. The Dixiecrats, by winning the South, could throw what promised to be a very close election into a three-way race in which no party had a majority. That election would then have to be decided in the House of Representatives, where the southern states numbered eleven of the forty-eight votes, with many persuasive and powerful politicians who, if Dewey and Truman were stalemated, might just be able to swing the election to my father as "the compromise candidate." Jean Crouch Thurmond was interviewed at length about how she would change the White House if she were First Lady. She promised that she would serve grits there.

When we returned to State in September, the campus was a hotbed of gossip and innuendo about "the president's daughter." Reporters, white reporters, from all over the country, as well as journalists from *Ebony* magazine, were snooping around. Lizzie Mae Thompson bore the brunt of the suspicions, but she never pointed a finger at anyone else, particularly me. I was worried that our college president, who had served as a go-between for my father and me, might now put two and two together and blow the whistle. I was aware that the president, as well as other academics, felt deceived and abandoned by "their friend," the progressive governor. But, as I have said, State was a very proper, dignified place, and they were not the types to sacrifice a student to get even, even with a traitor. Despite the gossip and the press attention, despite the horrible words our governor was spouting every day, the student body remained largely apolitical, if not apathetic.

Julius and I decided to move off campus because we wanted so much to be together, and I found a place with rent low enough that we could afford it. I have a friend, Katherine Dawkins, who was married to a man, Lamar Dawkins. They owned Lamar's Restaurant, a favorite hangout of South Carolina State University students. A delicious fried chicken lunch was only fifty-two cents. In addition to providing access to good food, Katherine was a beauty and a tennis star. She and Lamar were renting a big house from a white woman on Oak

Street, near the school, and they sublet a room to Julius and me. It wasn't a great room, just a bed they put in the large kitchen, which they rarely used because they had the restaurant. However, it was fine for us, our own "blue heaven," as the song went.

The daughter of a successful building contractor in Columbia who had worked on the state house there, Katherine must have had a lot of white forbears, because, after Lizzie Mae Thompson, she was one of the lightest-skinned girls on campus and considered one of the prettiest. She used to take me to a white laundry to do our clothes, and no one said a word. One day I tried going there myself, however, and the white proprietress asked me to leave. I was light, but not light enough. I never went back, even with Katherine. I "knew my place," though it would have given me the greatest spiteful pleasure to tell that laundress that my governor father was running for president. I have no doubt he was one of her heroes.

Julius had changed his career plans from medical school to law school. With no money, and given our desire to start a family, the medical route seemed to have an endless horizon, with the pot of gold at the end of the rainbow too far away. State had just started its own law school, under federal orders enforcing the "separate but equal" Supreme Court ruling. Rather than admit blacks to the sacred precincts of the University of South Carolina Law School, the state founded and funded a separate, if hardly equal, law school at Orangeburg. Julius was in the very first class. There was only one other student, so he knew he'd be getting plenty of attention. The presidential race had galvanized, if not radicalized, my husband. He vowed to use his law degree to try to correct the injustices advocated by my father.

Moving off campus gave me an extra sense of privacy and intimacy with my new partner in life. Now that he was going to be a lawyer, I sensed he was on a collision course with that other lawyer in my family, my father. It seemed inevitably hopeless to try to keep my secret from him, and, having our own place, tiny as it was, away from the college and all the snoopy reporters milling around, I felt less insecure about revealing the truth of my identity to him than I had before. Our love had only deepened and solidified, giving me a self-confidence I had heretofore lacked. I also had a deep need to share my secret with *someone*, and who better, if not my husband, even though he stood opposite from my father on just about every issue imaginable.

Still, the decision was anything but easy. I was filled with trepidation when I approached him late one night after dinner, and after we were both exhausted from studying. I invited him out onto the porch under a crystal clear Carolina sky with a full harvest moon. It was fall, but it was still balmy outside. We talked about our homework for a while. We both loved studying, and our books were among our strongest bonds. Then I segued into the combat zone. "It isn't Lizzie Mae Thompson," I said.

Julius knew exactly what I was talking about. "So what's your theory? Everybody's got one." Guessing who was the governor's daughter was the favorite game on campus that fall.

"It's not Lizzie." I said. "It's me."

Julius started laughing. I let him laugh a while. When I didn't join him, he stopped. He just looked at me. "You are joking," he said. And then his statement lost its conviction and became a question. "Aren't you?"

I just looked back at him and gave him a smile, a loving smile. "Will you hate me?" I wondered aloud, praying I already knew the answer.

He put a reassuring arm around me. "The only one who hates is *that* one. Why are you fooling with me?"

"I'm not fooling," I said, in the lowest voice I had, not wanting to alert Katherine and Lamar, who were sleeping. And then I told him the whole story.

"I guess I'm not going to sleep too much tonight," Julius said when I finished.

"Is this going to give you nightmares?" I asked him.

"It's just . . . crazy. It's hard to sink in."

"Do you hate me?" I asked him again.

"Honey, I love you." Julius cradled me in his strong, warm arms. Then he asked me the hardest question of all. "But do you love him?"

"He's my father."

"Is that a yes or a no?"

"You lawyer," I tried to tease him to make light of it all. But there was nothing light in Julius's countenance except the light of the moon, which illuminated all his concerns.

"Do you really think he loves you?" he asked me.

"He's been helping me. He doesn't have to . . ."

"Is that a yes or a no?"

"I wish we could all love each other," I blurted out.

"I wish you could teach him how," Julius said. "Then you would be some teacher. You'd win the Nobel Peace Prize."

"Try to understand," I entreated my husband.

"I'll never understand him," he said. "I'll always love you." He kissed me and we went inside. But we rarely if ever spoke about my father. As I told Julius, I wasn't even sure when I'd ever see him again. It wasn't as if it had been often, a few times in many years. He'd disappeared before, and he'd disappeared now. And if he became president, I tried to joke, I doubted that he'd invite us to the White House.

"That's why they call it that," Julius replied with a knowing chuckle. He seemed to accept that Strom Thurmond was my history, but that he, Julius, was my life and my future. Nor did Julius demand or suggest I go public with this history, much as it might have destroyed the man who was widely seen as the enemy of our people. He seemed willing to let the past be just that, bygones be bygones. And again, I saw the time-honored value of keeping my mouth shut. Strom Thurmond was one topic that could only get me into trouble.

My world was further turned upside down late in October when I got an emergency call from Mary in Coatesville. My mother was very ill, in a hospital. Could I come home? Mary wouldn't have asked me unless the situation was grave. I took the next train from Columbia and sat up all night in that dreadful, smoky coach. I didn't want Julius to come. I hadn't told anyone we had gotten married. That would create its own set of logistics and diplomacy, none of which I was prepared to deal with. This was no time for him to "meet the family." Most of the way I cried for my mother. I had never really gotten to know her, to spend the time with her I had wanted. I would have loved for her to have seen me in New York. I would have loved to have shown her State College and how I was fulfilling her dream of getting a higher education. I would have loved for my father to have been able to love her publicly. I prayed she would get better so that some of my wishes, fantasies, whatever, might come true.

I first went to Coatesville. Mary told me my mother was in the public hospital in Philadelphia, where she had been placed in the "poverty ward." Her kidneys were failing. She had gotten sick a month before, as she had intermittently for the last few years, which was why she had been looking so tired and drawn. She had refused to complain. This time, Mary told me, the doctors had little hope. It was "end stage" renal failure. There was no dialysis then or at least any that my mother could afford.

I told Mary that I had gotten married. She broke down, hurt that I didn't allow her to throw me a big wedding. I recalled Ethel Merman in *Annie Get Your Gun,* singing, "I want a wedding in a big church, with champagne and caviar. I want a wedding like the Vanderbilts have, a wedding that's big not small . . ." I didn't care about weddings. I was married and in love. Willie, Mary said, had been placed with a family who lived nearby. He was almost finished with high school. Mary said he was ready to go out on his own. He would be all right. Mary also told me that the man Carrie had been living with had left her. My mother didn't deserve to die all alone. I took the next train to Philadelphia.

I bought a bouquet of flowers at the station and took a cab over to the hospital, a large municipal facility. The white nurse on the ward was as cruel as a human could be. "She'll never be able to enjoy those flowers," the nurse said.

I found my way to my mother's bed on the ward. She looked terrible. She was gasping, her eyes bulging from her face in a mask of terror and pain. She was so young, far too young to be this way, yet she was now as frail as an old woman. Each breath seemed as if it might be her last. I think she recognized me, but I couldn't be sure. I tried not to fall apart. I told her how much I loved her. I told her about my marriage, about Julius, how wonderful he was. I told her about State, about how well I was doing, how she was my inspiration for learning, for being. I told her Julius and I were trying to start a family, to give her her first grandchild. I did not mention my father. I couldn't.

Carrie's eyes closed. Her gasping continued. I sat there for two hours by her bed, just holding her hand, stroking her brow. She kept breathing badly, but she didn't open her eyes again. Finally, visiting hours ended. The mean nurse told me I had to move on. I handed my mother's flowers to an elderly black woman in the bed across from her. The woman smiled with enormous gratitude.

I took the night train back to Coatesville. Mary and I were about to return together the next morning when we got the call that my mother had passed away. She was thirty-eight. We had her funeral at Mary's Baptist church, rather than Carrie's Pentecostal one. There was no shouting or testifying, only gentle hymns and many tears. I went to the open casket and took one last look at my mother. I had thought I would have a lifetime with her to make up for our lost time and my childhood spent without her. Now she was lost forever, but I would never forget her.

A week after I lost my mother, my father lost the presidency. He lost by a lot. He and his Dixiecrats carried only four states: South Carolina and the Deep South—Alabama, Mississippi, and Louisiana. It did not speak well for South Carolina to join the most backward, most racist, most violent states in the nation. The image of the state as "progressive" was sacrificed on the altar of my father's political ambitions. Still, over a million Americans voted for my father, which was a huge number of people. A lot of Americans, and not only southerners, had responded to his message of racial hatred. I'm sure he got votes in Coatesville. He would have never gotten mine. Truman won the election, in a last-minute upset over Governor Dewey, and as governor, my father went back to politics as usual, urging South Carolinians to close ranks behind the president, against whom, only weeks before, he was nearly threatening to go to war to protect the South's pernicious racial status quo.

On a cold, dark day in December, I was studying in the library, when I got a message to go to the president's office. I had no idea what he might want, other than ask me to do some secretarial work, which I had done for that office several times before as part-time employment. Imagine my astonishment to see my father, sitting all by himself in that big office. President Whitaker was nowhere to be seen.

"You have to forgive me for being so busy, Essie Mae." He stood up and shook my hand. I wanted to yank it away, but he had taken me completely by surprise. He offered me a seat. I nearly collapsed into the leather chair. "I have been looking after you. The president says you've been doing just fine. I understand you've gotten married." That surprised me, too. I had told the school when I moved off campus. I suppose as governor my father had total access to student records, especially mine. "I understand he's an outstanding young man. I started that law school, you know? I wanted him to have a good place to go."

Was he trying to bribe me to make amends? Yes, the law school was started during his term, but was he doing it for me? I refused to thank him. Instead, I blurted out, "My mother is dead."

His normal ebullience was knocked completely out of him. He sat stunned for a long time. "What did you say, Essie Mae? Did I hear you?"

"My mother is dead. She died in October. Kidney failure."

"Ohh . . ." he bleated, like a wounded animal. "Ohh . . ." He didn't cry, but tears filled his eyes. For the first time I had seen, the great orator was speechless.

After a long pause, he began to talk again. "Nobody told me."

"You were busy, sir."

"My God, what a terrible thing . . ."

I didn't want to give him the satisfaction of telling him how hurt she had been by his "dropping" her, though I could see he was genuinely moved. There was no satisfaction to be had. "She hadn't heard from you."

"I knew there was a man in her life . . ."

I noticed that he didn't say "another" man, he being the first.

"You got married, Governor," I boldly said, unafraid, for once, of being impudent.

"Not before she . . ." He let his voice trail off. He was implying my mother had taken up with George before he took up with Jean. I had no idea who came first; I realized he might be telling the truth. I declined to press the issue, to argue with a lawyer, a judge. It was possible he sought refuge in Jean Crouch only after it had ceased to be available with Carrie Butler. I tended to doubt it, but it did blunt my implacable hostility, enough to prevent me from addressing the outrage of the age difference.

Instead, I completely changed the subject. "How could you have said all those terrible things?"

"What things?" He pretended he had no idea what I was referring to.

"About 'Negroes.' " I used his disdainful term.

"Essie Mae, there is no man in this country who cares more about the Negro than I do. I think you know that." He stared hard at me. I had hurt him, genuinely hurt him. He believed what he was saying. "Look around here. Look at your college. Look at my programs. I'm doing all that's humanly possible."

"All this stuff you said about keeping us out of your homes, your churches, your swimming pools . . ."

"Is that really where you want to go, Essie? A white swimming pool? We built a beautiful pool right here on campus."

"We can't even go to Edisto Gardens." The vast gardens, right outside of Orangeburg, were among the most famous in the entire country, famed for their roses, azaleas, and centuries-old cypress trees. It was for whites only. "That's like coming to New York City and being told we can't go to the Statue of Liberty."

"There's a big difference between Edisto and the Statue of Liberty, Essie Mae."

"Then Central Park."

"Essie Mae, Edisto is private property. The owners can do what they want. Private property is the essence of the American democracy. I know you're an A student in history. I shouldn't have to tell you that. Would *you* want the government telling you what to do with your property?" My father then launched into a defense of his offense against Harry Truman. "That's what this campaign was about. That man is like a Communist with that FEPC (Truman's proposed Fair Employment Practices Committee). He wants to tell employers how to run their business. He wants to send agents into every shop, every factory, to make sure Negroes are put there, whether they're qualified or not. That's the way Stalin does [it] in Russia, sending his spies everywhere. You don't want the federal government in your life. Then we're all slaves. Do you want that in your country, Essie Mae?"

"I want black people to have jobs."

"So do I, Essie Mae. That's why I love this school, which gets Negroes *qualified*. I'm working on a lot of educational reforms. Essie Mae, I'm a schoolteacher! I believe in education. That's the way to go. We've come a long way. We're going to go a lot further. But it takes time."

"The backs of the buses, the railway coaches, the colored balconies at the movie shows . . . It's not fair."

"It's the *South*, Essie Mae," the governor spoke with finality. "It's the culture here. It's the custom. It's the way we live." I could tell the "we" didn't include me. "You don't go to England and tell them to get rid of the queen and the royalty. That's not fair, either, but it's the custom. They got rid of the royalty in Russia, and what do you have? Communism! A police state. It's no different from Hitler."

And neither are you, I wanted to say. What I did say was, "Hitler said the Jews were inferior. You said the Negroes (I often used his terms) are inferior."

"That is completely untrue, Essie Mae. A terrible falsehood! Where did I say that?"

"I don't remember. It seemed . . . If you don't want them around white people, then that means they're inferior."

"Not inferior. Different! Different! Imagine! To compare me to Hitler. Not that I haven't heard it in that campaign. I heard everything. But to hear it from *you*. Essie Mae . . . You can't change the South."

"You don't *want* to, sir."

"Oh yes I do. I'm changing it right now, by having you here, getting a fine education, to get you a fine career. There's nothing in this country you won't be able to do, Essie Mae. Nothing at all. Nothing your husband won't be able to do."

"We can't get served at the counter at Woolworth's."

"Why would you want to? The food's no good. I bet these restaurants right over here are much better. They serve good fresh food. I know they do. You can't get a vegetable at Woolworth's. I've never seen spinach, green beans at the five and dime. What do you want, a hot dog that will kill you?"

"I guess I want the choice, Governor."

"I think the Communists are putting these ideas in colored people's heads, that they're missing something wonderful at Woolworth's luncheonette. You're too intelligent to be taken in by that nonsense, Essie Mae. Much too intelligent."

For a moment, I couldn't help being flattered by his backhanded praise.

"Stand up for what matters, not hot dogs at Woolworth's. I'm standing up for the Negroes. Ask your president here. He knows what I'm doing. The future of South Carolina depends on the amelioration of the condition of the Negro. I love this state. But give me time. Give me a chance."

"A lot of Negroes, Negroes here, are hurt by what you said."

"That's politics, Essie Mae. You're in the heat of a campaign, you get misquoted, taken out of context. Look at the *deeds*, not the words. They made me sound like I thought lynching was no problem, but you saw that I prosecuted the Willie Earle case."

"You lost."

"This is the South, Essie Mae," he kept repeating. "The party was called the States' Rights Party for a reason. The South has had enough problems with the federal government. Reconstruction left terrible scars on this region that still haven't healed. Southerners are ultra-sensitive about Yankee interference, telling them how to live their lives. It'll all work out in time, but change takes time. Imagine if your husband tried to force you to kiss him. You'd say no. You'd resist. But if he gave you time, let you get to know him . . . see? You end up married. It all works out."

Given his own marriage, my father's choice of analogy was highly unfortunate. It made me extremely uncomfortable. "Are you sad that you lost?" I again changed the subject.

"I never expected to win. I never expected to run. It was quite an experience, quite an honor. I was trying to make a point for the South, that the South has to be respected, that there can't be another Reconstruction, that the federal will can't be imposed. I wasn't against Negroes. I was against Washington. Maybe I spoke too strongly, maybe I got too passionate. If I did, then I'm sorry. Washington was simply using the Negro issue as a wedge. I guarantee I care more about the Negro than Harry Truman. Just look at my record. Study John C. Calhoun, Essie Mae. Our greatest South Carolinian. You'll understand exactly what this campaign was about."

My father got up to leave. "I've got a year of work to catch up on. I promise to be in better touch," he said, but did not invite me to visit him in Columbia or meet his new wife. "I'm terribly sorry about your mother," he added, trying hard not to choke up. "That is shocking news." He handed me another of his envelopes. "This is for your marriage," he said and shook my hand. It seemed weaker than his hello greeting. Then he leaned in to me and, in a near-whisper, said, "I truly cared for that woman. She was a wonderful person. A wonderful woman . . . I can't . . ." Then his voice trailed off into silence.

"Good, bye, Governor," I said. He reached out to hug me, but this time I simply couldn't let him and left him standing alone in the office.

Outside in the twilight, I opened the envelope. It was stuffed with hundred-dollar bills. Benjamin Franklin seemed to be smiling at me, again and again. I knew there was no easy way to hide this enormous amount from Julius, who was so principled that he might force me to give it back. Should I give it back myself first? I pondered. Was it right to take money from Strom Thurmond? For all his bluster, for all his racist campaign posturing, I somehow couldn't dislike him the way I wanted to. I'm sure it was the genuine grief he felt, but could not express, over my mother. Even though on the surface he had it all, high office, a perfect wife, health and wealth and power, I—and only I—knew how deeply conflicted he had to be. I knew he loved my mother. I believed he loved me, after his fashion. It was an unspeakable love, forbidden by "the culture and custom" of the South, as he called it. The money was speaking it for him. It wasn't hush money; it wasn't a bribe. It was the governor's own outpouring of love and shame and frustration. He had no other way to demonstrate his affection.

I thought about Strom Thurmond's own strict, fiercely tough mother and his father and The Pitchfork. I understood better that he had an election to try to win, a chance to become president of the United States. I was captivated by the mere notion of being the president's daughter, just as Jean Crouch Thurmond was captivated by the notion of serving grits in the White House as First Lady. I could understand how he might say just about anything for a chance to win. He was an arch-southerner, to be sure, but he was also only human. He had gotten carried away. I might have as well. Actually, I concluded, Strom Thurmond had already come a long way. I would forgive him, as the Bible says to do, and as my heart told me to do. I wanted to see how much further he could go. I would hide the money around the house, in jars, under the mattress, and save it for a rainy day. I wouldn't tell Julius. I wanted to let sleeping dogs lie, and this money might have just set the hounds barking.

In the public sphere, Strom Thurmond set out right away to try to make amends, to the blacks of South Carolina, and, I'm certain, as a gesture to me. He pardoned a black man facing what seemed an unfair manslaughter conviction. He led a campaign to raise funds for Benedict College, an all-black private school that had fallen on hard times. He declared April 5 Booker T. Washington Day. He gave a strong speech to the right-wing American Legion warning that he would never tolerate the Ku Klux Klan or any other vigilantism that targeted blacks. He stirred up a hornet's nest of white backlash when he appointed a black Charleston doctor to the state hospital board. This was the very first time in post-Reconstruction history that a black man had been appointed to any public position in South Carolina. "Thurmond Appoints Negro!" was the headline, and I could just see my father grinning like a Cheshire cat when I read it.

Julius, for one, didn't trust anything Strom Thurmond did. Though he generally avoided the subject, just as I did, to keep the peace, sometimes with friends we couldn't avoid the subject of politics. He never tried to pretend that he had warm feelings toward this father-in-law he would in all likelihood never meet. Julius thought the governor's gestures to blacks were nothing but political fence-mending, too little, too late. I wanted to give my father the benefit of the doubt, though I wasn't about to argue with my husband, for fear of seeming like a turncoat.

I may have exposed my sympathies, conflicted though they were, while watching Truman's inauguration on the television. Truman and his vice president, Alben Barkley of Kentucky, were on the reviewing stand waving at all the dignitaries riding by. My father and his wife passed the stand, and my father, trying to bury the hatchet, took off his hat and waved it at the two leaders. Truman icily looked the other way, but when he caught a glimpse of Barkley starting to wave back to the governor, Truman grabbed his VP's arm and held it down. I could see how my father was humiliated by the very public snub. "That was vicious," I said without censoring myself.

"That was great," Julius exulted. "Bravo, Harry!"

CHAPTER SEVEN
Dear Senator

I NEVER IMAGINED myself as a college dropout, but when I'd found myself pregnant with our first child, that's what I had to become. This was before day care. You simply couldn't be a mother and a student at the same time. So in the fall of 1949, I took a leave of absence to start our family, while Julius remained in law school. I decided to go to Coatesville to have our child. I had my family there, I knew the hospital situation, and I had plenty of support. Furthermore, although I loved the college and my friends there, I was happy to take a breather from the South. I wanted the best medical care I could get, and what passed for "separate but equal" in South Carolina was anything but. The day I left Julius to go home to Coatesville, Orangeburg was celebrating its renowned annual Grand American Coon Hunt. I took this as an omen that it was high time to say at least a temporary farewell.

As before, I was relieved to be back in the North. The southern custom of strict separation of the races didn't seem natural at all to me, even though my father insisted that it was down there. Born a southerner, I wasn't sure I could ever *be* one. President Truman's civil rights campaign had helped blacks turn a new corner in their integration into and respect by the American mainstream. Everywhere I turned there was black achievement. Ralph Bunche won the Nobel Peace Prize for mediating the original crisis in Palestine that led to the foundation of Israel. He was the first black to be so honored. Another black, Gwendolyn Brooks, was the first black to win a Pulitzer Prize for her poetry. Jackie Robinson won the Most Valuable Player award in major league baseball. Nat King Cole had the number one record, "Mona Lisa," while Mahalia Jackson's gospel concert sold out Carnegie Hall. Ethel Waters became a huge television star with her show *Beulah*. The Naval Academy admitted its first black midshipman.

One of the biggest films was *Pinky*, starring Jeanne Crain as a light-skinned black trying to pass for white. Black was all the rage in 1949 and 1950. Of course, this was all happening in the Northeast, where I was living. Orangeburg was so benighted and becalmed, I wasn't sure the news was getting down there. Even if it were, I had the feeling my schoolmates were too constrained by the "know your place" southern system that my father embodied to stir themselves to the achievements they were capable of if only they lived elsewhere.

Julius was different. He was burning up in Orangeburg, eager to get that law degree and turn the South upside down. I was terrified about an ultimate confrontation with my father, who to Julius was the ultimate adversary. Fortunately, my father's political fortunes seemed to be coming to an end. In 1950, his gubernatorial term expiring, he ran for the United States Senate. If he could be the South's candidate for president, I think he assumed that winning a Senate seat would be a foregone conclusion. However, this time he faced a powerful opponent, a man who was a far bigger, more devout racist than my father could ever pretend to be in his worst incarnation.

Olin Johnston, the incumbent senator, was himself a former South Carolina governor. Unlike my privileged father, Johnston, at fifty-three—five years my father's senior, was the son of a sharecropper and had worked as a textile assembly-line worker as a young man. He got past a flat feet disqualification to fight in France during World War I, albeit without the medals my father won in World War II. Johnston, too, was a consummate campaigner and politician, serving numerous terms in the state legislature before ascending to the governor's mansion. Even though they both had folksy styles, Johnston, the earthy man of the people, was able to paint my father as an aristocrat, at least relatively speaking, which was a liability in any election.

My father responded by painting Johnston as a Truman man. Johnston had stuck with the Democrats, rather than the Dixiecrats, and my father tried to make him seem like less than a true southerner for so doing. In return, Johnston played the "race card." Asserting that my father was "soft on Negroes," Johnston trotted out all sorts of evidence, the hospital board appointment, the pardon, the school support, everything except *me*. For some reason, the "secret daughter" rumor that had come up during the presidential campaign had evaporated. I'm sure Lizzie Mae Thompson was relieved. I know I was. I was surprised that Johnston did not dredge it up. He even attacked my father for inviting the black governor of the Virgin Islands to stay at the governor's mansion in Columbia. The man, a Truman appointee, had spurned the invitation, so my father lost on both fronts.

The two candidates, governor and senator, squared off in an endless series of debates over barbecues around the state. Several times the two men nearly came to blows, especially over my father's insinuation that Johnston had not stood up in the Senate against Truman's campaign to fully integrate the armed services. To Senator Johnston, calling him "soft" on affronts to racism was worse than calling him soft on Communism. Johnston riposted by calling my father the worst sort of liar, and my father said "Let's go outside." In the end, no punches were thrown, but it hurt me to see my father using race to try to beat a racist. I guess all's fair in love and politics.

In the end, my father lost the election by 30,000 votes out of over 300,000 cast. The Korean War had just broken out, and it was felt by some that Johnston, who stood firmly behind Commander-in-Chief Truman, benefited from this. Other political analysts felt that the 30,000 votes that beat my father came from black voters. Even though my father never once used the N-word, in contrast to his opponent's endless offensiveness, blacks in South Carolina, the ones who voted, would not forgive my father for his Dixiecrat candidacy. They preferred a Truman man to a Pitchfork man.

My baby was born in Coatesville. He was a beautiful boy. We named him Julius, after his father. I always thought of Julius Caesar; I hoped he would grow up to be a leader, just like I believed his father was about to become. After all, it did run in the family. I moved back to Orangeburg, so big and little Julius could be together. We arrived soon after the election to pack up and move to Savannah, Julius's home. He had graduated from the law school in June 1950 and had decided the cheapest place to live and start a career was the one he knew best. He wanted to be an activist lawyer. He wanted to change things. He felt the South needed him much more than the North did. I would have loved him to have gone to Philadelphia, or Washington, D.C., but not necessarily back to New York. That was too fast, too competitive. But Julius preferred Savannah, and it did seem that a smaller town like that was the best place to raise our son and the other children that we knew would be coming along.

Sometime before we left, my father showed up in a black car with his driver. I was a full-time mother, but occasionally I would go to the school library and read or take out books. He had called our house to say he was coming, and I met him again in the president's office. His term as governor would soon be up. He had no judgeship or other post waiting for him. He told me he was moving to Aiken, the town where I was born, to open a private law practice. I felt sorry for him. Was Strom Thurmond already a forgotten man?

He had noticed Julius's picture in the yearbook, one of the two graduates of the first class at State's law school. Strom Thurmond was proud of him. "He's a good-looking young man, Essie Mae. Very handsome. He looks a little Spanish."

"He's half Indian," I said. "On his mother's side."

I told him about baby Julius. I thought of saying, "He looks a little like you," but I knew that would have made him awfully uncomfortable. He never once referred to the baby as his grandchild, never asked if he could drive over to our house and see him, never asked to meet my handsome husband, his son-in-law, the graduate of "his" law school. I suppose it was just as well, given their adversarial political positions, but it would have been nice if my father had asked.

Because he had nothing to lose now, I hoped that he might get more personal with me, but he kept it cool and formal. The most he would do was urge me to go back to school. "You need that education, Essie Mae, as much as your husband needs his." But that was as close as he would get, like a guidance counselor or the teacher that he was. As much as I wanted to "belong" to him, I never felt like a daughter, only an accident. I had read that Oscar Wilde called homosexuality "the love that dare not speak its name." So it was with whatever the emotion was between my father and me. Something, some strong feeling, was definitely there. That was what was drawing him to me, and me to him. But that feeling was all bottled up. We both felt it, from opposite sides of an invisible wall. It was segregated love.

"Are you going to miss it?" I didn't want to call him Governor any more. I had never called him father. So I didn't call him anything.

"Of course I will, Essie Mae," he answered reflectively. "I've been a public servant most of my life. It's been a long time since I had a private life. I hope I know what to do with it."

"Maybe you can have some children yourself now." That was as personal a comment as I had ever made to him, but as a new mother, I couldn't contain my own emotions at the joys of parenthood. It was a gospel I wanted to spread.

He didn't answer.

"Senator Johnston reminds me of Cole Blease," I said.

"How do you know about Cole Blease?" My father was surprised at the reference. By now, I was getting insulted that he assumed I knew nothing. But fathers could be like that, particularly fathers of black people.

"You told me to study Calhoun. Blease, like Tillman, followed in his footsteps, wouldn't you say?"

"My God, no, Essie Mae!" He was appalled that I had mentioned the two men in the same breath. Coleman Blease, the South Carolina governor and senator who succeeded Tillman as the champion of the "poor white trash" in the World War I era, was to me the predecessor and inspiration of the victorious and profane Olin Johnston.

"My father tried to prevent that demagogue from getting elected. He managed the campaign of his opponent. We lost that one, too," he said, shaking his head.

The main difference between the cultivated Ben Tillman and the wild man Cole Blease seemed largely one of degree and couth. Every other word out of Blease's mouth was "nigger." He opposed black education as "a ruination of perfectly good field hands." He advocated mob violence, pardoning countless Klan types, setting a record 1,700 pardons in his term as governor. In one rape case, he released the convicted assailant of a black woman on the grounds of "Why would the man rape someone he could have for a quarter?" He made the amazing comment, "I have serious doubt that the crime of rape can be committed upon a Negro." Blacks to him were comparable to "the order of the lower animals. Adultery seems to be their favorite pastime." I guess what offended my father was not so much the theory of black inferiority, which even Calhoun espoused, but Blease's lack of hope for the Negro. My father, a true believer in education, was deeply sincere in his confidence that black people could make great strides in society. He just wanted to keep them separate.

"I suppose South Carolina must have a weakness for demagogues," I said.

"The world has a weakness, Essie Mae. That's what I'm most worried about. The Communists. That's what I'm most sorry about, not being in Washington to fight them. And that's the biggest danger facing us today."

"What about states' rights?"

"Fighting Communism is the one thing the federal government must do, but I'm afraid of how deep the Communists are there. You see what Senator McCarthy is saying."

The witch-hunts had begun, and my father missed not being on the front lines of this modern Inquisition. The "bomb" had the whole world in terror. Spies were being unearthed here and in Europe; Alger Hiss was just convicted, as was British scientist Klaus Fuchs. Paul Robeson's passport had been revoked because of his suspected Communist affiliation. Robeson had made the near-treasonous assertion that blacks were treated much better in Russia than they were in the United States. A lot of black people were attracted to Communism because of its dedication to equality. Suffice it to say, this was not a popular position to take in this emerging time of the Red Scare. I didn't begrudge my father his Cold War hard line. He was a patriot who had risked his life fighting Hitler. Joseph Stalin was fiercely scary, as was the Communism he had brutalized his country into.

He handed me another envelope. "For your baby," he said. "And try to go back to school as soon as you can. Get that degree. It's your passport." I knew he had been displeased when I had dropped out, but he never tried to make me feel like a failure over it. He knew about love; I hope he did. He reached out and hugged me, not letting me even think about turning away as I had the last time. This time, miraculously, he kissed me on the cheek. He had never done that before. Maybe he felt he had fences to mend with me, and it was to show how much he did care. Then he left me in the office and went down to his car and drove away. I was numb. I knew it was my father riding off into what seemed like the sunset of his career. Yet, with my mother's passing and the shock of my father's campaign style, my emotions for him had been drained out of me. All I could do was stare at the huge wad of money. He was a distant father, perhaps a false father, but he was certainly a generous one.

Aided by my father's nest eggs, we settled into Savannah, which was about a three-hour drive south of Orangeburg, right on the coast. Savannah was the most beautiful place I had ever seen, laid out in elegant squares draped in moss, lined by stately mansions and town houses of the antebellum elite, shaded by magnolias and palms. Horse-drawn carriages clip-clopped down the spacious, gracious streets. The city was frozen in another, gentler era. Despite my time at Orangeburg, because we were so restricted about leaving campus, I had never been to Charleston, which, like Savannah, was also a city of great charm and history. But we had plans. We had lots of plans.

We first moved into the home of Julius's parents, whom I had not met before. His mother was blind; his father, who now was a truck driver, was totally devoted to her, caring for her like a little baby. Julius had a sister, a social worker, who also lived in the house. It sounds crowded, but there was plenty of room. Compared to sleeping in the kitchen, as we had in Orangeburg, our room, where little Julius slept with us, felt like a suite at the Waldorf-Astoria. While we were in an all-black neighborhood, the houses were all quite grand, ancient, and charming. They were the homes of rich whites once, before General Sherman took the city. He didn't burn it, the way he did Columbia and Atlanta. It was too pretty for even a rebel hater to destroy.

I loved walking around Savannah, getting to know it. Julius knew Savannah, so he loved getting away from it. His hobby was deep-sea fishing, off the lush nearby sea islands. He had a tiny boat that reminded me of the one in Hemingway's *The Old Man and the Sea*. I would get seasick, so I sat on the shore and prepared the fish fry that would inevitably follow. One Sunday we attended the First African Baptist Church, right near the waterfront in the heart of the rich, white district. The stately old church used to house a white congregation, but a freed slave bought it long ago and rebuilt it in brick as a black house of worship, the first brick building to be owned by blacks in Georgia. While First African was a cultural experience, our normal place of worship was the First Congregational Church of Savannah. We rarely missed a Sunday.

In many ways, Savannah at first seemed like a vacation. Unfortunately for Julius, it was too much of a vacation. Starting his law practice proved far more difficult than he had imagined. He thought that since there were so few black attorneys, he would have the city to himself. There was a reason for the number. Almost all the blacks in Savannah were too poor to afford lawyers. Although he was admitted to both the Georgia and South Carolina bars, and affiliated himself with the top black lawyer in town, a man called Mayfield, there was simply not enough paid work to support us. So Julius began doing pro bono work for the NAACP, criminal defense cases, some futile discrimination suits, welfare claims. He wasn't changing the world yet, and he was impatient.

To help out financially, I took a job as a secretary in the public relations office at Savannah State College, which was Georgia's counterpart to my alma mater at Orangeburg. Later, I got an even better job as assistant to the president, Howard Jordan, a South Carolina State alumnus who had a soft spot for Orangeburg people. A kind woman named Mary who came in to look after Julius's mother did double duty as babysitter. The two colleges were of the same vintage, founded under the Morrill Land Grant Act, but Savannah State, whose original name was Georgia State Industrial College, seemed grander—lots of red brick Georgian buildings with those southern plantation columns. There were elegant circular drives and lovely landscaping, with moss draping everything.

As at Orangeburg, the students were impeccably dressed, very polite, very serious, and largely apathetic when it came to politics. They knew "their place" was not behind barricades, not if they wanted to enter the black bourgeoisie, which most of them did. I didn't begrudge them that, although Julius did. Considering the slave cabins that stood everywhere as a reminder of where their forbears had come from, the comforts of the bourgeoisie seemed most attractive.

Eventually, we got our own place, a duplex apartment in a newer all-black neighborhood near the college. What other kind of neighborhood existed in the South? The minute a black family moved into a declining neighborhood, the whites would flee and create suburbs. We enjoyed having much of Savannah to ourselves. Our friends were the people Julius had grown up with, doctors, funeral home owners, realtors, all somewhat prosperous, none rich. We entertained each other at our homes. For a city with a black population as large as Savannah's, there weren't many places to go. Savannah was tightly segregated, and most of the blacks there were of the "plantation school," never wanting to push matters, to open new doors for themselves. There were a few black cafes, a few roadhouses to hear jazz and dance, but it was a long way from Seventh Avenue. It was great for kids, though, and in 1950 our second son Ronald was born.

Sometimes, the utter complacency of black Savannah would provoke me into action. I was usually very self-effacing. First, I was a woman, who wanted to be a lady, and ladies weren't loud, pushy, or, that hated word used by whites, "uppity." Second, I was black, or at least assigned to that category, so I felt second class and hence not entitled to speak my piece. Third, I was illegitimate and harbored a shame over my birth that stifled me, despite the fact I knew it wasn't my fault. Finally, I had had a big secret to keep, and as the illegitimate daughter of a famous white supremacist, I was under a lifetime gag order.

Nevertheless, there were times then that tried my soul. I would take a bus to work at the college. Black people were always required to sit in the back, or to stand in the back, even if there were plenty of empty seats in the white section in the front. Since most whites had cars, there were very few whites on the bus, just a lot of empty white seats. One day coming home from work when I was pregnant with Ronald, I was so tired I felt like I needed to sit down or I would faint. There wasn't a white person on the bus, but the back was filled with black rush hour standees. I plopped down in the last row of the white section. Seeing this in his rearview mirror, the driver screeched to a halt, sending several standees to the floor. He stormed back to me. "Go to your place, lady."

"This is my place."

"Whites only."

I wanted to tell him my father ran for president on the "whites only" ticket. "Can't you see I'm pregnant?" I went for sympathy.

I didn't get it. "All I can see is that you're in the white section, and you ain't white. Now move."

"Then give me my money back. I'll get off."

"No refunds, you. Move!"

"No. I just want my money back."

"You damn . . . woman . . ." the driver spat, and skulked back to his seat. I stayed in mine. The other blacks looked at me as if I were Mahatma Gandhi. I was quite pleased with this little victory.

By 1953, Julius had hit a professional wall. Nothing was happening for him in his career, nor in his hopes of effecting change. Julius's sister had married her childhood sweetheart and moved to California. She sent back endless glowing reports of this American Eden that was her new home in Los Angeles. She kept pushing Julius to move west, and one day he decided to do it. Before we left, I felt impelled to say farewell to my southern roots. I took a long bus ride to Edgefield to visit my relatives in Old Buncombe. Nothing had changed there; it seemed nothing would *ever* change there. Then I took a shorter bus ride over to Aiken to bid good-bye to my father.

Aiken was less than twenty miles away from Edgefield, but it felt like another universe. What it most resembled that I had seen was one of the aristocratic towns along Philadelphia's Main Line: Bryn Mawr, Paoli, Haverford. There were all gated mansions, manicured lawns, and country-club white people riding horses down the city's tree-lined streets. There were black servants everywhere in maid's and butler's uniforms, none of the poor unemployed derelicts who lay around the typical southern squares. I was one of the only black people *not* in uniform. This was the kind of place where a black person not in uniform might be stopped by the police. But I didn't see any police. None were needed in a perfect place like this. My father's new law firm, Thurmond, Lybrand, and Simons, was in a manicured building right across from the post office, but I didn't think about going in. I remembered how my mother and I had just walked into his office in Edgefield, but that was Edgefield, and that was before he was famous.

It occurred to me that if my white half had been the lowest common denominator, then I might be living in one of these gated mansions, riding horses, sipping juleps at the country club, instead of skulking around this exclusive paradise, my own birthplace, feeling like an intruder. I had to wonder why in the world my mother was taken here, of all places, to give birth to me. I supposed it was simply to get out of Edgefield, out of the radar of scandal. Twenty miles in those days was a long way. I imagined that a black midwife delivered me; I was certain that I wasn't born in any hospital. I was born an outsider, and now I was back as one, in this most inside of towns. If I were truly my father's daughter, I could have been one of the Aikenites, an insider, not an interloper. But I wasn't.

I found a pay phone outside of the post office and called the law firm. A secretary put me through to my father. I had called a week before to plan the visit.

"I'm here."

"I'll pick you up."

I told him I was at the post office. He told me to wait on the street outside. There was nobody there, no witnesses, when his car pulled up. It was a dark Ford, nothing fancy, even in this fancy town. My father was definitely not pretentious.

"This is some place," I said, as we drove around aimlessly. He had never taken me to a restaurant or any public place. I was sure he wasn't going to start now.

"Full of Yankees," he said. "Southerners don't have this kind of money. Yankees and their horses. There's my bank."

My father proudly pointed out another manicured building, the Aiken Federal Savings and Loan Association.

"I thought you were a lawyer."

"Lawyers make the best bankers," he said. "They can read all the fine print." He told me a little about his life here. He had this law practice, which handled everything from murders to divorce, but made most of its money in eminent domain cases. Nearby was a federal nuclear reactor facility known as the Savannah River Plant. The Atomic Energy Commission had to purchase private land. My father's firm went to court to get the owners better prices than the government wanted to pay.

"That's a perfect job for you," I said.

"Why, Essie Mae?"

"Because you hate the federal government. You get to fight them for a living."

"I hadn't thought of it that way."

With all the money he was making from this practice, my father had set up the bank. We rode by his new house, which seemed like a cottage compared to the neighboring palaces. As I said, he wasn't pretentious.

I asked him if he had plans for a family.

This time he answered the question. "I'd love one," he said. "But my wife has some health problems." Deep inside, I was a little hurt—even though I had brought the subject up. Here *was* his family, after all, right in the seat next to him. He asked a few perfunctory questions about my children, but nothing more. His grandchildren, if he had wanted them, were just three hours away. I hated not existing.

The subject changed to politics. Ever fearful of Communism, my father had committed the heresy of supporting his wartime commander General Eisenhower, a Republican, against the Democrat Adlai Stevenson, in the 1952 election. Although he had bet on the winner, for a white hero like himself to vote for the party of Lincoln, the "Negro Party," as the GOP was known in the South, was an act of political suicide in South Carolina. "I'm not in politics anymore, Essie Mae. You have to vote your conscience."

He drove me to the bus station and said good-bye. He told me he thought I would enjoy California. "It's wide open out there," he said. I wasn't sure whether he meant the spaces or the segregation situation. I didn't press it. He repeatedly urged me to finish college and handed me an envelope to that end. He hugged me and kissed my cheek and said how much he'd miss me. I waited for the Edgefield bus, then dutifully trudged to the back of the coach. The envelope was packed with more of those Benjamin Franklin notes. I doubted anyone who ever rode this bus carried this sort of money. California, I supposed, must have warranted this display of affection.

All the money in the world couldn't have bought Julius and our two sons decent accommodations on our trip across the country. We drove across the green and lush Deep South and then Texas, which, for all its barren plains, was just like the Deep South as far as blacks were concerned. There were motels all along the highways, but blacks were barred from most of them, nor could we use rest rooms at many of the gas stations, for fear of being victimized by Klan types. There was an informal "network" of black travelers who had told Julius what rest stops and service areas were "safe" for us, which often meant a nail-biting long ride in which we often came close to running out of gas before we arrived at a safe harbor.

Throughout the trip we sometimes had to improvise, sleeping in the car, that sort of thing. It was tough with the two young boys, but they were good and didn't complain, which may have been a genetic trait they inherited from my long-suffering side of the family. In big cities like New Orleans and Dallas there were "colored only" motor courts where we could catch up on sleep and bathing, but it was more the Mary and Joseph experience of no room at the inn until we reached New Mexico. There were very few blacks there, and people seemed happy to receive us, to take our money. There were lots of Mexicans, and maybe they thought Julius was one of them. It was smooth sailing all the way across that endless southwestern desert to Los Angeles. The whole trip lasted about a week, but the trials and tribulations of being black voyagers in a white world made it seem like a month.

Our first impression of Los Angeles was the surfer shacks along the then-deserted Pacific Coast Highway in Malibu. The ocean was beautiful and blue, and those shacks represented the freedom of the endless summer that was L.A. Eventually, those shacks became the beachfront palazzos of Santa Monica, where the stars lived then. Hooray for Hollywood, I sang to myself. We had finally made it! The City of Angels immediately lived up to all the stories Julius's sister had regaled us with. I had never been in a place that wasn't a humid steam bath, so the eternal spring weather was a miracle. There were huge mountains, which I had also never seen, right up to the Pacific Ocean. The orange groves, the palm trees, the night-blooming jasmine, it was a little like the South, but minus the muggy heat, much neater and more spacious, and, above all, the biggest difference was that the blacks were living like white people. There were no Old Buncombes, no shantytowns, no slave cabins, just sprawling ranch houses, like you saw on the televison shows that were made out here, or Spanish Colonial stucco houses, or Craftsman-style wooden bungalows with swimming pools and palm trees and ocean vistas and nice cars.

Julius's sister and her husband, whom we stayed with, lived near Hollywood. They had friendly, white neighbors; friendly, Japanese neighbors; and friendly, Mexican neighbors. Everyone seemed to get along. We'd eat at drive-ins with waitresses on roller skates, at taco stands, at coffee shops, at Creole restaurants when we'd get homesick for fried chicken. The clientele at these establishments was generally mixed.

There were no colored balconies. We'd go to the movies and see *From Here to Eternity* or *Mogambo* and sit where we wanted, excited by the fact that we might spot the stars of these films in real life when we walked outside. Of course, most blacks weren't rich, and most whites did have more money than we did, but out west we felt we had a chance, a more equal opportunity to do well, than we had back east. There was none of the pressure you felt in New York, none of that eastern rat race, none of that southern hatred. There were vast spaces, endless vistas, zero claustrophobia, enough for everyone without having to fight someone else for short supplies. Los Angeles went on forever, and we were thrilled to be here. It was indeed wide open. I finally understood what my father meant.

As I got to know Los Angeles better, I saw that there were indeed all-black neighborhoods. But there were no slums, no urban blight like in the east. Blacks, poor blacks, may have been living in tiny wooden houses in Watts, but they had the same cool air, the same bright sun, the same palms, the same Pacific. If you were going to be poor, it was a lot easier being poor out here than it was in Harlem. The southern blacks had called their immigration to the Northeast their exodus to the "Promised Land." Los Angeles held far greater promises, in my eyes. I was thrilled that when I gave birth to our daughter Wanda that first year in Los Angeles that she would grow up a California girl.

Julius quickly found a job in the suburb of Downey at North American Aircraft. The aviation industry was one of the big businesses out here, and it hired lots of people, blacks and whites. Julius worked as a drill press operator. It seemed like a terrible comedown for a lawyer, but he saw it as only a stopgap position until he could take the California bar and qualify as an attorney in the Golden State. The bar course was very expensive, so he was working to save up for it. Meanwhile, the money at North American was very seductive. Julius quickly rose to become a shop steward and kept making more and more. It wasn't a fortune, but it kept him from wanting to take any time off to study for the bar. Because the segregation factor and other inequities of the

South weren't at all obvious in Los Angeles, Julius may not have felt as pressing a need to "save the world" as he had back in Dixie. Whatever, he postponed resuming the legal career that had thus far held only promises for him but no tangible results. He also gradually began drinking and became increasingly depressed. There was trouble in paradise, though it took several years to become apparent.

I would call my father at his law office every few months, just to say hello. He would send me money by cable that I would go down to get at Western Union. His bank must have been doing well, because he would send a thousand here, a thousand there. It was very generous of him. I opened my own bank account and put it away for our children's future. I wanted to give it to Julius, but he was still so idealistic that I was sure he would refuse the money of the racist Strom Thurmond, even if it meant his getting off the assembly line and back to his dream. That money would have felt tainted to him.

Nineteen fifty-four was an amazing year, both for America, and for my father. In May of that year, the Supreme Court handed down its decision in *Brown vs. Board of Education,* declaring that segregated public schools were unconstitutional under the Fourteenth Amendment. Separate but equal was over, at least according to the law. I was glad to be out of the South when that ruling came down. The news made it clear that the entire region was up in arms and was planning to fight back and not honor the Court's decision. In California, as in Pennsylvania, the schools were "mixed." The problem was not ours.

In the midst of South Carolina's anti-*Brown* mobilization—which was known as "massive resistance," as opposed to Gandhi's "passive resistance"—the senior senator from South Carolina, Burnet Maybank of Charleston, who would be running as the shoo-in Democratic candidate for reelection that fall, dropped dead of a heart attack at his summer home in the North Carolina mountains near where Julius and I had gotten married. The state Democratic Party, right after the funeral, decided to nominate one of their own, Edgar Brown, Sol Blatt's co-head of the infamous Barnwell Ring, to take Maybank's spot on the ballot. The party fiat seemed to shake Strom Thurmond out of his cushy Aiken hibernation. Mentioning the Barnwell Ring to my father was the same as showing a red cape to a bull. It represented all that was undemocratic about the Democratic Party in his state. So he came out and denounced the actions of this old boys' club and announced that he would offer himself as a write-in protest candidate on the November ballot.

No one took my father very seriously this time. No write-in candidate had ever won a major election. The entire Democratic apparatus came out for Brown. Senator Olin Johnston, the man who had beaten Strom Thurmond and sent him packing to Aiken, endorsed Brown, as did former president Harry Truman, still the party's grand old man and still the man who vanquished, then humiliated, Strom Thurmond. But this time my father got the last laugh, pulling off an upset even bigger than Truman's had been. Campaigning as a grass-roots outsider, a man of the people, Strom Thurmond came out of his political grave and trounced the Barnwell ringleader, getting nearly twice the votes as Edgar Brown. My father, the senator, was now going to Washington to take on Big Government, to walk in the giant steps of his idol, South Carolina's greatest senator, John C. Calhoun.

When I reached him in Aiken to congratulate him, he was the happiest I had ever heard him. He was so happy that he insisted, "You come see me in Washington, you hear?"

I wasn't sure I heard him correctly. Maybe he forgot who I was. Maybe he confused me with some white well-wisher. Maybe he said that to everyone, without meaning it, a politician's empty greeting. For some reason, however, I took it seriously. In the back of my head, I began making plans to visit my father in his new office on Capitol Hill. How could anyone who was the daughter of a senator not want to do the same thing?

I took these plans more seriously when a month or so after the election I got a Christmas gift wire of 1,000 dollars. It was my father's equivalent of a victory cigar. I decided it was high time I tell Julius that he should get off his high horse and let me help him get back into the law. We were safe in California. There was no Klan to harm us; the fear of race fanatics was not present. Few people in California even knew who Strom Thurmond was, other than a right-wing southern politician. Interracial marriages, while not a huge trend at this point, were definitely not unheard of out here. In the South, biracial children were forced to live as blacks and as second-class citizens; here they weren't forced to do anything but follow the American Dream. My father had just beaten a real ring and the racists behind it who were far worse than my father. Everything was relative, certainly in the South. My father was going to the Senate, where he could do the whole nation some good. I wanted to go see him, and I wanted to take Julius with me.

We had moved to our own small house by then, a rental on Hobart Street between Hollywood and downtown. We had a TV, a dishwasher, a view of the Hollywood sign in the distant hills, and three beautiful children. Plus, my father was a senator. Was this not the American Dream come true? Julius didn't think so. When I suggested to him that he and I go to Washington and open a dialogue with my father, he refused flat out. "Waste of time," he said. "Just because he's going to the Senate doesn't mean he's got religion. He'll just use the place as a pulpit of hate."

"Not if he gets to know real black people, people like us. It'll make him see the light." My pleadings for a bridge to understanding fell on deaf ears. Julius thought my idealism was unrealistic. "You know, if it wasn't for him, we wouldn't have met," I commented.

Julius began laughing. He thought that one was funny. "Now you're giving him credit for fate. Come on." Julius stopped laughing when I revealed to him that my father had been sending me money that I had saved and wanted to use for him to quit North American Aircraft and get back to the law, however long it might take to pass the bar and start a practice. He seemed insulted, just as I had feared.

"I won't take his money. Neither should you," Julius bristled, and an argument, one of our rare ones, began to explode.

"He's my father. Don't you think he owes me something?"

"Don't fool yourself. He's not your father."

"Yes he is."

"Not where it matters. Don't dignify that man by calling him your father."

"But that's what he is. I can't help it. He's my father."

"Then let him say it," Julius challenged me. "Let him testify. See what I say?"

"He can't . . ." I sputtered. "It's the South."

"Those are *his* excuses, not yours, woman! Let him say it."

"He won't. He can't," I said.

"Then you say it."

"I'm saying it. I'm saying it now."

"To whom?" Julius asked, like the lawyer he was, the lawyer he wanted to be. He was taking his years of rage, of frustration out on me.

"I'm saying it to you."

"Say it to the world!" Julius ordered me. "Say it loud! That would set the cat among the pigeons. That would change the world."

"Are you crazy, Julius?" I asked my husband.

"Do you realize how much good you could do if you let this out?" he pressed me, grabbing my arm for emphasis.

"That hurts."

"You're covering for that man, aren't you? You're taking his bribes. It's not money to help you, or us, or anybody but him. It's hush money, Essie. Don't be stupid."

"I'm not betraying my father, Julius. Don't ever ask me to. And don't get any ideas yourself."

He didn't reply for a long time. Then he said, "What do you call what he's doing to you?"

"I call it the best he can under the circumstances. He's a southerner, Julius."

"So am I," my husband said with a pained look and walked outside to be alone. I didn't dare bring up Strom Thurmond for over a year. The fight didn't really change our marriage, for we truly loved and respected each other. But it did change Julius. His drinking gradually escalated, and I sensed a mounting frustration in him, which I didn't dare address for the sake of avoiding discord. Blessed are the peacemakers, I rationalized to myself, though I remained filled with doubt, especially after seeing my father in action in his new position.

As my father took his place in the Senate during the next few years, there were many occasions when I was deeply embarrassed for him and for myself. Maybe Julius was right about him. Maybe as a daughter I was too forgiving. Maybe I had filial blinders that prevented me from seeing the out-and-out racist at whom Julius was glaring daggers.

A case in point was my father's role in the creation of what became known as "The Southern Manifesto." If the 1954 *Brown* decision was a slap in the South's face, the 1955 Montgomery, Alabama, bus boycott was a stab in its back. The first mass protest was led by the young Reverend Martin Luther King, Jr., from Atlanta, a graduate of the Crozer Theological Institute in West Chester, near Coatesville. The Montgomery movement stirred my heart. I had been one of those back-of-the-bus riders who hated it, and now Rosa Parks and other abused blacks had finally had enough and said so, bringing Montgomery to its knees. I guess southern whites had had enough of this "uppityness" and looked to my father, as their voice in the Senate, to stop the liberal madness.

The 1956 document, signed by nineteen of the twenty-two southern senators (Lyndon Johnson of Texas did not, nor did Albert Gore and Estes Kefauver of Tennessee) and the vast majority of southerners in the House, basically declared war on the *Brown* decision as an "abuse of judicial power" and called for a return to the "separate but equal" status quo ante *Brown*. It stated that the states had the right, by any lawful means, to resist integration ordered by the federal government. My father, in touting his manifesto, once again put his racist foot in his states'-rights mouth, calling the white people of the South "the greatest minority in this nation." He also bemoaned that "outside agitators," the South's favorite euphemism for Communist sympathizers, were out to destroy "the harmony which has existed for generations between the white and Negro races." Oh, daddy! I despaired.

Nineteen fifty-six was also the year our fourth child, Monica, was born. With Julius's North American earnings and the liberal credit availability to aircraft workers, we were able to buy our own residence in the suburb of Compton, in a new tract house development called the Joy Homes. Like us, there were many first-time black home owners, and it felt very empowering to own our little piece of the rock that was California. That summer, while Julius worked (he never would take a vacation, especially with the new mortgage at hand), I took all four children to Coatesville to see Mary and the rest of the family. That was when I decided to call my father on his invitation. The Southern Manifesto might have chilled my interest in seeing him if it had been my first exposure to his racist bombast. But it wasn't, and I knew that he'd say it was just politics, and that the Negro had no better friend than he, and that included Reverend King. To my surprise, when I called the Senate and reached his office, my father got right on the line. I told him I was in Coatesville and wanted to say hello. And before I could say it myself, he repeated his invitation. "Come see this big office, Essie Mae. And bring your children."

I thought four kids might be too much for me, and for him. So I decided to take a day trip to Washington on the train, which took only a couple of hours each way, and show Strom Thurmond his oldest grandson, Julius, now seven. We got off at Union Station and took a cab to Capitol Hill. Because we were early, I asked the driver, who was black, to drive us around, to see the Lincoln Memorial and the Washington Monument. Washington was a beautiful city, and I had only caught glimpses of it from the train on my journeys to the South. Now I got to see it up close, and its white marble majesty really, forgive the cliché, made me proud to be an American.

So did my father. His whole staff at the Old Senate Office Building knew I was coming in, though I assume they thought I was an old family friend from Edgefield. They gave me a royal welcome, oohing and aahing over little Julius, who was getting taller and handsomer every day. Whether they noticed any resemblance to their boss, I'll never know. Nor did the boss himself make any such comment, though his face certainly lit up when he saw him. He took

Julius into his arms and embraced him, lifting his grandson over his head to show off for him how strong he was. Now I know that as a politician Strom Thurmond had a lifetime of experience kissing babies, but not black babies, and not his own grandchildren. Julius wasn't really a baby, but the love Strom Thurmond showed for him was totally genuine, and the man was deeply moved. I wished that I had had the chance to show him my other children when they were young. That might have humanized our stiff relationship.

The Senate office was very grand, filled floor to ceiling with law books and history books. The first thing I noticed were the American and Confederate flags hanging behind his desk. You could take the boy out of Dixie, but you couldn't take Dixie out of the boy. But he was so loving to my son that I couldn't get disgusted with him. There were lots of framed awards, degrees, magazine covers, including *Time*, and countless framed photos of every member of his family, with numerous shots of his father and of his wife Jean. I wished mine, and my children's, could have had a place of honor as well. That would have been nice. But it wasn't realistic, not then, not for the man I came to think of as "President of the South."

I noticed a set of barbells behind his desk.

"Every morning I exercise an hour at home," he said. "Then I come here and lift these, after I walk up the stairs to work. I always walk to the Senate chamber, never take the train. I don't believe in elevators." He stood up, did some high kicks, knee bends, and stretches. He reminded me of the Rockettes at Radio City in New York. "Just because you're in an office doesn't mean you can't get exercise." Then he opened a large dresser, which turned out to be a medicine cabinet stocked with row after row of vitamins and mineral supplements, wheat germ, and many bottles of mineral water. "Water up here isn't pure like South Carolina's. Have to drink this." He opened a bottle called Poland Springs. "Roosevelt's favorite," he noted. "Do you think I look fifty-six, Essie Mae? Tell the truth."

"No way, sir," I said with a laugh. He was doing something right. He could have passed for someone twenty years younger. In the 1950s, before the Swinging Sixties and the rise of the Youth Culture, a man of fifty-six would have been considered an elder statesman. My father may have worked at the statesman part, but the elder was anathema to him. He told me how he rode bicycles every weekend in Rock Creek Park and was introducing legislation to build bicycle paths all over the country. "Exercise and diet, that and eight hours of sleep every night. That's the key to longevity," he asserted, as he had before. "Of course if you eat well, you'll sleep well. You are what you eat." He then gave me his inevitable nutrition lecture. Today, he was on a protein kick, decades ahead of Dr. Atkins. "Try to avoid bread, Essie Mae. You'll lose weight if you stick to meat and vegetables. And no potatoes, French fries, even baked potatoes." He always managed to make me feel fat. I didn't take it as a warning, but as a critique. I hadn't lost the weight from having Monica, and I knew it.

"But she's worth it," I told him.

"I'm sure she is, if she's anything like her big brother here." The senator playfully pinched Julius's cheek. "Your children deserve the best."

At that he gave me another envelope and a big hug and kiss and had his driver take us back to Union Station and see us onto the train. He had given us several thousand dollars this time. Whatever he stood for, however he segregated me from his real life, I couldn't help but like having a senator for a father.

CHAPTER EIGHT

Days of Rage

IN 1959, WE sold our house in Compton and moved back to Coatesville. It seemed that we were the first family in those days to leave California and go in the opposite direction. Disneyland, Hollywood, and surfing had captured the American imagination, and the whole country was getting infected with California fever. But my aunt Mary had gotten very ill, and I wanted to care for her. Julius, whose own mother was an invalid, could understand. Moreover, at North American Aviation he had hit a ceiling. He was earning good pay, but it was clear he wasn't going much higher, off the line and into the executive suite. Besides, he didn't really want to become a corporate man. He wanted to do good, and corporations in the 1950s weren't the place for that. He still hadn't studied for the California bar. Perhaps he feared he wouldn't pass. Somehow, he had a block against doing it. I thought a return to our roots might reanimate his legal dreams.

Mary had diabetes and heart disease. She was only sixty, but she was like an old woman from the weight of her illness. Like my mother Carrie at the end, Mary could hardly breathe. Her wasting away brought back terrible memories. I didn't want to put her in the hospital, so I used all my old nursing training to care for her at home. Because he was not a member of the Pennsylvania bar, Julius took a job as a social worker, but right away we knew it was temporary. If he was going to be back east, he wanted to be home in

Savannah. The Civil Rights movement was heating up in the South, and for a conscience-driven aspiring activist like my husband that was "where the action was." President Eisenhower had been forced to send thousands of army troops to Little Rock to integrate the schools. Martin Luther King was in the news almost every day planning a protest over segregation. I knew Julius could hear the siren call.

Mary died about six months after we arrived. With the savings I had hoarded from my father, I was able to buy her house at a very low price from her estate. I would fix it up and rent it as an income property. My father had frequently extolled the virtues of real estate, and now I had a chance to own property. The experience was very solid but quite strange. It was the first time I had ever felt like a capitalist. Julius stayed for about a year until 1961, when he went to Savannah. Pennsylvania wasn't for him. I stayed on with the kids to work on the house, getting it ready to rent before joining my husband in Savannah. Meanwhile, I took a nursing job at the nearby Veterans Administration Hospital.

I visited my father in his Senate office several times when I was in Coatesville. As much as he had enjoyed little Julius, I never took any of the children again. With Julius at home, there was much more tension over my father, who continued to help financially. With four children and little work, we needed some help, and I appreciated deeply what he did, his politics aside. I didn't want to have a row with Julius, who clearly did not approve of my relationship with my father, so I never mentioned Strom Thurmond. Still, it was hard to avoid hearing about him, as he was constantly in the press as the key southern bulwark against Communism and against integration. I did my best to be away from the television when Julius watched the evening news, for fear of seeing my father railing against Reverend King and getting into a big argument that no one could win.

In 1957, my father set a record, which still stands, for the longest filibuster in congressional history. For over twenty-four hours, he stood on the Senate floor cataloging what was wrong with President Eisenhower's proposed new civil rights law. The law seemed fine to me, guaranteeing voting, educational, and employment rights for blacks, but my father saw it as a federal assault on his sacred states' rights, a desecration of his beloved John C. Calhoun. Most Americans, like Julius, believed that states' rights was nothing but a euphemistic front for racism and segregation. My father would deny this to his death, insisting that he was acting on principle, the sacred principle of Calhoun, who himself admitted that he saw the blacks as an inferior race that must be protected but not exploited. My father obviously shared Calhoun's paternalism; he never saw it as racism, even though the rest of the country did. The daylong filibuster was regarded as a far more prodigious display of bladder control than statesmanship. Both houses of Congress passed the civil rights law by large majorities. My father seemed like an anachronism from the Old South, a throwback, a laughing stock. Rather than hate him, I pitied him.

I pitied him far more when his wife died in early 1960 of a brain tumor. She was only thirty-three, a year older than I was. Now my father had lost not one, but two, of the women he loved far before their time. Small wonder he lost himself in his work, though it was a shame that work was segregation. I'll never forget reading about a particular speech he gave soon after his wife died. I cut it out and saved it; I think to prevent Julius from reading it.

> Just as there are in this country two main and quite distinct cultures, a northern culture and a southern culture, so there are in this country two different species of genus segregation . . . Segregation in the South is open, honest, and aboveboard. Northern segregation is founded on hypocrisy and deceit.

He called southern segregation "human," which was one of the worst uses of that adjective I ever heard. Then there was the 1960 Presidential election, Kennedy versus Nixon. At the Democratic Convention, my father had supported Lyndon Johnson over JFK mainly because the Texas Senator was not a Yankee, though in time my father would come to see Johnson, who would champion black rights, as the worst sort of turncoat scalawag. At the Convention, after Johnson lost, my father refused to cast South Carolina's votes for

Kennedy to make it unanimous. Just as he had voted for the Republican Eisenhower in 1952, he voted for the Republican Nixon in 1960. There was historical precedent for this nearly a century before. Just as the Old Democratic South had backed the Republican Hayes to end Reconstruction, Strom Thurmond urged the "New" Democratic South to back the Republican Nixon to end Lyndon Johnson's attempt to revisit Reconstruction.

Once Kennedy was elected, my father decided that the new President was soft on Communism. This was before the October 1962 Cuban Missile Crisis. When Julius left for Savannah, I went down to Washington to see my father. The staff gave me a warm welcome. Apparently, the senator enjoyed receiving his constituents. There was nothing aloof about him. I must have been viewed as just another back-home voter. He was on a rampage against President Kennedy for trying to "muzzle" certain generals who were perceived as making inflammatory "nuke the Commies"–type right-wing military speeches that were considered an impediment to Kennedy's diplomatic efforts on the international front.

"You can't be too right-wing in the cause of freedom," he said, presaging Barry Goldwater's famous remark that "Extremism in defense of liberty is no vice" by three years. My father and the Arizona conservative Republican were apparently close friends. "The Russians are putting missiles down in Cuba. We've got to stop them," he warned, many months before that warning was taken seriously by the administration and the world nearly went to war.

"He's soft on crime, too," he railed against JFK. "He's in with the Mafia."

"He doesn't seem the type," I said, defending the fair-haired prince of Camelot. I liked JFK, but I didn't dare say it.

"His best friend's Frank Sinatra," my father said with a sneer.

"Frank Sinatra's a singer, not a mobster." I liked him, too. Now he was off-limits as well.

"He's their boy," my father said, using a word that had slavery and racist connotations for me. "Anyone who works in Las Vegas works for them. Joe Kennedy, too. He made his liquor fortune in Prohibition with the Mafia. He has that Merchandise Mart in Chicago. That's all Mafia. That's dirty money. Filthy."

"Kennedy was a war hero, like you," I tried to defend him. "You'd think he'd be on guard against the Russians."

"He's a lightweight. All that boy has is his hair and his lovely wife. She and Jean were the two beauties of the Senate. They were becoming friends . . ." His voice trailed off, and the belligerence drained from him.

"I'm sorry about that, Senator. I know it's hard."

"Yes it is, Essie Mae. We know what that is." The "we" made me feel special; it made up for the "boy." Everything was relative with my father. Like his diet, like the Cuban missiles, like the Kennedy underworld connections, history would prove that Strom Thurmond wasn't as crazy or fanatical as he might have sounded at the time. By the time I settled back in Savannah in 1962, the civil rights movement was reaching its crescendo, and Julius was at the heart of it, working as a staff attorney in the local office of the NAACP while trying to reignite his private practice with Mr. Mayfield, the one local black lawyer he had been associated with in the early 1950s. The idea that lawyers get rich is a recent one. In Savannah, Julius's clients were so poor that they sometimes could not pay him at all. But Julius wasn't in it for the money; he truly wanted to do right and do good.

One of Julius's cases involved a white man who threw lye in the face of a little, black boy whom the white man caught peering at him through the posts of a fence. The little boy was blinded. Julius was able to get the boy a large judgment, but it didn't make up for his loss of sight. Despite the victory, Julius was depressed. I did all Julius's typing for him, and he served his own papers. Once a white man had Julius arrested for trespassing. He refused to believe Julius was a lawyer, and even if he was, the man snarled, "I won't have no nigger serving me papers." I had to bail Julius out of jail on this one. Even though the trespass charges were dropped, and he won the case against the white racist he had served, he didn't feel any satisfaction in his vindication.

When Julius was visiting friends in South Carolina, the car his friend was driving was stopped by a policeman in a small-town speed trap, the kind that were always rigged. There was no radar then, no proof, no appeal from the judgment of the local lawman, who was *always* right. This lawman, however, didn't count on there being a lawyer in the car. When Julius protested that his friend was under the speed limit and that he was a witness to it, the trooper pulled Julius out of the car and beat him to the ground. He then wrote out the ticket and sped away, leaving a battered Julius to the care of our friends. When I found out what had happened, my first instinct was to call my father. That evil cop, that South Carolina cop, had no idea what trouble was about to rain down on his brutal head. But then I thought better of it. The last thing Julius wanted was any assistance from my father, even to correct a grave injustice. Julius felt, wrongly I believed, that Strom Thurmond was incapable of doing anything helpful as far as blacks were concerned. Though I grieved for my husband's victimization, once more I kept my mouth shut. Seeking my father's intervention might have caused even more pain at home than Julius suffered on that mean backroad.

Although Atlanta was only five hours away and may have been the nerve center of the civil rights crusade, Savannah seemed like a sleepy outpost of Reverend King's empire of activism. Every day I'd see men on the chain gangs fixing the roads. That's what Savannah reminded me of, the chain gang of life. It was a museum city imprisoned in its own history, incapable of change. Birmingham, Montgomery, Greensboro, that's where the changes were going on. Savannah was too locked into its own time warp to escape. The whites liked it that way, and the blacks didn't comprehend any other way. Julius was deeply frustrated that his efforts were falling on deaf ears. In 1964, our oldest son Julius, then fifteen, became one of the first black students to integrate the high school in Savannah. There were no protests, nor were there any troops. The white people in Savannah were as enervated as the blacks.

That summer we decided to move back to California, which we all had loved so much. We wanted to do the best for our children, and we felt California was the place for them. Even though the Savannah schools were now mixed, I didn't want to raise my children there. Nor did I want to go home to Coatesville, not with both of my mothers gone. Besides, there were massive race riots in Philadelphia that year in retaliation to police brutality. The Bull Connors (the brutal Birmingham police commissioner who sent attack dogs into a black sit-in) of the world weren't confined to Alabama. I wanted a fresh start, far from the South, far from the East. California was the land of fresh starts and clean slates. I had been happy there before and had been sorry to have been forced to leave.

Julius needed to stay in Savannah until he could settle the remainder of his cases there. I decided to make the trip with the children. I thought it would be a great adventure for them. Before we began our cross-country drive in Julius's old, black Dodge that he had purchased from our minister, I went up to Coatesville to say good-bye, and I stopped in Washington, too. Strom Thurmond's biggest headline that far in 1964 involved the wrestling match he had gotten into outside of the Senate chamber with Senator Ralph Yarborough, who was from Texas but was considered a liberal in the Lyndon Johnson mode, a mode my father would characterize as "turncoat." Both my father and Yarborough were sixty-one, but my father, physical fitness fanatic, was far leaner and meaner. He pinned the liberal Democrat to the marble floor and wouldn't let him go until he hollered "uncle." Once more, I cringed at my father's behavior and how the public saw him. However, in the South the people saw him as a champ, and I guess he really cared only about how southerners felt. Yankees, to him, didn't count.

"I'm sick of fighting the Democrats," he told me when I was in his office. Given his grudge match with Senator Yarborough, he must have meant it literally and figuratively. "We're way better off with the Republicans." He told me he vastly preferred the Republican front runner Barry Goldwater to the Democratic incumbent Lyndon Johnson, though he did tell me that he found "First Daughter" Lynda Bird Johnson extremely attractive and couldn't understand why she would waste her time with tanned actor George Hamilton. I had the feeling my father wanted to date her himself, regardless of his attacks on her father, regardless of the huge age gap. He was relentless in that way, in pursuit of a woman, in pursuit of a political result. Now he was relentless in his hatred of the Democrats. He went into a litany of Democrat atrocities:

The Democrats cowardly backed down from invading Cuba during the missile crisis and lost a great opportunity to free our hemisphere from the Russian threat. The Democrats were plunging us into a pointless war in Vietnam. The Democrats were turning America into a welfare state. The only thing he didn't say was that the Democrats were soft on segregation.

I said it for him.

"What was that, Essie Mae?"

"The Democrats are soft on segregation."

"I never said that," he bristled.

"Only a million times, Senator." I was leaving for California. Somehow I felt liberated. I would speak my mind for once. And Julius's mind, as well.

"You say black people are inferior."

"I never said inferior. I said different."

"Then what am I?"

"Are you all right, Essie Mae? What's gotten into you?"

"If you mean what you say, how could you . . . how could you . . . love . . . my mother?"

He didn't speak for the longest time. He just looked like the wind had been punched out of him. It was a question he never expected to be called to answer. And he didn't. He kept silent. He poured some water from a Poland Springs bottle. He offered me a glass.

"No, thank you, sir."

"You should drink at least three full glasses a day."

"Do you look at me as a Negro, Senator?"

"I look at you with a lot of pride, Essie Mae," he said, always knowing how to flatter his way out of a tight corner. This time it wouldn't work.

"I hate to say this, sir, but do you realize how black people feel about you?" I asked him point blank, amazed at my own boldness.

"I'm dedicated to the improvement of the Negro race . . ." He was trying to turn this into a campaign speech. I wouldn't let him.

"Black people *hate* you, Senator. My husband *hates* you. I tried to speak up for you. But he hates you. Almost all black people do. They don't see you as a friend. They see you as the enemy. Their worst enemy. Is that the way you want to be looked at?"

He sat silently again, astonished at what I was saying. He wasn't angry. He didn't think I was being "uppity." He was just stunned.

"More and more black people are going to be voting. They want you out of office. Do you want them to turn you out, sir? Because if you don't, you better change your ways."

I stood up to go. He stood up. He had the envelope waiting. At first I refused to take it. He pressed it into my hand. "You'll need this in California."

"No thank you, sir."

"A little spirited debate never hurt anybody. Essie Mae, I'm glad you spoke your mind. I surely speak mine." He flashed a smile at me, putting the envelope back into my hand. "Now you go back to school, like I've been telling you. Just do it." And then he hugged me and kissed me good-bye. "I'll miss you," he said.

"Y'all come back now, you hear?" my father's pretty secretary drawled at me as I left to be chauffeured back to Union Station. I didn't know if I would ever be allowed back. Even though he was polite, that was the way politicians were, never showing their true feelings, and Strom Thurmond may have been the most guarded politician of them all. I may have just seen my father in person for the last time, I thought to myself. The envelope had thousands of dollars, hush money, Julius had angrily called it. There's an old southern expression, "Hush your mouth," which means to keep your trap shut. I would never go public with my secret, I thought, but at least I hadn't "hushed my mouth" with my father this time. And I was glad that I hadn't.

I would like to feel that my candor with my father had some good effect. Some time later, when he made his big "coming out" speech as a Goldwater Republican, he never mentioned the word "segregation." He made a few of his obligatory references to states' rights and the "judicial tyranny" of the Supreme Court and creeping socialism, but he didn't make it black and white as he always previously had done. He didn't use the word "Negro" in a hostile or even paternal sense. He took a high road, talking foreign policy, highlighting the Communist threat, denouncing Vietnam, attacking inflation, worrying about old people, fixed income people, plain people, who could be black or white. I felt he was talking to me, using this speech to show me that he could change. I knew now that I would see him again, and that his days as the point man for the repudiated doctrine of separate but equal might be coming to an end.

When my children and I drove cross-country, with all our belongings in a U-Haul behind us in 1964, it was a far easier trip than it had been in 1953. Now there were lots of chain motels, Howard Johnsons and Holiday Inns, where black people could get a night's sleep. The thrill of the trip for little Julius was getting to drive. Even though he was only fifteen and was a year away from his license in Georgia, he already knew how and promised me he had great skill behind the wheel. Given the endless distances, I decided to let him share the wheel with me, and the other kids lived vicariously through Julius's navigation. However, somewhere in a Texas rainstorm, we did skid off the road into a ditch. Some very nice motorists saw our plight and helped us get the car back on the road, and no harm was done, except maybe a little to my son's ego.

We had a fine time. The children loved the desert, they loved the big mountains, they loved seeing the Pacific and eating tacos and being in the West. "The West is the best," they all agreed. Like Reverend King said, we were "free at last." We were totally exhilarated by the time we reached Julius's sister's house in Los Angeles, where we would stay until Julius came out and found us a place of our own. His sister, however, greeted us with the darkest expression. She didn't seem to want to hear about all our adventures. She was raining on our parade. When she asked me to step into a back room, away from the kids, I understood why. She had just gotten a telephone call from Savannah a few hours before our arrival. Julius Williams had died of a heart attack. His law partner hadn't seen him for several days. They had to break into the house, which was locked. They found Julius's body in our bed, all alone.

I had to walk outside to compose myself and take it all in, before I could destroy all my children's joy and exuberance with this horrible news. If only I had stayed behind until Julius was ready; that was my first thought. Julius had suffered from asthma. So many times he'd wake up in the middle of the night in a coughing fit. I'd wake up with him, massage and slap his back, until his breathing returned to normal. It always worked. I worried that he had been drinking, that he had woken up with one of these spells and was all alone, and possibly too incoherent to call for help. Poor, poor Julius. I loved him so much. He was only forty-six. He was brilliant, and everything he had dreamed about was ahead of him, ahead of us. He was going to take the California bar. He was going to change the world. And now he was gone. What a tragedy. Julius's heart, the heart that had stopped, had already been broken by the assassination of John F. Kennedy, by the viciousness of Governors Ross Barnett and George Wallace, by the hatred he saw all around him, by the slaying of civil rights martyrs Goodman, Cheney, and Schwerner in Mississippi, maybe even by my failure to repudiate my father. And now my heart was broken by losing him.

I went back in and told the children, who were even more shocked than I was, particularly coming exactly at the close of our joyous trip. What a roller coaster, to go from total happiness to total misery in seconds. We just sat there crying for what seemed like hours. And then I had to unpack from the trip and pack to fly back to Savannah the very next day. Because Julius's sister was coming as well, I left the children with a family friend, Mrs. Pinkney, until I returned. I've never seen sadder faces than when I left them with her. They looked like orphans, being exiled to a home, but it would have been too much to drag them onto a plane at this point. I promised them I'd be back soon to take care of them and kissed them all good-bye. I had never felt more protective of them in all my life. I knew I would have to do double duty as mother and father now, but through my grief, I never doubted that I could rise to that challenge. There was no choice. I was thirty-nine years old. Again, my life had taken a major turn.

When I got home from Savannah and laying Julius to rest, I called my father to tell him my bad news. Even though the two men had never met, and Julius regarded my father as the enemy of the black cause, I felt part of the tragedy of Julius's premature death was what the two men might have eventually accomplished together, had they been brought together. I realized now how deeply I'd always hoped to make the match, but now the time, which I thought I had plenty of, was gone.

"I'm sorry about your husband, Essie Mae. He was one of our first law graduates at State. It's a shame his life was cut short. He would have been a credit . . ."

I couldn't bear hearing him say "to his race," so I interrupted him. "A credit to America," I said.

My father was actually very kind and sympathetic, talking about how he had felt when his wife Jean had died so young. My mother had died young, too, but he didn't mention that. He did, however, insist on sending me some help, which he did in the form of several money orders in envelopes with a Washington address I didn't recognize. There were no letters within. Again, he was being cautious, and I would have been an awful ingrate to second-guess his generosity.

Back home, my children pulled together in the most inspiring way. Young Julius more than lived up to his name, becoming the man of the house. Tall, strong, and confident, as well as someone who could fix anything, he became the guardian of his younger siblings, allowing them to flower. Ronald, our resident genius, seemed to study all the time, but always took out time to tutor his brother and sisters and made sure they did their homework, and did it well. Wanda was our creative interior decorator and Monica our gifted chef. Meanwhile, I went to work teaching business classes at local trade and parochial schools while going back to college at California State University in East Los Angeles to complete my degree. I rarely got home before nine, but my family took care of each other so well, I didn't worry. And weekends together, from museum trips to flea market searches to Sunday services, were always happy events. It may sound like a too-good-to-be-true television family—but the hovering secret of Strom Thurmond, which none of my children knew, would have kept the show off the air.

I rented a small house for a while, but soon I used some of my husband's life insurance to buy another piece of the California Dream, a pretty ranch house with a driveway and a swimming pool, shaded by big palm trees. We even had a view of the ocean. It was our own resort, located in the elite black neighborhood called View Park.

View Park was like a black Beverly Hills. Along with adjacent Baldwin Park and Ladera Heights, View Park was about as good as a neighborhood could get for African-Americans of the time. It had nothing in common with Watts or South Central, which, in their turn, had little in common with Harlem except poor people. Compton, where we had lived in the Joy Homes, was more lower middle class, a big step out of Watts, but by no means fancy.

Our new neighborhood was as safe as Bel Air, and the home owners couldn't have been prouder. After all, they had worked hard to own these homes, and they were going to make them showcases. My father, I reflected, could have used View Park as a case study in segregated self-sufficiency. It was interesting to me that the Los Angeles neighborhoods weren't more mixed, as they had seemed when we had originally moved there. We had a few Asian neighbors, a few Mexicans, a few whites, but this was largely the black bourgeoisie. Not that we turned our backs on our brothers and sisters in Watts. The black churches of Los Angeles, which were still located in the old South Central district, were filled every Sunday with worshippers from the "good addresses," and the collection plates that were passed were filled as well.

The Watts riots of 1965 made me rethink exactly what kind of racial paradise I was living in. "It can't happen here" was what most of the people I knew thought. Perhaps we were too insulated. Even during the height of the conflagration, which was triggered by the alleged racist brutality of the largely white Los Angeles Police Department, while black clouds of acrid smoke hung over the city, there was never any fear that our neighborhood was in danger. Los Angeles was simply too big, too spread out. Unlike the crowded eastern ghettos, violence could not help but dissipate over our endless spaces. Nonetheless, the damage was monumental, dozens killed, thousands injured, millions of dollars of property—most of it belonging to white landlords and shopkeepers—destroyed. It was a warning that California was not immune to the rage at the inequality in our land of plenty. I knew I had to do my part to turn that anger into effort. I began to finish school. I registered to vote, which I had not done, out of fear and intimidation, in South Carolina and Georgia. It gave me such a sense of power, of participation, of pure citizenship. That voter registration reaffirmed my Americanness, which I felt I had lost, or at least misplaced, when I was in the South. At the same time, I became a Democrat, though I never told my father, not that he asked. I also joined the NAACP.

I was fulfilling my father's wishes, and my own, by going back to college. I went part time, slowly but surely, and received my BA in business education in 1969. That was one of the happiest days of my life. I only wish that I had had a parent there to share it with. My father did send me a stunning diamond-and-emerald necklace and matching earrings. Having me receive my degree, he later said, was one of his happiest moments. Teacher that he was, he had always urged me to complete my education. I was thrilled that my children saw my graduation, and it set a good example for them. Under Ronald's tutelage, and a bit of my own, each of them turned out to be a good student.

In my part-time teaching, my initial subjects were typing and shorthand, but once I had my degree, the fact that I also had a nursing background enabled me to teach courses in the burgeoning medical-business field. I was always able to get jobs, good jobs, all around Los Angeles. I taught English as a second language to students from all over Central and South America as well as Asia. I was very flattered that so many of my students would want to come up to me after class and ask more questions. Their desire to learn was so gratifying that I was even later getting home to my own family. But my children understood and supported me totally. Eventually, I rose to become a guidance counselor. Helping others plan their careers, the way I would have liked to have been able to plan my own, was what gave me the most satisfaction. My father was right; that degree was a passport. During the period of the completion of my education and my immersion in my teaching career, the only thing that seemed to be missing was a social life. But there was no time for it, nor did I miss it. My social life was my family, my professional life was my students, and I felt completely fulfilled.

Strom Thurmond turned out to be right about a lot of things, though segregation wasn't one of them. However, by the next time I saw him in Washington in 1968, he was sixty-six years old and was becoming one of America's elder statesmen. Despite Barry Goldwater's ignominious defeat by Lyndon Johnson in 1964, the only five states he carried beyond his own, Arizona, were southern states delivered to him by my father—South Carolina, Georgia, Alabama, Mississippi, and Louisiana. At home in South Carolina, Goldwater was the first Republican to carry the Palmetto State since the Reconstruction era. That's how much my father was an icon there, a prophet in his own country.

Now in 1968, Richard Nixon looked to my father to redeem himself from his heartbreaking photofinish loss to JFK in 1960, an election my father claimed the Mafia had stolen for the Kennedys in Illinois at the last minute. Strom Thurmond had come through for Nixon, who went on to defeat the relatively liberal Democrat Hubert Humphrey. The Republicans had been deeply concerned about the seriously racist independent campaign of Governor George Wallace of Alabama. They therefore looked to my father to save the South for them. I think one of the reasons my father backed off from his notorious hard-line position against true racial equality was that when he looked in the mirror, he may have seen George Wallace. That cruel reflection of the atavistic "nigger hater" may have sobered him up, as did the assassinations of Martin Luther King and Robert Kennedy, as well as the student revolts at Columbia and other fine schools, including my college, whose name had now been formally changed to South Carolina State.

In February of that year the students, who had been cowed into political apathy when I was there, finally had caught the protest fever of the times. Their goal was simple; they wanted to be able to use an all-white bowling alley, All Star Lanes. But South Carolina was not used to protest, and the massing of black students stirred up the white paranoia. To quell this display of black power, the governor of South Carolina (a Democrat) called out the armed forces of SLED, or State Law Enforcement Division. An army of riot police, with guns, nightsticks, tear gas and storm trooper–style leather jackets and boots, descended on Orangeburg. At the end of the showdown, three students had been killed and nearly thirty more badly wounded. Because it was a small, black school, the tragedy barely made the press. But I know my father was aware of it, and just like the Willie Earle lynching when he first became governor and before his ambitions sent him careening to the right, he was deeply ashamed.

As Bob Dylan sang "The times, they are a'changin'." My father was getting old, but not too old to realize he had better change as well. He loved being in office, in power, too much. In the November election, Strom Thurmond carried South Carolina for Nixon, along with the more moderate rest of the South, save for Texas, Arkansas, and the four other Deep Southern "Goldwater" states—the "axe-handle" states as Californians called them, referring to a favorite weapon of violent racists. Leaving the axe handles to George Wallace and the equally inflammatory Georgia governor, Lester Maddox, my father now became the hero of the party of Abraham Lincoln.

Heroes are entitled to their idiosyncrasies. My father's was an obsession with beautiful, *very* young women. When I saw him, his "secret" courtship with a twenty-one-year-old former Miss South Carolina named Nancy Moore was breaking in the press. Like the late Jean Crouch, Nancy was a pert and perky college girl, a true Southern belle who had the crown to prove it. The sleek Nancy, a Duke graduate who also attended the University of South Carolina Law School, grew up in Aiken, where her father was a scientist at the Savannah River nuclear plant. She was definitely well groomed, a gifted pianist who came close to winning Miss America and who had become an effective spokeswoman for the state. I remember first seeing her pictures in the Los Angeles papers, even before my father publicly courted her, with Jim Nabors, who played Gomer Pyle on the hit shows *The Andy Griffith Show* and *Gomer Pyle, USMC*, and who later was revealed to be the secret love of my own heartthrob, Rock Hudson. Beware of heartthrobs.

Like Jean Crouch, Nancy Moore had been hired as my father's administrative assistant, and, from there, love conquered all, though my father drew the line at standing on his head for her, at least not in the presence of photographers. He had learned a lot of lessons, except the humility of his maturity. How in the world could he have the audacity to marry someone a third his age? This wasn't a generation gap; this was the Grand Canyon. But he got away with it, and instead of becoming the laughing stock of politics, he became a role model, and not just for aspiring dirty, old men. Only in Hollywood and Washington could a man get away with this and enhance his popularity.

Nancy had left his employ to plan their Christmas wedding by the time I got to Capitol Hill in 1968.

"Congratulations, Senator," I said when I shook his hand. We always shook hands when we first saw each other, and it always hurt. I somehow hoped that he would invite me home to the wedding, but that was unrealistic. I never asked him, but I assumed he never told either of his wives about me or my mother. Imagine what these southern belle child brides would have done. I myself had told no one but Julius, not even my children. It's not that Strom Thurmond ever swore me to secrecy. He never swore me to anything. He trusted me, and I respected him, and we loved each other in our deeply repressed ways, and that was our social contract. I would have loved to talk to someone, but I couldn't.

"See what diet and exercise get you?" He showed me a silver-framed picture of his beauty queen in her tiara. He was as cocky as a schoolboy who had just gotten lucky with the homecoming princess.

"Doesn't she want children?" I asked him, perhaps impertinently, as he seemed taken aback.

"Who says she doesn't?" my father replied. "I think she'll make a fine mother." Again, there was the cockiness of a young stud totally confident of his breeding abilities, even if no one else in America was. He wasn't going to marry a baby; he was now going to have babies of his own. The sheer audacity, I guess, was what got him into this office.

I couldn't help feeling a twinge of jealousy. I somehow fancied being his only child. Even though I was a state secret, I knew as a parent how much you loved your children. Now I saw myself having to share that love with a new generation, one that he could have photo opportunities with.

Aside from a trophy wife and a trophy president, my father was equally proud of his role on the all-powerful Senate Judiciary Committee in derailing the nomination of the great jurist Abe Fortas as our next chief justice to replace Earl Warren. Throughout the South for years I had seen bumper stickers that read "Impeach Earl Warren," the integrationist villain behind *Brown vs. Board of Education*. Now he was stepping down, and his position was the legal football in the big game between liberals and conservatives. Thurmond wanted President-elect Nixon, not the scalawag lame duck President Johnson, to appoint the next chief justice and steer the Court toward conservative waters. To do so, he had to block the nomination of Fortas, a Memphis-born child of poor Jewish immigrants who was already on the Court and considered its most brilliant mind.

"I got 'im," my father boasted, as if he had just shot a raccoon at the Orangeburg Hunt. It crossed my mind that my father might have been anti-Semitic, but I crossed it off. Yes, he hated Sol Blatt, but not as much as he loved Barry Goldwater. He had grown up among too many Jewish merchants in Edgefield to feel xenophobic toward them, and he had seen them prosper far too much to regard them as inferior, as he may have with blacks, until they had a fair chance.

My father's problem with Fortas was that he was Johnson's man. He needed ammunition to beat him, and he found it in Fortas's softness on pornography. The candidate was bigger on First Amendment freedoms than my supposedly straitlaced father, although my father's growing reputation as an aging Casanova put the lie to his personal Puritanism. More damning to Fortas was a special seminar my father's investigators had found he had given at American University for captains of industry whose corporations might have cases coming before the Court in the future. This was a conflict of interest. It didn't seem that grave to me, but my father was grasping at straws, which in this case he turned into kindling. In the end, Fortas withdrew his nomination, and Nixon eventually appointed the conservative Warren Burger to be the chief.

"The chief justice has to be above reproach," my father said. But was my father above reproach, with his secret black daughter? Wasn't this as relevant as Fortas's students? I never asked. I felt by now the statute of limitations had run on our secret, as to whether it was right or wrong. A secret was a secret, and so it would remain. Why did I continue to keep it? By this point, sheer loyalty to my father was the answer. I didn't want to do anything that would damage his political career. I was in awe of my father for a lot of reasons: his power, his lineage, his perseverance, his affection for me, after his own fashion. I felt honored to be his daughter. I liked the idea of changing him, and I believe I did, but I certainly had no interest in hurting him or dishonoring him in any way.

This was my first visit to my father after which he did not give me one of his thick envelopes. I thought that maybe he was getting forgetful in his seniority, but several weeks later, I was contacted by a lawyer named Thurmond Bishop, who was my father's nephew by his sister Martha. Thurmond informed me that he was taking care of his uncle's finances. He asked me to fly to Atlanta so that he could give me money that his uncle had placed in his care for *my* care. So not very long after I had just returned from the East Coast, I turned around and flew right back out again. If my father wanted to help, wasn't that what fathers do? After all, these were his grandchildren. If he didn't see them, didn't "claim" them, which is the southern expression in regard to a "back street" family, then why shouldn't he assuage his guilt, or duty, or honor, or whatever, by helping out?

Hartsfield Airport in Atlanta was not the pleasantest of places to meet my white cousin, not that Thurmond Bishop ever embraced me as kin. Our meeting was strictly business. We established a rendezvous spot in front of a gift shop near the Delta Air Lines ticket counter. Thurmond was nervous but extremely polite. He was tall and thin and in his mid-twenties and resembled his uncle in a rangy, gangly way. His courses in law school had surely not prepared him for this assignment. He handed me a very large cashier's check and a file of telephone numbers and addresses where he could be reached.

We didn't even sit down for coffee, thus perpetuating the Thurmond tradition I had with my father of never sharing a meal, even a Coke, in public. This was Atlanta, after all, and blacks and whites rarely were seen breaking bread together.

Thurmond Bishop told me he would be my contact should I need any assistance, and that he would be in regular contact with me over future "disbursements." He said he had just finished law school and was taking care of all the Thurmond business. He was the third generation of Thurmond lawyers and knew he had a powerful tradition to live up to. They liked to keep all their legal matters "in the family," he said. He didn't tell me why we were going through these much more formal channels, after so many years of my dealing directly with my father. I assumed it was because my father was starting a new life with Nancy Moore and did not want any details of our relationship to leak into the idyll that would be their marriage. Or maybe he was afraid that the FBI had put him under surveillance. This was a time of great paranoia in the government, and any great man couldn't help but be too careful to keep damaging secrets from his real or potential enemies. I wasn't insulted by my father's secrecy, but rather grateful for his generosity. As I grew more mature, that was increasingly becoming my style, to try to look on the bright side.

Thurmond Bishop and I had a cordial but somewhat awkward conversation about his new law career and my new teaching career. He kept staring at me, as if in a trance. "So *this* is my first cousin?" he seemed to be asking himself. "What on God's earth was my uncle up to?" The young lawyer thanked me for taking this long trip. I thanked him for taking care of business, and I asked him to thank his uncle for his ongoing kindness. I don't recall either of us using the word "father." The concept was too hard for him to handle and for me to articulate. We shook hands. Thurmond's grip was normal, not the vise of his uncle. He went back to his gate to catch his return flight to Columbia. I went back to my gate to catch my return flight to Los Angeles. I was on the ground less than two hours.

The fact that Thurmond Bishop was handling his financial affairs did not, as I had feared, distance my father from me. It actually made us closer. Now my father would call me every month or so, just to say hello. One day he astonished me by calling to say that he was coming to Los Angeles for a speaking engagement and wanted to meet my children. He never called them his grandchildren, only "your children," but he had rarely called me his daughter, either. In this case, though, his action was speaking far louder than any words. I was extremely excited. His desire to connect was a major breakthrough.

My problem now was what to tell the children. I thought about not telling them at all, only that I was taking them to hear Strom Thurmond speak. However, I realized that they would have never gone. Julius was now nearing twenty. He had Black Panther posters on his wall, sported an Afro, and read books like *Soul on Ice*. James Brown's "Black is Beautiful: Say It Loud, I'm Black and I'm Proud" was constantly blaring from the stereo in his bedroom. His younger brother Ronald remained the studious one, wanting to become a doctor, but he idolized Martin Luther King and would have had a natural distrust of any Republican, much less the "King of the South" that was his grandfather. My daughters were barely teenagers, but they, too, had a black awareness and a black pride. They all had Afros. Even I had an Afro. I got it at the Lady Coiffure on Santa Rosalita Street. For me, it was a matter of style, but for my children, one of pride. Go hear Strom Thurmond? Come on, mom. Who's next, George Wallace? Why not George Lincoln Rockwell?

Strom Thurmond had recently made news by hiring his first black aide, Tom Moss, a former meat-packing plant union organizer and NAACP voting drive leader. I was delighted that my father had made what was, for him, a radical change. Of course, the "Yankee"-dominated press lampooned the appointment as sheer tokenism. A third of South Carolina's voters were black, and Strom Thurmond, the crafty politician, was only doing what came naturally—to a white supremacist. I was sure that my children, who were very interested in current events and loved watching the news, would concur in this popular view. The bottom line was that I was going to have to sit down with them and bring them into our family secret. I wasn't looking forward to it.

I assembled the children in the living room one night after dinner. "Did you ever think of why you're all so light?" I asked them.

"Daddy's mama was an Indian, wasn't she?" Monica volunteered.

"But what about me?" I continued.

"Your mama was an Indian, too," Wanda added, laughing.

"Mom, can I go watch TV?" Julius asked. "*Laugh-In*'s about to come on."

"*Laugh-In* can wait a minute, Julius." He fidgeted in his chair, bored to death. "What if I told you I had a white father?" I tried to wake him up.

"No big deal," he said, yawning. "But we know your father, so what's the point, mom?" They had met Mary's husband many times and assumed he was their grandfather.

"What if I told you Grandpa wasn't your *real* grandpa?" I paused and got no response. "Because he isn't."

They still seemed bored. "A lot of people from the South had white fathers," Ronald said. "You mean Grandma . . . fooled around?"

"Your grandma wasn't your real grandma, either." Then they woke up.

"Who was your daddy, then?" Wanda asked.

"He still is."

"Then where is he? Do you know him?" Ronald wondered.

"I do."

"And your mama?"

"She passed. Years ago. Before you were born."

"Can we meet this guy?" Monica asked.

"You can. I want you to."

"How come you waited this long to tell us?" Wanda asked.

"I wasn't sure you were ready."

Julius was still lethargic. "I'm ready for *Laugh-In*, mama. Can I be excused?"

"Where does he live?" Monica was far more interested than Julius was.

"In Washington, D.C. He's a senator."

Julius came to attention. "What's his name, Teddy Kennedy?" Julius liked to joke.

You wish, I thought. I took a deep breath and let it out. "Strom Thurmond. Remember, Julius, when we went to see that senator in Washington when you were little? That man wasn't just your senator. He was your grandfather."

"Gross!" Wanda exclaimed.

"Come on," Ronald gasped. "That's not funny."

I went through the entire story to my wide-eyed family. They were at rapt attention. Not one of them believed that Strom Thurmond loved my mother.

"You're fooling yourself, mom," Monica said. "I'm sure he took advantage of her."

"Don't talk ugly, Monica."

"That's what rich, white men do to their servants," Ronald reinforced her. "She was scared to death of him. She had no choice."

"She loved the man," I insisted.

"Do *you* love him?" Wanda put it to me. "How could you?"

"We wouldn't be living here right now if it weren't for him," I tried to reason with them. It was just as hard as when I tried to reason with my husband. "He's been good to us."

"Let the man be a lot better," Julius said, his voice crisp with rage.

"He *is* getting better. And he'll be better still if he sees who his kin are and how special you all can be." I had to play all my "mother" cards, my guilt cards, to calm them down. In the end, good kids that they were, they agreed to come.

Strom Thurmond addressed a full house at a large Christian church on Wilshire Boulevard. It was an entirely white crowd, and they cheered his conservative message of less government, lower taxes, and stronger military defense. There wasn't a word about segregation, a word that would have offended black people, if there had been any besides us present. My family and I, with our Afros, were the only black people there. The whites must have thought we were the Jackson Five.

Afterwards, in the congregation hall, we stood in a long line with countless well-wishers. My father was a little stunned when he saw us and our hair. Yet he kept his cool, as always. He shook everyone's hand, mine included. It wasn't some emotional family reunion. There were too many people around for that, and, besides, he preferred things this way, just as if he were out on the stump, charming for votes. Once the line had finished its respects, he came back to us. We spent a half hour together. He introduced us to his local handlers as "some dear old family friends" from Edgefield. He asked each of the children about their schooling, and couldn't resist his standard plugs for diet and exercise. He mentioned how good the strawberries and the cantaloupe were out here and warned them to watch out for the lard in the Mexican food.

"He thinks we're *fat*," Monica whispered to me.

"No, he doesn't," I reassured her. "He does that to everybody."

He didn't tell Julius he had played with him as a boy. He probably didn't remember.

Eventually, his aides hustled my father to his next appointment. I wished he had been able to visit our house, to spend some real time with us, to see how the "black Thurmonds" actually lived. Another day, I hoped.

"Y'all come see me in Washington," he said in farewell, insisting that if any of us needed anything, to call him and he'd "fix it up." He probably said that to everyone, but the thought was appealing.

"Can we really go to see him?" Wanda asked me, wide-eyed.

"I have," I said. "So can you."

"He didn't seem so bad," Ronald admitted. "I thought he'd be an old redneck."

"Are you sure we're blood?" Julius puzzled. "I don't see it."

"I do. A little," Monica said, and a new debate began. The consensus, though, was that my children would accept their grandfather for whatever he was, mainly because what he was now wasn't what he used to be. They assured me they would preserve the secret.

Julius the jokester kept playing with the payoff concept. "That guy must own half of South Carolina, and he bought it when it was cheap a hundred years ago."

"He's not *that* old," Wanda defended him. "Leave him alone." I could see she felt something for her grandfather.

Strom Thurmond turned out to be as good as his word. Wanda went to visit him in Washington and received the red carpet. When Ronald decided to go to medical school, his grandfather arranged for him to get a commission in the Navy that paid for his entire education. He did lots of smaller favors for our family. And he continued, through his nephew Thurmond Bishop, to send us money, perhaps not as much as Julius would have liked, but to me an extremely generous amount as a token of his affection for us. I flew back East every year to pay my annual visit to Coatesville and to my father in Washington. It was fortunate that I enjoyed airplanes.

Just as he was helping us, my father, who was legendary in South Carolina for his "constituent services," began lavishing his "Mr. Fixit" political magic on his black constituency. In addition to creating jobs and righting ancient wrongs, from the schools to the polls, the Senator continued to recommend black people to key state offices as well as to his own personal staff. One of his beneficiaries was my old boyfriend Matthew Perry, who had gone on to become one of the top black lawyers in the South, as well as the chief counsel of the state NAACP. My father appointed Matthew in 1974 to the U.S. Court of Military Appeals. By doing so, my father was the first southern senator to ever recommend a black for any federal judgeship. He might have done the same for my Julius if he had lived.

"He's a fine man, that boyfriend of yours. He may make it to the Supreme Court," my father told me on a visit to his office.

"How did you know I went out with Matthew?" I asked him.

"That's my job, Essie," my father said with that Cheshire cat smile. "Knowledge is power. If you liked him, then I knew he was all right."

"That was a long time ago," I said.

"Good judgment doesn't have an expiration date," he answered.

I noticed that my father was looking weird, but it took me a while to figure out what it was. Then I got it: his hair. There was not only more of it, a lot more, but it was also the strangest color, a kind of orange, instead of its normal brownish gray when I last saw him. It was so ugly I thought of Agent Orange, the toxic defoliant they used in Vietnam. I later learned that once again my father was way ahead of the health and beauty curve. Inspired by Senator William Proxmire of Arkansas, he had gotten hair implants. He wanted to have a youthful mane to match his still youthful physique. I never visited him without his reminding me of his Olympian workout regimen and that Spartan diet of his.

"Don't you crave fried chicken?" I had to ask him.

"I crave feeling young more than I crave feeling full."

He was obviously feeling virile. He had fathered a daughter, Nancy, and a son, Strom, Jr., and would sire still another son and daughter. I would have liked to meet them. Instead, he showed me their baby pictures. I never asked him if he had told his wife about me. I was sure he hadn't.

I had gotten remarried myself in 1970. Just when I had reached a state of contentment that I didn't need a social life, love walked right in. I met James Stoner at a dance at a parochial school where I had been teaching. A priest introduced us. James was tall, handsome, a great dancer, and a wonderful cook. He had just retired as a baker. He also had that wonderful deep voice that I was so susceptible to. He was sixty-two; I was forty-four. Maybe I shouldn't have been that hard on my father on age differences, I reflected. What mattered was shared emotions and feelings. James and I dated for one year. The kids loved him, especially because of the elaborate meals he would prepare.

Our marriage, alas, lasted only one year. James would fall asleep in the living room watching television, then complain that the children were making too much noise and waking him up. He soon moved back in with his brother-in-law, which was where he had lived before we met. He moved back east and met another woman. He lived with her, though he never got divorced from me. When he died at eighty-two, I got his Social Security. It was a windfall I never expected.

Whatever happened in my personal life, I never failed to find refuge in religion. I became an active member in the Congregational Church of Christian Fellowship, not far from my home. Julius had been an Episcopalian, but he didn't go to church very often. I had traditionally been a Baptist but I decided I preferred the Congregational style, in which the congregation has the final word, unlike the Baptists or Methodists, where the minister runs the show. Sundays were my favorite day of the week.

We were all getting older. As I reached my fifties, I was beginning to feel it, to accept the fact that retirement was not that far away. I unfortunately developed adult-onset diabetes, which runs in the Thurmond family. Two of my father's sisters suffered from that as well, though my father and I never discussed this as a "family" problem. I had to inject myself with insulin every day. I lost a lot of energy. Not so my father. He told me he would rather expire than retire, and that as long as he was vigorous, he would continue to run for office. I wasn't sure the voters of South Carolina would agree with him, but with each election, his opponents would make an issue of Strom Thurmond's advancing age. Each opponent would lose. However, 1978 appeared to have the makings of my father's Waterloo.

He was now seventy-six, and the man who wanted to replace him seemed to have all the right stuff. This was Charlie "Pug" Ravenel, a thirty-nine-year-old progressive Democrat who styled himself as a "Southern Kennedy." Like the Kennedys, Ravenel had gone to Harvard, where he had been the star quarterback of the football team. He'd been nicknamed "the Gambler" as much for his high-risk plays as for his evocation of Gaylord Ravenel, the suave riverboat gambler in the musical *Showboat*. Pug Ravenel was anything but a southern aristocrat, though. His father had been a shipyard worker in Charleston. He had won a scholarship to Phillips Exeter Academy in New Hampshire en route to Harvard, then Harvard Business School, and then had gone on to success as an investment banker on Wall Street.

"Carpetbagger" was the only word my father had for him, despite the place of his birth. "He's a Yankee with a southern accent. Look where his campaign money comes from. Wall Street and Park Avenue," my father scoffed. Four years before, Ravenel had moved back from New York to run for governor and was disqualified by a court ruling that he had not met the state's residency requirement. Now he was back, with a vengeance, and with President Jimmy Carter in his corner. He challenged my father to debate him, but my father wanted to avoid a talking contest.

"I'm running on my record. Let him run on his, if he has one," was Strom Thurmond's retort. His campaign strategy was designed by Lee Atwater, who would become notorious as Ronald Reagan's stop-at-nothing pit bull. Atwater would parade out my father's children wearing T-shirts that said "Vote for My Daddy," and stage endless photo opportunities with his beauty queen wife to show how vital my father actually was, hair plugs and all. Strom Thurmond grew Elvis-style sideburns, donned a Stetson hat that made him look like a hipster cowboy, slid down fire poles, went jogging for the press. At the same time he was presenting my father as a poster boy for the Fountain of Youth, Atwater attacked Ravenel's New York *Social Register*, Ivy League support base, playing the carpetbagger card over and over. In the end, my father won a resounding victory, one he was never in doubt of, even if I was. Pug Ravenel, who went back to banking, later served nearly a year in prison for financial misdoings. Years later, he was granted a pardon by President Clinton.

And so it went, year after year, the unsinkable Strom Thurmond, going on and on as the Grand Old Man of southern politics. As the country became more and more conservative in the Reagan years, his position in the party and his stature as an icon continued to grow. No more was he seen as the racist redneck, but as the dominant figure of the region that was coming to dominate the American political scene, the voice of the New South, with the echoes of the Old that provided soothing traditional reassurance to a cautious nation. We would have Carter from Georgia, Clinton from Arkansas, the Bushes from Texas, all southerners. Despite Clinton's liberalism, my father saw him as a good old boy just the same and regarded him as a friend. Perhaps they bonded over their attraction to young women. Whatever, the Dixiecrat had become a solon. He was one of the chief champions of Clarence Thomas's controversial nomination to the Supreme Court. It didn't matter that Thomas was a conservative Republican. He was a black man, and my father was right behind him, 100 percent. Ben Tillman must have been turning over in his grave.

The older my father got, the more reflective he became about his own father, although not about my mother. I thought he might want to have some closure in his life, and make peace with her memory and how he felt about her. Maybe he did, too, but he kept putting off that day of reckoning. The man sincerely believed he was going to live forever, so, for him, time was not of the essence. Into his nineties he still bragged to me that he ran every morning, swam every week in the Senate pool, kept those barbells by his desk, and made me punch him in his hard, flat stomach to prove to me he was in fighting shape. He got a little repetitive, but a man that age, in that shape, had to be forgiven a lot.

He became more personally generous to me as he got older. By now he was constantly traveling the world as head of the Senate Armed Services Committee, touring military bases in Germany and Turkey, conferring with Anwar Sadat in Egypt, revisiting the Normandy beaches he had stormed on D day. He made a special point to tell me when he visited Africa, as if that showed how "enlightened" he had become. We never discussed apartheid. He had amazing stamina, flying to China and back for a weekend. Wherever he went, he would bring back souvenirs, little trinkets, letter openers, bookmarks, keychains, plastic jewelry, decorative tiles that he would always give to me in a "care package" when I came to see him at the Senate.

In the past he had been even more thoughtful. He had given me a dictionary to give to Wanda when she finished high school. He had given me those expensive jewels when I got my BA. When I went on and completed my MA degree at the University of Southern California, that was icing on my father's cake. For that milestone, he presented me with a string of genuine pearls and a diamond-encrusted giant pearl pendant. In the box was a note that said "Congratulations" and nothing more. There was no signature, no "love." Secrecy had to take priority over affection. But that jewelry was the high water mark. As the years went by, pukka shell necklaces were the rule, which he would collect whenever he visited our military bases in Hawaii and the Pacific and always give to me. From my perspective, it was the thought that counted.

Strom Thurmond did romanticize his father. He was my grandfather as well, but I never embraced his memory. I couldn't, because the ghost of Ben

Tillman was always standing behind him, with his pitchfork aimed at me. But I humored my father's own filial piety. In his office in the Senate, a special place of honor held a framed letter from his father upon young Strom's graduation from Clemson in 1923. He read it to me on every visit for the last twenty years of his life, and gave me a copy each time I was there. I didn't dare say I already had one. To him, this letter was as sacred as the Magna Carta. It read:

> Remember your God.
> Take good care of your body and tax your nervous system as little as possible.
> Obey the laws of the land.
> Be strictly honest.
> Associate only with the best people, morally and intellectually.
> Think three times before you act once and if you are in doubt, don't act at all.
> Be prompt on your job to the minute.
> Read at every spare chance and think over and try to remember what you have read.
> Do not forget that skill and integrity are the keys to success.
> Affectionately,
> Dad

I wish he, as my father, had written me a letter like that for my souvenir files, for my own wall of honor. But Strom Thurmond was the most punctilious man who ever lived, and he would have never taken this perceived risk. He was a military man, from Clemson cadet to decorated soldier to chairman of the Senate Armed Services Committee, the best friend the soldiers and sailors of America could have. He was his father's son, following every rule to the letter, by the book. The one time in his life that he broke the rules was with my mother, his one and only walk on the wild side. I was Exhibit A, proof that Strom Thurmond had soul. But by the same token of his eternal caution and propriety, I was proof he dare not present. That's why, even at the end of his life, he never stepped forward to celebrate our relationship. He must have been thinking of his legacy, his posterity. The southern gentleman in him that prevented him from forsaking me also prevented him from embracing me—and all the glory that embrace might have brought him. He would always be a conservative, in war and in love.

CHAPTER NINE

Reckoning

THE LAST DECADE of my father's life was filled with glory. It was counterweighted with tragedy. In 1991, Nancy Thurmond sought a separation from my father. Many South Carolinians, dubious of this May–December romance, believed that Nancy had married my father thinking that he would soon pass away, and that she would "inherit" his Senate seat, as had another bright and ambitious southern belle, Lindy Boggs of Louisiana, when her powerful husband died in a plane crash. When my father lived on, and on and on, the word was she got depressed and simply couldn't take it any more. "I suppose she wanted her freedom," he said to me in a rare moment of helplessness.

Then, in 1993, my father's eldest daughter, the half-sister I had never met, was killed in a Columbia intersection by a drunk woman driver. Nancy Moore Thurmond was only twenty-two. She was just about to graduate from the University of South Carolina, and was planning to follow in her mother's pulchritudinous footsteps by entering the Miss South Carolina pageant as Miss Aiken. She had her own designer jewelry company, Designs by Nancy, and was planning to go to law school and become a part of the great Thurmond legal tradition. The night she died, she was walking to the apartment of her boyfriend with a chess set she had just bought at Eckerd Drugs.

What a tragic waste. The drunk driver was a lawyer herself who represented bar owners seeking liquor licenses. My father detested alcohol. He had often pressed for higher liquor taxes and had spoken of the horrors of drunk driving on the Senate floor. Now his worst nightmare was coming true. I thought he would use his immense power to punish his daughter's killer in a torture worthy of Torquemada of the Spanish Inquisition. But the restraint he showed in his darkest hour made me respect him a great deal.

The press, which had never been kind to my father, inflamed the issue by suggesting that young Nancy had been contributorily negligent by jaywalking. The possibility was also raised that she had been drunk herself. I felt very badly for my father when the poor girl's body had to be subjected to an autopsy. There was no alcohol in her; she, like I, was a nondrinker, her father's daughter.

The public still had the feeling that the drunk driver, who admitted to having been to four different bars that evening, was being railroaded because the victim was Strom Thurmond's child. Ultimately, the jury convicted the woman and gave her a two-year prison sentence, out of the possible fifteen for a drunk-driving felony. She served one year. In a sense, the light verdict was a judgment against my father. The people of South Carolina may have always elected him, but tremendous resentment brewed under the surface. I read in the papers that he broke down at his daughter's burial at the family plot in Edgefield's Willowbrook Cemetery, just across the road from Old Buncombe, a road that black people still, figuratively, did not cross. Vice President Al Gore, whose relatively liberal senator father had been described once to me by my father as a "pinko" for supporting Harry Truman, attended the service, as did many other national dignitaries.

I had never seen my father weep. I would have liked to; it made him much more human. And I would have liked to have been there to comfort him, to put my arms around him, something I had never done. Nancy was my family, too, and I couldn't help but regret being deprived of my right to mourn her. I wanted to join my half-brothers and half-sister. I wanted to meet them, to hug them, too. The younger sister Julie was a diabetic. I had become a diabetic. Two of my father's sisters were diabetic. It ran in the family, *our* family. I wanted to speak with them about it. The Thurmond boys seemed perfect, one a tennis star, both lawyers-to-be, both surely with their own hidden problems that I as a guidance counselor, not to mention a sister, might be able to help them with.

I had helped many students over the years find a career or a college or a change of direction in life. It was deeply satisfying to help these students with personal and emotional problems, so they could focus on their educations. I thus considered my academic career a great and gratifying success. I had changed many, many people's lives. In that sense, I had realized my own dreams and goals of changing the world. I had changed *their* worlds, and I was sure for the better. I would have loved sharing the wisdom of my years with my other, "secret" family. But I was excluded. All I could do was call my father on the phone and offer my condolences, which he received graciously, as he would from one of his valued constituents. I didn't fault myself for wanting to be different. I *was* different.

A couple of years after this tragedy, the press reported that my father's estranged wife Nancy was herself arrested in Aiken for drunk driving. The papers said she made the grave mistake of trying to bribe the arresting officer; the incident was videotaped by the patrol car. Nancy was locked up for the night in the Aiken County Jail. She later lost her license, went into rehab, and then admitted a twenty-year ongoing addiction to alcohol and diet pills. Being perfect in the public eye wasn't as easy as it seemed. The state's maternal role model, the author of two model-parenting books, *Mother's Medicine* and *Happy Mother, Happy Child,* had tumbled off her pedestal ignominiously. Press vultures, always looking to say the worst about a Thurmond, had one more field day when Nancy admitted publicly that she, too, might well have drunkenly taken the life of someone else's innocent child. Again, I felt sorry for her, and I felt sorry for my father, both bereaved and humiliated by the "demon rum" he so abhorred.

Strom Thurmond detested scandal. Mr. Straight Arrow, he detested the mere suggestion of impropriety. So it was one of the unkinder cuts that right in the middle of losing his wife and losing his daughter, my very existence was coming out of the closet to haunt him. "Thurmond and the Girl from Edgefield" was the headline of a several-page 1992 *Washington Post* "Style" section story that attempted to "out" both my father and myself. I refused to give an interview, and I was heartened that all my sorority sisters from Orangeburg declined as well, but the tone of the piece implied that I had been bribed by my father to keep silent, and that for all his changes, he was still Simon Legree. "He's a man descended from slaveowners—that's how he came to know black people," was how the article ended, on a quote from a local black lawyer, obviously no fan of the senator.

In 1998, the writer of the article, Marilyn Thompson, collaborated with South Carolina political writer Jack Bass on a very unauthorized biography *Ol' Strom,* which reiterated the accusations of the "illegitimate black daughter" and the cover-up. Jack Bass even showed up at my house in Los Angeles. I tried to be as polite as I could, telling him, as I had told Ms. Thompson years before (she was on this case like the dogged Inspector Javert in *Les Miserables*) that we were "family friends," which was technically true. We were family, and we were friends, but I wasn't trying to split hairs. I wanted them to go away. I valued my father's privacy, and I valued my own. Neither when the article nor the book appeared did my father mention the story to me. He never had asked me to cover anything up, and he didn't these times either. The only family response that I was aware of was that one of my father's sisters chided the *State* newspaper in Columbia, which reprinted the article, for publishing "trash." Once I did ask my father how to deal with the press. His answer was simple: "Ignore them."

When both big Julius and little Julius had goaded me to go public with my heritage, they both assumed that the revelation would destroy my father, personally and politically. They wanted him out of the Senate and out of our black hair, and I was the one to do it. I always thought they were wrong, and I was right in so thinking. Strom Thurmond had more lives than a litter of cats. He was a political Superman. If there were a kryptonite that could destroy him, Essie Mae Washington-Williams was not it. Of course, I wasn't sure, though, and I wasn't about to risk being wrong. But in 1972, W. W. Mims, the eccentric owner and editor of the Edgefield *Advertiser* and a man who had a perennial blood feud with my father, printed a front page, full-page headline charging that Strom Thurmond had "COLORED OFFSPRING WHILE PARADING AS A DEVOUT SEGREGATIONIST." Mims was compromised in his objectivity by presenting himself as a write-in candidate in that year's Senate campaign, which my father won in his usual landslide. Mims's "scoop," which he tried to promulgate all over the state and nation, didn't make a dent in my father's popularity, nor did the *Post* article or the biography. My father, as attorneys would say, was "judgment-proof."

The last time I saw my father was in 1999. For the first time in his ninety-seven years, I sensed he was failing, though he continued to put on a brave face. He was slow, frail, and, above all, his handshake was weak. The year before, I had sent him a Father's Day card. I had been sending similar cards and notes to him for years at this point, and other little letters as well, congratulating him when he won the Presidential Medal of Freedom, things like that.

The cards would be simple things, flowers on the front, poetry inside: "We hope your day is as happy as it ought to be for you. We hope you'll just enjoy it, doing the things you like to do." And I'd sign it "Essie Williams and family." It was something that could have come from any constituent, and there was no way it could have gotten him into any trouble.

On occasion, his office would send a note of acknowledgment, a form letter they would send to any well-wisher. I never had received, nor did I expect, a personal, written acknowledgment from my father himself. That was too risky for him; that could be proof that could be used against him. But this time he sent me a personal note of thanks. It was very simple: "Dear Essie Mae, Thank you for your kind remembrance on Father's Day. Affectionately, Strom Thurmond." But it was clear that it had come from the man himself, not some staff letter-writer. To me this letting down of his guard was proof that the end was near.

Sometimes, in blustery moments, my father would boast that he was going to live to be 120. He didn't say that now. I was seventy-four myself and retired from teaching. I couldn't believe where the time had gone. He asked the pro forma questions about my children, though he still never would refer to them as his grandchildren. Ronald, in whom my father took special pride in sending through medical school, had settled in Seattle, where he had become a successful emergency room physician. He had married and divorced and was remarried. His first wife was the daughter of one of the Tuskegee Airmen, the famous black flying squad during World War II. His second wife was white.

Ronald had been our family's Moses in leading the way to the cool, green, and racially harmonious Pacific Northwest. Julius moved there and went to work as a bus operator for the Metropolitan Transit Authority. As I said, he loved to drive even as a teenager. Then Monica, who was so high energy that she had run her own karate studio while working at the Bank of America as a teenager, moved there and became the director of a battered women's shelter, Polly's Healing Center, and an accomplished fund-raiser for worthy causes. Only Wanda remained with me in Los Angeles. Another highly motivated businesswoman, she had founded her own consulting business in information technology, Ocean Crest Technologies, and it was doing very well.

All my children had their own children, and I loved the whole big bunch. Since so many of them are in the Washington state area, I have been tempted to move up there, which is about as different from South Carolina as a place can be. I marveled to my father that I had thirteen grandchildren, by implication his great-grandchildren, whom he had never met. If only he had said, "Bring them all down to Edgefield. Let's have a real family reunion while I'm still on this earth." Instead, he told me to fry things, if I had to fry at all, in canola oil, which was lowest in saturated fat, and to be sure to add fiber to my diet. He offered me a large jar of Metamucil from his still-overflowing medicine cabinet behind his desk. I told him I had plenty.

Now that the Soviet Union had imploded and the Cold War was over, my father didn't have the Communists to rail at as his Enemy Number One. Nevertheless, even at our last visit, he went on about military preparedness and about how many enemies America had in the world and how vigilant the country needed to be. "There are still Communists," he warned, "the Chinese, the Arabs, and they're out to get us." But at this point in his career as the longest serving senator in American history, he was more tuned in to the micro than the macro view of politics. He wanted to help South Carolinians, whether that meant getting an appointment to West Point, or helping them defend an IRS audit, or sending funeral condolences. Strom Thurmond was a man of the people, his people. When I was with him, his aides would be buzzing in and out with little favors for the "little people."

"Do you need anything, Essie Mae?" he would invariably ask me at the end of our visit.

"No thank you, Senator," I'd say. "It's all taken care of."

I never thought I wouldn't see him again. Just before I had last visited him, he had made a big show of citing his health regimen in volunteering to back up astronaut/Senator John Glenn on the space shuttle. He led the vote to impeach President Clinton in the Monica Lewinsky affair, with his critics suggesting that Senator Thurmond, who had reportedly groped his fair share of staffers and even female senators, should not be casting stones. But my father's flirting days were over. The death of his beloved sister Gertrude, still a spinster in 2000, seemed to rattle him. When he collapsed on the floor of the Senate, I called him with great concern. He assured me it was nothing, just "too hot," and reminded me of his twenty-four-hour filibuster on that same floor. "I'm not going to disgrace myself by dying there," he said, concerned for his image until the end.

After a few more blackouts, however, my father, unable to live alone as he preferred, moved into a suite at Walter Reed Army Hospital and was chauffeured back and forth to the Senate by male nurses. In 2002, after his gala 100th birthday celebration, he finally retired from the Senate with great fanfare. Alluding to my father's legend as a ladies' man, a Marilyn Monroe impersonator sang "Happy Birthday" just as the real Marilyn had sung to JFK.

"I love you all," he told his colleagues in his farewell address, "especially your wives." This was when Senate majority leader Trent Lott of Mississippi put his foot in his Republican mouth by saying of my father's 1948 Dixiecrat campaign: "We're proud of it. And if the rest of the country had followed our lead, we wouldn't have had all these problems over all these years either." My father's name was still a buzzword for white supremacy, particularly in connection to his rabid presidential bid, and Democrats came after Lott's hide, forcing him to resign.

When he moved back to Edgefield in early 2003, I accepted the fact that my father was coming home to die. A special suite was created for him at Edgefield County Hospital. He was driven around on occasion to wave at the constituents whom he loved and who loved him back. I called him once there, but I'm not sure he knew who I was. I might have come to visit had I thought the controversy surrounding my presence would not have disturbed his peace. There was one more burst of fanfare in June of that year when his daughter Julie presented him with what the press called "his first grandchild." Once more, my feelings were hurt, but that was the name of the game we had been playing for the last six decades.

On June 26, 2003, my father passed away. The leaders of the country paid their respects at Columbia, where his new statue stood in a place of honor in front of the Capitol, the very building General Sherman once tried to burn to the ground. Then my father was taken to the family plot in Edgefield's Willowbrook Cemetery and laid to rest next to his daughter Nancy. Two flags, American and Confederate, stood proudly in equal stature above his grave. Those two flags, waving in death, were the story of Strom Thurmond's life.

I tried to feel at peace with the passing of my father, but I couldn't. If life was a game, then Strom Thurmond had won it, big time. He lived 100 years, with almost perfect health. He had enormous success, wielded inestimable power, and served his country with great honor both at war and peace. He had beautiful wives, beautiful children, a beautiful life, as well as a prominent place in history. Why was I so unsettled, so discontent? It was because he and I had never really made our peace. Yes, he had changed, and so had the world, but he and I had never so much as sat down together for a meal. We had never said "I love you" to each other. We had never confronted the reality of our relationship. Too much remained unsaid. I was so grateful just to have a father that I had never been brave enough to risk losing him by rocking the boat. Now I was seventy-eight years old. This was no time to start rocking.

My daughter Wanda refused to let me off the confrontation hook. She became my gadfly. "He's gone now," she said. "What have you got to lose?" She beseeched me to consider writing a book. Astute businesswoman that I had raised, Wanda also brought up the issue of my father's estate, which still felt unmentionable to me. "It's probably worth millions, if not tens, or hundreds, of millions," Wanda said, "Think of the real estate he must own."

I did, though I didn't want to. I remember my father's deep interest in real estate, how he was fascinated with the details of valuation, his expertise in those eminent domain cases that surely made him one of the top real estate attorneys in the South, how proud he was of me when I bought my home, how he went through the details of my mortgage to make sure I was getting the very best deal. "Just hold on to it no matter what you do. Property is the best way to get rich in this country. Just buy and hold. You sell your children before you sell your land," I remember him joking. A joke that hit close to home.

"A hundred years," Wanda went on. "That's a lot of time to accumulate property. Think of what it must be worth. Why shouldn't we get part of it? Shouldn't we be heirs, too?"

"Not if he doesn't want us to be," I answered, trying to defend the late senator, and thinking of the conservatism and strict construction of his idol John C. Calhoun. A man could leave his money to whomever he wanted.

"That's the point, mama," Wanda would not relent. "I'm sure he *wanted.* He just *couldn't.* Not the way things are down there. You may have rights you don't even know about."

I didn't really want to know. There had been all these lawsuits in the papers about blacks seeking reparations for slavery, about Jews seeking stolen art from the Nazis. They were all noble causes, but they seemed like endless, impossible journeys. The last things I wanted in my life were lawsuits and publicity. I remembered how uncomfortable, how queasy I felt whenever journalists had come snooping around. I wanted to get on with the rest of my life, to live quietly, to avoid the storm.

Wanda wouldn't let me. "It's too big to let go, mama. You owe it to yourself. You owe it to us. You owe it to your country."

"Don't get so dramatic, honey."

"This *is* dramatic."

While I was trying to make believe that this sense of unfinished business would pass over time, Wanda refused to let sleeping dogs lie. She began consulting Los Angeles lawyers about the possibilities of a challenge to the Thurmond will. Of course, she didn't mention who the descendant was, attorney-client privilege notwithstanding. That would have been too hot for most lawyers to touch. Even with the anonymity, none of the lawyers she consulted would take the case on contingency. Lawyers are notoriously risk averse, and speculative will contests regarding illegitimate children are particularly risky. Then, through a high school friend, Keith Webster, she was introduced to a local lawyer named Frank K. Wheaton, who struck her as far more creative than all the stuffier lawyers she had met with.

Frank was creative because he was in the entertainment business. He had been a broadcaster and actor himself before going to law school. He had represented such sports heroes as Lakers forward James Worthy and Olympic runners Florence Griffith "Flo Jo" Joyner and Bob Beamon. He also had important white clients like my comedy hero Milton Berle. Much more importantly, he was willing to take the case on a contingency. That made me instantly suspicious when Wanda told me she had found the right man. Just meet him, she begged me, to explore possibilities, and nothing more. If I decided I didn't want to go forward, Frank Wheaton was the one lawyer that we could trust to forever hold his peace.

What sold me on Frank Wheaton was his voice, a deep, reassuring baritone that inspired not only confidence, but hope. It was a preacher's voice, minus the fire and brimstone. In fact, in his acting days Frank had made a good living doing voice-overs in many national commercials. I had always been a goner for voices, though this time I got the sense that the substance matched the sound. Frank was a poor, self-made kid from Compton, one of the toughest black neighborhoods in Los Angeles. He was both a believer in, and an example of, the American Dream, and after he heard me reluctantly tell my story, he asserted that I was a far bigger example, the best he had ever seen. Like Wanda, he urged me to tell my story, which he guaranteed would be an inspiration to blacks and whites alike. He felt if anyone could help bridge America's racial divide, I could. I laughed and told him he was quite a salesman.

He laughed back. Then he turned serious and told me how hard a case we would have in challenging the Thurmond will. The Thurmond family would surely deny Strom Thurmond's paternity of me. I would have to undergo DNA genetic testing. Even if science proved to be on my side, the law was not. South Carolina had no automatic right of inheritance for children, as some states do. Just as I had thought, South Carolina was pure laissez-faire on what a person could do with his estate.

"Like states' rights," I observed, writing the whole matter off as a lost cause.

"What about *human* rights?" Frank Wheaton replied. He felt the state law could be challenged, just like *Plessy vs. Ferguson* had been challenged, and overturned by *Brown vs. Board of Education.* Leaving me out of his will, just like leaving me out of his life, had been a massive injustice, Frank asserted. He was willing to go out on the shakiest of limbs to challenge it, but he couldn't do it without me. I had to be prepared to weather a violent storm and a perilous journey, he warned me, before we could reach the Promised Land. It took me a week to decide, but I didn't want to end my life carrying this secret to my grave. I wasn't a black Joan of Arc as Frank was trying to inspire me to be, but maybe I could help someone by telling my tale. "The truth shall set you free," and I wanted to die a free person.

In August 2003, we crossed the Rubicon. Frank realized he would be playing the black David to the white Goliath of the southern legal establishment. Luckily, he was associated with a very WASPY Pasadena law firm, Scolinos, Sheldon and Nevell. Also in our corner was Harry Scolinos, the senior partner of the firm, who had been stationed in the military in South Carolina and was intrigued, rather than terrified, as most lawyers would be, by the prospect of taking on the sacred cows of Dixie. He therefore allowed Frank to correspond on the firm's letterhead, which would have the effect of showing a cross to the vampires of the South Carolina bar and winning the respect and courtesy for Frank that he might not have found as a sole black practitioner.

Armed with white armor, Frank wrote to my half-brother Strom Thurmond, Jr., whom our father had appointed, at twenty-eight, to be United States Attorney for South Carolina in 2001, making him the youngest man ever to hold the post as the federal government's top gun in the state. Some locals had cried nepotism, but not too loudly. Such was my father's absolute power on his home turf. At first, Frank got no reply. A month later, he received a terse letter from the Thurmond family lawyer, J. Mark Taylor, telling Frank, in so many words, to drop dead. Taylor wrote that the family was by no means certain of the paternity issue, that the estate had a value of only $200,000, and that, in any event, Essie Mae Washington-Williams was not provided for. Case closed.

But not for Frank, who saw the fact that the Thurmonds were not vehemently denying my assertion that I was their sibling as a major crack of the door. That was the good news, if grasping at such straws was good. The bad news was that the South Carolina statute of limitations on challenges to estates over paternity issues was a mere six months. Furthermore, all such claims had to go before the family tribunal in Aiken County, where my father's will was registered. And still further, the family tribunal in Aiken was a panel of arbiters, who didn't have to be lawyers. This was a vastly complex matter, and these locals weren't about to challenge the sanctified memory and racial purity of the man they regarded as their savior. "It's worse than a kangaroo court," Frank told us glumly.

The kid from Compton was not a quitter, but these were times that would try any lawyer's soul, assuming the lawyer had one. Accepting the necessity of local counsel to sort through the arcana of Palmetto jurisprudence, Frank contacted no fewer than twelve prominent black lawyers, all of whom politely turned him down. This was a hornet's nest no one wanted to stir up. Finally, my alma mater, South Carolina State, came to the rescue. The college's general counsel was a young man named Glenn Walters, who had graduated from

State and then from the prestigious University of Virginia Law School (founded by Thomas Jefferson, who had his own secret romance with his slave Sally Hemings). Walters loved the case, especially because I was a State girl. He was too young to be afraid of my father's long shadow. He relished the challenge of changing the laws of inheritance for the benefit of secret children.

Even with Glenn's assistance, the Thurmond lawyer J. Mark Taylor would not budge, nor would he even respond. As months went by and the time on the statute of limitations ticked down toward its December expiration, Frank Wheaton knew desperate measures were necessary. He had to take off his lawyer's hat and put on his Hollywood director's visor. It had to be Showtime.

Frank planned a media campaign and began to organize a press conference at which I would "come out." To that end, he located Marilyn Thompson, the *Washington Post* writer who had done the 1992 article as well as the coauthor of the unauthorized Thurmond biography. She had been obsessed with the story for nearly two decades. He offered her an exclusive in return for front page coverage in the *Post*. It was arranged that the story would indeed appear in what was known as the *Post*'s "bulldog" edition, which was the Saturday night issue of Sunday's paper of December 14. For this dogged reporter, whom I had done my best to avoid, this was the scoop of a lifetime. I did speak to her, though I was still very guarded and had a lifetime of caution. I'm not sure I helped her very much, but it was enough for a bombshell.

Aside from that interview, Frank kept me sequestered from everyone. He knew the value of the element of surprise. He also knew the power of the press, which descended on his home the minute the contents of the upcoming *Post* story leaked out. Fox News immediately assembled a panel of separately talking heads, including Frank himself, Nancy Thurmond, and Armstrong Williams, a prominent black Washington, D.C., columnist who had grown very close to my father during his "transformation" into the "friend of black South Carolina" in the 1970s. Nancy Thurmond said she knew absolutely nothing about me, which I don't doubt was the truth. My father was a master of secrecy. But Armstrong Williams broke the tie, saying he fully believed what Frank Wheaton was asserting, that Strom Thurmond was my father.

CBS called immediately. I was "real." Dan Rather wanted me on *60 Minutes*, the television equivalent of my father's cover of *Time*. Rather was planning to fly right out. Frank and my family were all very excited. Still, in a matter of days the statute of limitations was going to expire. What good was all this posturing if the Thurmonds continued to stonewall? "They won't stonewall *60 Minutes,*" Frank assured us all. "The only thing that could knock us off the air is if they find Saddam Hussein."

That very day they captured Saddam Hussein. I have never seen such a depressed group of people as we were. The game was over, lost on a freak shot at the last second.

A few hours later, one of the CBS producers called. The two producers, Mary Mapes and Dana Robertson, had been relentless. Mary told Frank that Dan Rather still wanted me. I meant more to him, and to America, than Saddam Hussein, she told Frank. The only catch was that Dan couldn't fly to California. Could we come to New York the next day? And so we went. The next day, just before the limo picked Frank up for the airport, he got got a call from the Thurmonds' lawyer, J. Mark Taylor. Rushing, Frank told Taylor he had no time, but Taylor insisted he listen to the statement about to be released to the media by Strom Thurmond, Jr. Taylor read from the statement, and all Frank remembered, before dropping to his knees to thank "God and Essie Mae," as he said, was that "the Thurmond family wishes to acknowledge the genetic heritage of Essie Mae Washington-Williams."

I was sitting in an airport coffee bar when Frank came back in tears. I first thought it was more bad news until I saw him smiling through. They were tears of joy. He embraced all of us, me, Wanda, my grandson Jason, and we all thanked God for His infinite kindness. I would say relief, more than anything else, was my immediate dominant emotion. I sat there stunned for a long time. Despite all the noise of the terminal, all the announcements, I was in a zone of blissful silence. I was totally relaxed, totally loose, almost floating. After a lifetime of denial, the truth was out, and I was free. The Thurmonds were publicly acknowledging me as their blood relation. My history could now become American history. I would have liked to see a plaque at that coffee counter as the spot where Essie Mae Washington-Williams was "released."

The next twenty-four hours were a blur of airlines and terminals. Five of us flew cross-country to New York. There were Frank, myself, Wanda, Jason, and Frank's childhood friend Van Adams. Van was trained as a chiropractor and helped me with warm, soothing massages throughout the five tense days in New York. The next day, as Frank handled the press, I remained sequestered at the hotel until I was taken to the CBS studio to meet Dan Rather. Mr. Rather took southern hospitality to a new level. He couldn't have been more supportive. From there, it was back on the plane. I would have loved to see the city, but all we saw was the studio and the inside of black-windowed limousines to and from the airport. There were no flights to Columbia, so we had to fly to Charlotte and be driven south to Columbia to be on time for our momentous press conference.

Glenn Walters had arranged a mini-army of twelve burly bodyguards to protect us from irate Klansmen or other white supremacy types. Frank, ever the showman, had planned to hold the conference in front of my father's statue at the Capitol, the statue that listed the names of his four children by Nancy, but not mine. But that would change now. That and a lot of other things. I knew change was coming. But it was getting near winter in Columbia, and the weather was cold and blustery and rain was threatening. So Frank at the last moment changed the venue to the grand ballroom of Columbia's grandest hotel, the Adam's Mark. There were 400 seats, and the next morning all of them were filled with press from around the world. There were countless television trucks creating a monumental traffic jam. If ever there were a media event, this was it.

Frank asked me if I was nervous, and my honest answer was that I was not. A great weight had been lifted. The truth had set me free. So after an eloquent introduction by Frank, I made the long march from the back of the ballroom to the raised podium. It was like winning an Academy Award, with the press in as big a frenzy. But I was ready. I talked from the heart. I hope that my husband Julius heard me, and that my father heard me as well.

There were a lot of tears in that audience, black tears and white tears. I felt it was a wonderful moment for South Carolina. It was bigger than I would have ever imagined. After I made it through my speech, the crowd roared, and there were countless dozens of people standing, waving, and crying. Afterward, Frank conducted a careful question-and-answer session with the national and world press that might have gone on for hours had the CBS stringer not signaled to bring the conference to an end. Instead of leaving the back way, through the security exit we had planned, Frank decided I should walk back to our suite through the main entrance of the lobby. It was as if the waters were parting. I felt so much love. Frank told me he encountered two women who he was certain were Thurmonds sobbing uncontrollably. "You're relatives, aren't you?" he asked them. They didn't answer, but he could tell they were there to wish me well, even if they couldn't say it. Silence tended to run in the family.

In a way, my life began at seventy-eight, at least my life as who I really was, without the subterfuges of the previous sixty-five years. I may have called it "closure," but it was much more like an opening, a very grand opening. I was on many television shows, so many that children stop me on the street and ask for my autograph. I have developed a friendship with Nancy Thurmond. It's strange to call someone my stepmother who is decades younger than I, but that's what she is. As mothers, and as Thurmonds, we have much more in common than might meet the eye. We both love to talk, and we talk about everything. We often speak on the phone, and I try to see her whenever I go back to South Carolina, which has been frequent.

I have had the dinner with Strom Thurmond, Jr. that I always longed to have with his father. We didn't talk politics or race at all, just family—his family and my family, which is now "our" family. He's a "fine young man," as my father might have said. I've also had lunch with my half-brother Paul and I'm looking forward to meeting my half-sister Julie. I know that more, and deeper, dialogue will follow as we get to know each other. The key thing here is that the great divide has been bridged. Meanwhile, the South Carolina legislature voted to add my name to my father's statue, albeit at the bottom rather than the top of the list of his children. Whatever the placement, I'm honored to be there. As for the estate, Frank Wheaton and Glenn Walters are still on the case, which will surely profit from the dialogue that has come to take place with the family.

One of my greatest honors was to have been granted an honorary doctorate by South Carolina State, for my thirty years of teaching and guiding students, at graduation ceremonies in May 2004. I received a standing ovation at the school's new football stadium. I couldn't help but think of the straight-hair requirement back at Coatesville that kept me from being a cheerleader and made me make the turn that found me accepting the cheers of thousands. I also visited Charleston for the first time. I spoke at a scholarship fund charity event at the once whites-only and still very exclusive Francis Marion Hotel on State Street. I also spoke at an all-black Baptist church in North Charleston, where the mayor presented me with the key to the city. That was the dichotomy of Charleston; that was the dichotomy of my life.

I visited Edgefield and Aiken, escorted by my father's dear friend Bettis Rainsford, a true pillar of that community. Mr. Rainsford, a dedicated historical preservationist, took me to visit the building that housed the law office where I first met my father. We also took a wonderful tour of my father's birthplace, warmly welcomed by the young family that has bought the great white mansion and lovingly preserved it as a living shrine to the boyhood of Edgefield's favorite son. We toured Old Buncombe, where my mother and her family grew up. It hadn't changed much since I first visited there in the early 1940s. And then we crossed the big road where all those huge plantation houses still stand to visit my father's grave in Willowbrook Cemetery, a green and serene slice of heaven where, over Strom Thurmond's resting place, the American and Confederate flags continue to flutter softly and peacefully together in the gentle southern breezes.

I had lived my life as an African-American. Now things had changed. Not that I wanted to live the rest of my life as a white person. I wanted to live out my days as an American, with all the delicious complexity that term has come to imply. My visit to Charleston, our most historic city, has also slaked my thirst for history. To that end, I have applied for membership in both the National Society Daughters of the American Revolution (NSDAR) and the United Daughters of the Confederacy (UDC), to which I am entitled to join through my father's lineage. In wanting to join the NSDAR, I was inspired by the efforts of the Black Patriots Foundation to address its dismay that written history had marginalized black involvement during the Colonies' struggle for independence against England. In the 1980s, the visionaries behind this Foundation commenced a lawsuit against the NSDAR that ultimately compelled it to identify and honor the thousands of black soldiers who had fought for America's freedom in the Revolution. I would be honored to join the NSDAR to encourage the rich dialogue between blacks and whites that, without participation of the descendants of *all* our country's patriots, would otherwise not take place.

As for the UDC, many people have raised the question of how a black person could consider joining a society that honors a past of racism. The answers are much more complex than the question. First of all, the United Daughters of the Confederacy is anything but a racist cabal of ancestors of slave owners. It is not the Simon Legree Society. The Confederacy was composed of many great Americans: Judah P. Benjamin, Robert E. Lee, Lucius Lamar, Wade Hampton. These were hardly Klansmen, just as the Civil War was hardly a battle to the death over slavery alone. There were many black slave owners as well, many free people of color who supported the Confederacy. There were also slaves who fought and died for the Confederacy. Were they forced by their masters, or were they loyal to their masters' cause? Or were there other compelling reasons that led them to fight and die in this terrible war? I wanted to join the UDC to find the answers, to learn more about this key conflict that defined America and continues to define us. I've lived my life believing that knowledge was power, and certainly empowering. I want all the knowledge I can get. And I want my children and my grandchildren to connect to all aspects of their heritage, whether patriot or politician, slave or slave owner. The past, and all of its lessons, must not be denied.

Second, many of those who decry my joining the UDC tend to categorize me as a black person. They may make the more subtle argument that anyone who's lived through and supported the civil rights movement should never join any organization associated with the abridgment of those rights. To them, the Confederacy, as well as its flag, are old times in Dixie that *should* be forgotten. But what really bothers these critics is that a black person would consider honoring the Confederacy that perpetuated the enslavement of his or her ancestors. Such labeling is as racist in its own way as the Confederacy itself. I am every bit as white as I am black, and it is my full intention to drink the nectar of both goblets. History is complex, and mine is as complex as it gets. That's why I want to join these organizations, to explore and try to comprehend all the fascinating complexities, tragic as well as joyous, of my life, and of my country. In my past lives, as defined by my genealogy, I was a slave and I was a master; I was black and I was white; I was a Roosevelt progressive and I was a Dixiecrat; I was for Kennedy and I was for Nixon; I was the glorious president of the South and I was a lowly maid in Edgefield. Above all, I transcended all these internal contradictions to become a real person, my own person, a simple person who loves America as the wonderful place that has allowed me to discover, and to be, exactly who I am.